Father Factor

A Note about the *I Speak for Myself* series:

I Speak for Myself ® is an inclusive platform through which people can make themselves heard and where everyone's voice has a place. ISFM®'s mission focuses on delivering one core product, a "narrative collection," that is mindset-altering, inspiring, relatable, and teachable. We aim to deliver interfaith, intercultural titles that are narrow in scope but rich in diversity.

Please be sure to check out our website, www.ISpeakforMyself. com, to learn more about the series, join the conversation, and even create an *I Speak for Myself* ® book of your own!

Sincerely,

Zahra T. Suratwala and Maria M. Ebrahimji

Co-Founders, *I Speak for Myself* ®

BOOKS IN THE SERIES

Volume 1: *I Speak for Myself: American Women on Being Muslim*

Volume 2: *American Men on Being Muslim: 45 American Men on Being Muslim*

Volume 3: *Demanding Dignity: Young Voices from the Front Lines of the Arab Revolutions*

Volume 4: *Talking Taboo: American Christian Women Get Frank About Faith*

Volume 5: *Father Factor: American Christian Men on Fatherhood and Faith*

ISfM
I SPEAK FOR MYSELF

Praise for **Father Factor**

"*Father Factor* reads like a jigsaw puzzle. Each story adds a puzzle piece to this aggregated post-modern picture of fatherhood, sonship, and the quest for wholeness. Not till the pieces were nearly all assembled did I realize I had borne witness to history—a moment when disparate Christian men joined together in common struggle—the fight to face and forsake the mirages of "manhood" previously stalked and preserved by their forefathers. Transparent, funny, heart-wrenching, and often brutally honest, these men are on a quest to discover what it means to be a man—a Christian man—in the world today."

–Lisa Sharon Harper, Senior Director of Mobilizing at Sojourners and author of *Forgive Us: Confessions of a Compromised Faith*

"I love memoirs—who doesn't love a good story?—and these short narratives are a joy to read, a reader's delight, getting a glimpse into the lives of others. There is wonder, loss, love, joy, pathos, romance and laughter, a little cursing and a lot of praise. But there is more: these are exceptionally brave stories from many different sorts of men reflecting profoundly about God the father, their own fathers (for better or for worse) and their own particular journeys into fatherhood. This is not a self-help manual, but guys from all stages of life with learn much and be better fathers because of it. Highly recommended."

–Byron Borger, Hearts & Minds Books, Dallastown, PA

"I could not put this book down. It gave me whole new insights into both Christianity and fatherhood, and made me think long and hard about how my relationship with Islam impacts my relationship with my wife and two sons. In short, this book made me a better father, husband, and Muslim."

–Eboo Patel, author of *Acts of Faith* and *Sacred Ground*

"From creating life to enduring death, **Father Factor** takes us through the tumultuous, often humorous, sometimes heartbreaking journey of father-hood and faith. This is not a how-to manual; there are no lists of right and wrong, no simple strategies, no easy plans for becoming the perfect Dad. Instead, through this rich array of personal stories from fathering and being fathered, readers will feel inspired and challenged to examine their unique role as a parent, partner, and adult child as this book throws open wide windows for grace, forgiveness, and a Father's love."

–Jamie Wright, author/blogger of theveryworstmissionary.com

"Just as God has many names in the Hebrew Scriptures to represent the many attributes of divinity, so fathers have many unique titles and attributes as well. In the *Father Factor* you'll get to meet fathers, dads, daddys, and papas, all of whom share their personal experiences from a deeply spiritual perspective. This book is a rainbow of personal reflections on the essence of fatherhood. Although written from a Christian point-of-view it will be meaningful to people of every faith, in every culture. *Father Factor* is a gem reflecting the many facets of light from its wide array of authors."

–Rabbi David Zaslow, author of *Jesus: First-Century Rabbi*

"This book inspired me to pray for fathers, encourage fathers and believe in the important work of fathering! Pulling from culturally diverse and compelling experiences, *Father Factor* gives voice to the strong men of faith who are shaped the Father's love. This collection of inspiring stories affirms the various routes that fatherhood can take and shows that regardless of history or cultural context, men of faith can be powerful and vulnerable fathers. A true eye opener to the complexities and beauty of fatherhood."

–Christena Cleveland, author of *Disunity in Christ*

"The media makes many assumptions about men that are often superficial or inaccurate. Campbell's collection of personal reflections exposes these myths with challenging and complex narratives and is an important contribution to the ISFM series. Each story offers a shimmering refraction on the intricate relationship between fathers, their children and their faith. But the book's real value lies in the mosaic created when the stories are taken together and the seemingly small victories that emerge out of day-to-day life, sometimes from heartbreaking trauma and tragedy, are lifted into the light. It is humbling and inspirational to share in the stories of these men."

–Rev. Robert Chase, Founding Director, Intersections

Father Factor

American Christian Men on Fatherhood and Faith

edited by R. Anderson Campbell
foreword by Christian Piatt

White Cloud Press
Ashland, Oregon

The views and opinions expressed by each contributing writer in this book are theirs alone and do not necessarily represent those of the series' editors or I Speak for Myself, Inc.

White Cloud Press books may be purchased for educational, business, or sales promotional use. For information, please write:

Special Market Department
White Cloud Press
PO Box 3400
Ashland, OR 97520
Website: www.whitecloudpress.com

Cover and Interior Design by C Book Services

Printed in the United States of America
First edition: 2014
14 15 16 17 18   10 9 8 7 6 5 4 3 2 1

Library of Congress Cataloging-in-Publication Data

Father factor : American Christian men on fatherhood and faith / edited by R. Anderson Campbell ; foreword by Christian Piatt.
    pages cm
 Includes bibliographical references and index.
 ISBN 978-1-940468-20-4 (pbk. : alk. paper)
 1. Fatherhood--Religious aspects--Christianity. 2. Fathers--Religious life. 3. Faith. 4. Christian men--United States. I. Campbell, R. Anderson, editor.
 BV4529.17.F383 2014
 261.8'3587420973--dc23
                              2014030085

To my father, Robert Campbell, the man who taught me what it means to be a father in faith.

Acknowledgements

This project would not have been possible without the constant encouragement, support, and expertise of the I Speak for Myself series editors, Maria Ebrahimji and Zahra Suratwala. I have known Maria for nearly twenty years. She introduced me to the woman who later became my wife. She is the first person of a faith different than mine with whom I became fast friends. I was honored to follow the progress of the first volume in this series from conception through to release and humbled when I was approached by Maria and Zahra to design and edit this fifth volume. Thank you, ladies for trusting me with this work.

A few people warrant special mention in helping connect me to the men who contributed to this volume. Thank you Aaron Smith, Enuma Okoro, Christian Piatt, and Mark Strong.

Of course, none of this would be possible without the vulnerability and tenacity of the contributors who took on the audacious task of exploring two very personal aspects of their lives: fatherhood and faith. Thank you, gentlemen. It was an honor to work alongside you to tell your stories.

Contents

Foreword
by Christian Piatt

I grew up with a dad who was pretty clear about what it meant to be a man. It meant long hours at the office, building stuff on the weekends, drinking beer on the porch on Saturday evening, and providing for your family. Though less explicit, there was also the very clear message that guy-ness also required a fairly high level of toughness, emotional detachment bordering on aloofness, a hair-trigger temper, a skeptical mind and an approbation for aggression.

I was pretty sure I was a disappointment to him in a lot of ways. I was more into music and art than sports. I was too afraid of getting hurt to be effectively aggressive, and I was way too small for most of my young life to pull off the whole anger thing. I mean, who is impressed by an enraged chipmunk?

For those born after the Baby Boomers, we have borne witness to—and taken part in—a fairly historic deconstruction of male identity. Part of that has come from progress in gender parity. Part of it has come from advances in technology and increased specialization. And part of it is a natural by-product of a highly mobile, elaborately networked, and increasingly pluralistic national and global culture.

The thing is, although we have deconstructed much of what traditional culture has told us it means to be a man, and what it means to be a father in particular, there has been little offered to help us begin to reconstruct what those identities and roles look like. On the upside, there is a more fluid sharing of parenting roles between male and female, which actually can help contemporary families be more nimble and agile. On the downside, though, there's a general haziness about who is supposed to do what. The role of the postmodern father is perennially unfinished business.

The notion of a set of norms, rules, or values that apply to many of us seems arbitrary and desperate at best. At worst, it smacks of the kind of colonialist oppression from which many of us have endeavored to emerge.

There are those among us who feel that these ambiguities around our gender identity are at the heart of a larger social and moral decay. What is needed, they assert, is to reclaim our nostalgic gender roles with fervor and conviction, reestablishing ourselves as super-men, all for the greater good, of course. But if we have learned anything throughout the course of history, it's that we can't go back. And for most of us, it's not a past that we care to return to anyway.

There is a reason it is shocking to watch television shows like *Mad Men* and see the way gender roles played out just a few decades ago. The way women were treated not so long ago seems fairly unthinkable now. And really, when we talk nostalgically about the loss of traditional cultural roles, the only ones usually mourning such changes are those who directly benefited from things as they were.

So what are we left with, after all of this deconstruction? Fathering has become a more collective experience. Roles formerly held only by dads are now shared by mom, partner, aunts, uncles, neighbors, pastors, and even the media culture in which today's kids are so deeply enmeshed. The entire notion of "family" has been reimagined in innumerable ways, and although this has the potential to add richness to our experience of family life, it can also be confusing. Further, even as much as our new ideas about nontraditional family may feel right, we can't be sure of its impact on our kids until years, if not decades, later.

Many now believe there is no single template, no guidebook and no preexisting social expectation to dictate for us how we should act, what we should do, and how we should see ourselves. Absent any external, rigid, didactic normative systems to lend us a ready-made identity, we are left with personal experience, shared relationship, and the stories that emerge from the two. From these narratives, we find points of resonance and dissonance, of deep identification and this sense of things that are deeply true even if, paradoxically, those same truths may ring hollow for our neighbor.

The essays in this book provide examples of such a narrative-driven framework within which we can explore who we are and who we are to be. They are not prescriptive or particularly commanding in tone. On the contrary, many of them are vulnerable, revelatory, and lacking an authoritative voice, at least in the traditional sense. They tell stories of absent fathers, tragic loss, unexpected gains, and twisting, surprising, and often funny ways in which we try to discern who we are as fathers, sons, and spouses. They even affect our images of God, particularly as fatherhood butts up against our notions of God as "heavenly father."

But whereas in the past a man was valued more for his certitude, decisiveness, and firmness, we see an emergence of a new set of adjectives helping to mold the identity of postmodern males: authenticity, sincerity, humility, self-knowledge, and a healthy dose of irreverent humor. All of the same adjectives could be applied to this collection of touching and important stories.

Although each of the essays can certainly stand on its own, it can also be helpful to see the collection as a single work and search for the points of overlap, of tension and friction, or even contradiction. Singular authority was once a more precious virtue. Now, it is in those points where one set of ideals rubs against another that sparks are generated to ignite the flames of the wisdom and forge the character we seek.

We don't have to look or act the same. We shouldn't. It's not what the world needs from us, and it is certainly not what I believe the kingdom of God is meant to be like. If Pentecost is indeed our model for how a more perfect world should look, then our discussion about what it means to be a man in the twenty-first century should have a chorus of uncommon, unfamiliar, and unexpected voices, all reverberating in a sort of cacophonic harmony that, in its own strange way, works.

CHRISTIAN is the creator and editor of the Banned Questions book series, which include *Banned Questions About the Bible*, *Banned Questions About Jesus*, and *Banned Questions About Christians*. He cocreated and coedited the WTF: Where's the Faith? young adult series with Chalice Press, for which he also coedited the book *Split Ticket: Independent Faith in a Time of Partisan Politics*, and contributed a chapter to *Oh God, Oh God, Oh God: Young Adults Speak Out About Sexuality and Christianity*.

Christian's first book, *LOST: A Search for Meaning*, came out in 2006, followed by *MySpace to Sacred Space: God for a New Generation* (coauthored with his wife, Amy) in 2007. In 2012 Chalice Press published his memoir on faith, family, and parenting called *PregMANcy: A Dad, a Little Dude and a Due Date*. In August 2014 Jericho will release Piatt's first hardcover book, *postChristian: What's Left? Can We Fix It? Do We Care?*

Introduction

I was twelve years old when my parents divorced. For the next three years, my two younger brothers and I lived with our newly single father. As we watched him deal with the pain, frustration, shame, and uncertainty of a failed marriage, we saw a man deeply committed to his Christian faith. Our father ran to God, not away from him. That left an impression on each of us, shaping our views on both faith and fatherhood.

Talking about fathers and fatherhood can be tricky. As Christian Piatt noted in the foreword, "father" does not have a fixed meaning anymore. The word now encompasses birth fathers, foster fathers, stepfathers, fathers-in-law, grandfathers, uncles, male neighbors, aunts, even mothers, who all fulfill some portion of the "father" role in the lives of the young. At the same time, fatherlessness is reaching epidemic proportions in the United States. For those who do grow up with a father in the home, it is increasingly common for that father to be functionally absent due to the demands of his job. Worse yet are the scores of children whose lives might be better off if their father *was* absent, instead of heaping emotional, physical, and sexual abuse upon them.

For many people of the Abrahamic faiths, our understanding of God as Father is often shaped by our experiences with our own father(s). Sometimes we take the time to see how these two father concepts are intertwined, but often we do not. This book explores the intersection between faith and fatherhood, probing the resonance and dissonance created when men examine fatherhood in all its permutations, and how it is informed by and informs their faith.

This volume contains forty essays by forty men all under forty years old. They represent a wide variety of Christian faith perspectives:

Methodist, Presbyterian, Quaker, Mennonite, Pentecostal, Baptist, Church of God, United Church of Christ—and a whole host of different ethnicities: Korean, Mexican, Pacific Islander, Egyptian, Chinese, African American, and Caucasian. The contributors include ministers, professors, a real estate agent, an actor, nonprofit leaders, stay-at-home dads, and a call center representative, from locations as far apart as Honolulu, Hawaii and Paris, France, and from all points in between. Each one has a compelling story about faith and fatherhood.

Asher Gelzer-Govatos takes a hilarious look at masculinity and raising a toddler son and Shane Blackshear shares a touching letter to his unborn daughter. Chris Morris writes about having a child with a disability, while Andrew Marin tells us what it's like to not be able to have children at all. Drew Hart's essay on raising black sons in America will make you wonder if the Civil Rights movement ever happened and Bryan Blaise's story will make you glad it did. Tyler Johnson and D. Kyle Canty share what it is like to grow up as the child of a minister, while A. J. Swoboda and Jon Carroll share the challenges of parenting as a preacher. Your heart will be broken reading about how Guy Delcambre became a single father in one, unexpected moment, and it will be restored through Kurt Ro's story of grace and reconciliation with his father.

I should note that each of these essays speaks for itself. Some of the contributors here radically disagree with one another about what it means to be a Christian, though they all self-identify as such. Just because an author's essay appears in this volume does not mean that he endorses all of the others' views on faith or fatherhood in this book. And I think that is beautiful.

R. Anderson Campbell
Portland, Oregon, Fall 2013

The Burl of Greatest Price: Thoughts from a Not So Manly Father

by Asher Gelzer-Govatos

ASHER GELZER-GOVATOS is a cultural critic and writer who lives in Tulsa, Oklahoma with his wife and two children. He is the founder and editor of The Erstwhile Philistine, an online journal of faith and culture. By day he masquerades as a history teacher at a Tulsa charter high school. At any given point he is roughly 90 percent coffee.

Maybe it's the glasses. I tried wearing contacts for about a month once, but they made my eyes feel like someone had ripped them out, dipped them in lye, and then used them as decorative candles. So I wear glasses. And not small, discreet, investment banker glasses. Big, thick ones. Like Woody Allen had a love child with an 80's Dungeon Master.

Or maybe it's my physique, which can only be described as rugged when I'm lying on carpet. I somehow manage to embody the worst aspects of scrawniness while simultaneously being a bit on the *zaftig* side. I mean, I can open pickle jars okay, but that's about the extent of my physical prowess. My ability to throw a football downfield has not progressed since about the sixth grade. Once, under extreme duress, I did a pull up.

On third thought, it's definitely my utter lack of handyman credentials. Once I put a bookshelf together but somehow managed to put the back piece on backwards. It never got fixed. A fly on the wall as I put together my son's play kitchen probably thought he had stumbled onto a convention of sailors. All the pictures in our house hang at a slight angle, reminiscent of my Poindexter glasses as they sit on my uneven ears.

Whatever it is, whether these three elements—separate or combined—or an innumerable number of others (cries at movies that aren't *Rudy* but ARE *The Muppet Christmas Carol*—check; terrible at starting fires—check; does the cooking for the family—check) I cannot, by any standard measure, be considered a "manly" dad. I blame this in part on my upbringing. While other boys were tying Gordian knots and making hobo stew in Scouts, or being tricked into liking pain while playing Pop Warner football, I spent my time ensconced in books or practicing my beloved cello.

Not being a "manly" dad can be a bit hard. At least in certain (loud) sections of American Christianity today, you can hear repeated trumpet blasts about the "crisis of lost masculinity" that has infected the church. To hear tell, American Christian men are all pantywaists who spend their free time killing asteroids (or whatever it is you do in those gulldarned video games) while mooching off their parents. Twenty-something men need to reclaim their manhood, follow a shirtless lumberjack Jesus and sweep some unsuspecting, submissive Proverbs 31[1] woman off her feet, axe in one hand, bottle of scotch in the other. The role of the man, according to these voices, is threefold. First, be a rock your fainting wife can lean on. Second, raise up your children right, so the boys grow up to be MMA fighters and the girls marry astronauts. Third, smell continually of musk.

At the moment my concern over passing down these characteristics feels pretty remote. The only astronomical thing in my daughter's life at the moment is the amount of poop with which she fills her diapers. Even if I went through step by step, breaking down the complex parts

---

1. For the uninitiated, Proverbs 31 is the chapter of the Bible that talks about a wonderful wife who is industrious, provides for her family, and is praised for her hard work. In the mind of the many modern fundamentalist Christians, that translates to "a woman who stays at home, is very submissive, and makes wonderful baked goods for her children."

for her, I don't think she'd comprehend much of my varied rants on why she shouldn't date guys with ponytails, bass guitars, or names like Phoenix. My son likewise seems primarily concerned with running around the house at full speed, plowing into things. When he asks mommy to paint his nails too, he does not do it out of some subterranean desire to hop on the Goth bandwagon—he just sees something fun that mommy does and he wants in on the action. Still, I can't help but think of the future, and that gets me worried. The Jesuits used to say "Give me the child till he is seven, and I will give you the man." Five years away from that threatening deadline, and what do I have to show for my work so far?

On the plus side, my son has an obsession with balls that would make Sigmund Freud proud. He continually kicks one of his plethora of balls around the house, screaming with delight. Our backyard stands as a monument to the brave balls that have died in battle—basketballs tossed too hard, footballs with the stuffing kicked out of them. Extrapolating this fascination out twenty years or so, he should at least hold a dominant place in his rec league and church softball team, even if he falls short of his ultimate dream of being the token white guy on his high school basketball squad. These encouraging signs are balanced out by some dark clouds, however. In spite of best intentions, the written word still holds him in its thrall. He loves books—not quite as much as balls, but it's close. He will—of his own volition, not prompted by any outside force!—sit and consume book after book quietly and contentedly. That he cannot read does not bother him. There he sits, intent as some Egyptologist puzzling out a particularly difficult section of hieroglyphics, trying desperately to aid the baby bird as he quests to find his elusive mother.

Worse yet—and here is where I lie in the bed I have made—we bought him a play kitchen last Christmas, replete with pots, pans, and other reminders of his father's creeping domesticity. Often in the morning he will bring a pot to our bedroom replete with, gulp, eggs and a variety of condiments. To compound this terrifying state of affairs, he likes to help in the real kitchen. Every time he climbs up the step stool to help measure ingredients for pancakes, I see my dream of raising a well adjusted young linebacker go up in a puff of flour. His food proclivities extend well beyond the mere act of making it. At the table he expresses very little interest in the slabs of raw beef we routinely place in front of him, hoping to pique his interest in the animalistic urges of the true man. Instead he loves carrots—CARROTS!—and dairy. This would be alright if my goal were raising domesticated rabbits for future resale, but as part of an attempt at shaping a paterfamilias of the next generation? Clearly something has gone terribly awry.

And do not get me started on how much he loves his baby sister. How he dotes on her, kissing her frequently and with great tenderness. How he hugs her goodnight or enthusiastically includes her in his running tally of who's in our family (Mama, Dada, Bebe). How he will make goofy faces at her when she gets upset, or how he is the only one to make her really shake with laughter. It makes me sick to think of how nurturing he is. Sometimes I wake up with cold sweats in the middle of the night at the thought of my son winding up in the distinctly unmanly career track of a kindergarten art teacher. Or worse: What if he marries a high powered career woman and ends up as a stay-at-home dad? How can he radiate authority to his children if he forever scoots behind them cleaning their diapers?

When I start down these thought trails that quickly spin out of control, I like to stop for a moment and reflect on the gifts given to me by my own father. Now, my dad's a fair bit manlier than I am. He has a mustache that would make Tom Selleck cower in fear. He works out nearly every day and has stayed in great shape. But, on the whole, he's not what you would describe as a man's man. You would be much more likely to catch him reading an improving book than hunting muskrats with his bare hands. He never taught me to sharpen a blade, or start a fire, or bandage my own bloody stump after losing an arm in a bear attack. Despite these holes in my education, I can't help but admire the legacy he has left me. My father is one of the kindest, wisest, most encouraging people I know. Throughout my childhood he always encouraged me to follow my passions—whether an ill-fated flirtation with Little League or my more serious affair with the cello—pushing me to do my best while letting me know that, ultimately, I was doing these things because *I* wanted to. Starting in high school, he would write me encouraging little notes, now and again, anytime he saw me do something worth praising, no matter how small. Sometimes there was no specific trigger—he'd just write to say how much he loved me. He still sends me notes from time to time, to praise my skills as a father, a husband, a teacher, a son.

We talk often in the church about the love of a father, relating it to the love God has shown us. Usually those words contain more than a hint of sternness about them. A father loves his children, we assume, but he keeps them at bay, to toughen them up. And I do believe that sometimes God lets us experience the unpleasant consequences of our actions. But the Father's love that I have known has never been harsh or distant. It has first and foremost been *present*. It has been an encouraging love, dare I say a nurturing love. It has been concerned not with manliness but with servanthood. That reassures me. I know I'll make a lot of poor choices as a father. The period biopic of choice in our house will be *Amadeus*, not *Braveheart*. I'll probably encourage my son to try out for the Academic Team instead of the football squad. I hope with all my heart that I'll still kiss him goodnight for as long as humanly possible. But as long as I give him fleeting glimpses of the Father's love I have learned—and as long as I teach him to relish the taste of bacon—I think I'll have done more right than wrong.

Pulling Teeth
by Dan Stringer

DAN STRINGER is a pastor and social worker from Honolulu who grew up in five countries on three continents as the child of Presbyterian medical missionaries. He recently served Kailua Community Church as Associate Pastor of Adult Ministries and is currently pursuing a Master of Divinity from Fuller Theological Seminary. Dan is a graduate of Wheaton College (Bachelor of Arts) and the University of Hawaii (Master of Social Work) with seven years of experience in social services empowering low-income families and homeless veterans. He is married to Rebecca and blogs at danstringer.net.

My father wasn't always a jungle doctor.

By the time I entered kindergarten, he had grown a successful dental practice in downtown Honolulu, where patients appreciated his gentle touch and chair-side manner. My dad loved dentistry, but over a decade of fixing American teeth had failed to satisfy his desire to make a difference. His professional colleagues affirmed his skills and contributions, but Dad felt he wasn't taking full advantage of his gifts. He wanted more of a challenge.

An active church leader, he helped start a cluster of new churches meeting in suburban homes like ours, where friends appreciated his ability to explain spiritual concepts in simple language. A faithful husband and a playful father, he enjoyed living in Hawaii, but still wanted something more. As my dad understood it, his Christian faith demanded more.

The restlessness began in 1979, the year before I was born, when Dad discovered the value of his skills as an oral surgeon during a two-week mission trip to the Dominican Republic, sponsored by the Christian Medical and Dental Society. He could brighten many smiles in America, but overseas, he could save lives and train others to do the same. Dad was not content to pray for the global poor from a distance; he wanted to fix their teeth. Personally.

Following nearly a decade of prayerful discernment and discussion among trusted friends, my parents made a full-time commitment to international dentistry in 1987, signing on with the Presbyterian Church (USA) as mission coworkers to the Congo, then called Zaire. For the next twelve years, Dad lived his dream as an international missionary dentist. His young family of five would never be the same.

Before I turned seven, my suburban American childhood of the 80's was exchanged for the life of a third culture kid (TCK), a sociological term referring to children who accompany their parents into another society. Growing up in a "third" space that is neither your parents' passport culture nor the culture of the place in which you live, TCKs experience the feeling of being perpetually suspended between worlds, capable of surviving anywhere but fully belonging nowhere. From the ages of six to eighteen, I attended seven different schools in five countries (United States, Canada, Congo, Nepal, Philippines) on three continents. Even the most basic questions became difficult to answer. Where are you from? Where did you grow up? Where is home for you?

Not only a TCK, I was also *hapa*, a Hawaiian term for people of mixed blood, multiracial. My father, Ronald Bruce Stringer, was of British-German descent and grew up in Lafayette, California. My mother, Linda Sook Yee Wong, is a third-generation Chinese American and was raised in Honolulu. When they were married at Kalihi Union Church in 1977, both became the first in their respective families to marry interracially. Mom was supportive of her husband's adventurous humanitarianism, but to this day she readily admits we would never have left Hawaii had it not been for Dad's persistence.

All I knew was that our family was different. Though deprived of opportunities to put down lasting roots, my upbringing was richly diverse in experience. Thanks to my dad, I collected hockey cards in Quebec, swam in Congo's Lake Munkamba, played Little League baseball in Louisville, trekked the Himalayan foothills surrounding Kathmandu, and ate fried banana lumpia in Manila. Our family vacations included visits to England, Malaysia, Malawi, Singapore, Switzerland, Thailand, and Zimbabwe. I learned to identify flags from non-American places and hum the tunes of non-American national anthems.

More significantly, my upbringing taught me that Christianity did not begin in America, nor is American Christianity representative of the global Christian experience. My parents were evangelical Protestants, but we lived in a house rented from the Catholic Church in Congo. I later attended an international school in Kathmandu alongside Buddhist, Hindu, and Muslim classmates. I heard sermons in Tagalog and sang hymns in Tshiluba, growing to appreciate the privileges conferred by my U.S. passport while encountering a vast spectrum of reactions to my American identity, *hapa* or not. International Christianity was drastically unlike the Christianity I encountered in America. It was, quite simply, better.

In each new culture, my parents adopted portions of the local language, customs, and sensibilities. I watched as Dad cultivated relationships with colleagues from Canada, Britain, Australia, and Norway. He viewed his dental work as a natural expression of his faith, not merely an altruistic concern for the poor. Rather than swooping in as the foreign expert, my father understood how oppressed peoples could teach him more about faith, freedom, and God's nature than he could teach them about modern medicine, dental hygiene, and disease prevention. A true student of culture, he thrived at the kaleidoscopic intersection of diverse ethnic, economic and religious surroundings.

Most of my childhood friends were missionary kids, but not all their families considered my parents true missionaries. My parents seemed to challenge many of their peers' assumptions about the nature of mission work. After all, my father was not a pastor, bible translator, or evangelistic preacher. Instead, he performed oral surgeries, trained hygienists, resourced clinics, and promoted public health. Dad embodied his belief in Jesus by pulling teeth. His personal faith prompted him to take tangible action addressing poverty, disease and suffering on God's fragile, beloved planet. In doing so, he embraced an alternative way of being, joining God's mission in the renewal of all things.

Like any culture, TCK life is a paradox of flawed beauty. You can adapt to any environment without belonging to any one habitat. You find ways to fit in without ever fully blending in. Few people can identify with your story, which can make things lonely, or at least complicated. Transitions to and from your passport country are stressful, whether temporary or permanent. Relationships end abruptly. Changing schools, friends, languages, cultures, climates, countries, and continents takes a toll, especially on teenagers.

With its cataclysmic closure of familiar patterns, places, and relationships, high school graduation can feel like TCK Armageddon, although returning to America midway through high school might be even worse. There's no easy way to conclude a third-culture childhood. By following his dream, Dad had incurably complicated my upbringing, but I wouldn't trade those years for anything. I only wish he could have kept dreaming.

After I completed high school in the Philippines in 1999, my parents and two younger sisters returned to Hawaii while I attended Wheaton College outside Chicago. Amid our family's return to the American suburbs, a different kind of transition was also underway. Dad was diagnosed with CADASIL, a rare neurological disorder for which there is no treatment. His health declined dramatically. Each time I returned home, Dad was visibly worse. Over a period seven years, he slowly lost his ability to walk, stand, speak, write, and take care of himself. Hardest of all for Dad, he could no longer work with his hands. Dentistry was out.

When I got married in 2003, Dad attended in a wheelchair. The following year, my wife Rebecca and I moved from Chicago to help

Mom take care of him. As a TCK, I had relocated to and from Hawaii numerous times, but this transition was unquestionably the hardest yet. Rebecca and I exchanged our newlywed optimism in the big city for moving in with my parents, staying in my childhood bedroom, and caring for Dad, who was no longer himself. In an ironic reversal of roles, I learned to do everything for the man who once fed, bathed, and clothed me. At twenty-four I became like a parent to my fifty-five-year-old father, my once-invincible hero who could conquer anything. I had to brush his teeth.

Dad could no longer speak, but he wasn't done teaching me. I learned that God doesn't always make sense, that it's permissible, even beneficial, to express anger with him sometimes. Believing that God could work a miracle, we took Dad to receive healing prayers from a diverse range of individuals and churches. It seemed like everyone we knew was praying for Dad. I even drove him to a revival meeting featuring controversial televangelist Benny Hinn, but neither Dad nor I could stomach Hinn's repeated appeals for money. We left early and went for coffee instead.

The final lesson Dad taught me was to accept my wounds and sorrows. He wept openly and often. He wrote in his journal until his fingers stopped cooperating. A stack of Henri Nouwen books was never far from reach. Amid deep depression, frustration, anger, and disability, Dad found opportunities to laugh at himself, or anyone else that amused him. An incredible life condensed into fifty-six years, he died peacefully on October 11, 2005, two days after my twenty-fifth birthday. The funeral was standing room only. In homage to Nouwen, Dad's cemetery marker reads, "Wounded healer, now restored."

Less than two years after Dad's passing, I became a father. Theodore was born in 2007, followed by Vincent in 2009, bringing the same joy that once prompted my dad to write silly bicycle songs about me. The best part of early fatherhood is watching your children sleep, preferably both of them at the same time. God must love it when his children sleep.

Though my dad wasn't around anymore, I found myself instinctively repeating his parenting mannerisms and daydreaming about vocational aspirations. I didn't want to fix teeth in Himalayan villages, but I experienced a familiar restlessness and hunger to make a difference, perhaps as a social worker, church planter, or public advocate for Hawaii's most vulnerable. Pursing a graduate degree in social work kept me busy, but I felt there had to be something more on the horizon.

Then along came another transition, one I never expected.

Just before Vincent's first birthday, Rebecca felt a lump in his abdomen. After several weeks of tests and scans, our youngest son was diagnosed with an extrarenal rhabdoid tumor, Stage Four liver cancer from out of nowhere. The first fifteen weeks of aggressive chemotherapy helped shrink it, but the tumor grew back, spreading to Vincent's right lung. Believing that God could work a miracle, we took him to receive healing prayers from anyone who wanted to try. It seemed like everyone we knew was praying for Vincent. We even flew to Bethel Church in California where we had heard reports of miraculous healings. Everything medically possible was attempted, but my son wasn't healed.

The hardest part about being a father is watching your children suffer. I prayed my heart out, cried my eyes out, and screamed my anger at God, just like Dad taught me. I wrote in my journal, read Nouwen and drank coffee, desperately searching for comfort along my father's path. Only now *I* was the powerless father, barely thirty, wrestling again in the shadows of wounded sorrow. Vincent's name means *victorious*, but after six agonizing months battling cancer, it was time for another goodbye.

I will never forget driving Vincent home for the last time. We had shuttled him to and from the hospital countless times, but this was unmistakably the hardest transition of my life. On the evening of November 20, 2010, at the age of eighteen months, Vincent Wing Seun Stringer died peacefully in our bedroom. His funeral was standing room only. Buried next to my father, Vincent's cemetery marker reads: "Victorious in Jesus' arms."

Losing my dad and my son within five years of each other has left me wary of easy answers about death. When it feels like all I have left are memories and emotions, I remember Dad's authentic approach to the complexities of faith and suffering. My understanding of God is inseparable from Dad's example and influence as a suffering father. My understanding of fatherhood is inextricable from my experience of losing Vincent. When people ask me how many kids I have, I'm not sure how to respond. Should I say "three" to include Vincent or "two" to keep it simple? Once again, life's basic questions have proved the most difficult to answer for this TCK.

What kind of father is God? What are his dreams? What places captivate his imagination? Where does he work best? If God is anything like my dad, he's a wounded healer, familiar with sorrow and grieved by suffering. He is quietly influential, skilled at his craft, diligently working up close with gentle hands to renew his world. He speaks many languages, but does not carry an American passport. He's a long-term missionary, but not the kind people expect. If God is anything like me, he has watched his son suffer in horrible victory.

And just like my dad and me, God absolutely loves his children.

Even when they don't brush their teeth.

More Than You Know

by Drew Clyde

DREW is a pastor of HEADWAY, a new church in Loudoun County, Virginia. HEADWAY is simply a bunch of folks seeking to know and follow Jesus together. Before starting HEADWAY, Drew served two separate times as a director at Church of the Redeemer in Gaithersburg, Maryland. His first stint there was from 1998-2003 as the director of youth and young adult ministries. His most recent time there was from 2011-2013 as the director of outreach and small groups. The seven years between his two seasons at Church of the Redeemer were spent with Prison Fellowship, a national non-profit that serves prisoners and their families, as the director of Angel Tree Mentoring, helping churches develop mentoring programs for the children of prisoners in their community. His last four years at Prison Fellowship he was the national director of the Next Generation Initiative, leading the effort to engage 15—35 year olds in remembering and serving prisoners and their families.

Drew has a BBA from James Madison University and got about half-way through a masters in practical theology at Regent University. He has been married to his wife Dawn for fifteen years and they have five children: daughters Maddie, Ryan, and Devon, and sons Roba and Sean. They live in Leesburg, Virginia. Drew is a huge Washington Nationals and Redskins fan. He likes sports talk radio, the smell of new tennis balls, and Frosted Mini-Wheats.

I think I was made to have two children. We have five. It's tough to just roll with the chaos. I prefer things to be under control and quiet, but with five kids that's just not the case. Laughing, yelling, whining, arguing, singing, or crying is constant. "No running in the house!" is consistently ringing in my ears and coming out of my mouth. Five kids also doesn't allow for much "me" time or money. Food, clothes, and shelter almost put us in the red each month. Glasses and braces on all our children's faces aren't going to help remedy that. Don't even mention college tuitions and weddings.

It's really not that bad, though. In fact, it's very good. Having five kids is hard work and takes sacrifice, but it's worth it. There are those rare moments where I wonder what we were thinking, but we love our life and wouldn't change it for anything. My wife Dawn and I have three daughters: Maddie is twelve years old, Ryan is ten, and Devon is eight. Our two sons, Roba and Sean, are six and four years old. Four of our children were born into our family and Roba we adopted from Ethiopia in March of 2012 when he was four years old.

Our adoption story started long before I ever considered adoption. About seven years ago, I started saying that I was a "follower of Jesus" rather than calling myself a "Christian." At the same time, I started quietly asking myself the follow-up question, "Am I really?" I realized that "Christian" is a noun that everyone defines differently. But I was saying I "follow" Jesus, a verb, which is a whole different ballgame. I have to do what Jesus does and go where he goes for this to be true. My actions and attitude should reflect his.

As I paid closer attention to Jesus' life, I noticed his character and behavior. It got harder to say I was a "follower of Jesus" because now I felt like I was lying. I was forced to ask the hard question, "Do I really want to follow Jesus?" Being a "Christian" is kind of easy and has lots of perks, but following Jesus is hard. It's uncomfortable, it's dangerous, it's inconvenient. Jesus asks me to give up things I want to keep and tells me to do things I can't do. He requires full surrender and at times leads me into suffering and pain.

As I said above, I like things to be under control, and more specifically, under *my* control. I wanted to follow Jesus, but found myself struggling to put my money where my mouth was. I finally faced the reality that it's my actions that make the difference. It's in the "doing" that lives are changed, including my own.

I decided to start following Jesus, but quickly learned that it isn't a onetime decision. It's a moment by moment decision. At any moment, I can decide to pass Jesus and take the lead, fall behind, or veer off. There were times when I said "Jesus, that's too much to ask," but I continued to learn that everything he asks is good and necessary to experience the life of purpose and peace that he promises.

It also didn't take long for me to realize that I can't be like Jesus. I tried and failed. It became clear that Jesus is the only one who can live his life. However, if I can stop trying to act *like* Jesus and instead do what I've only recently come to understand, that is, let Jesus live his life through me, then I believe I will begin to *reflect* him with my attitudes and actions.

I also noticed in scripture that Jesus kept mentioning specific groups of people that he wanted his followers to help. He told them to remember prisoners, feed the hungry, look after widows, help strangers, visit the sick, and give to the poor. I also found him particularly concerned for children who don't have a family to care for them and it seemed that his ongoing strategy to help these people was through the actions of his followers.

Jesus was simply asking his followers to do what I learned to do when I was two years old: to *share*. When I have more and someone else doesn't have much, he asks me to love them by sharing. It's simple, but not easy. So, I started taking inventory of all the extra I had that others might need. I found some time, energy, insight, skills, money, and stuff in my possession. I also found that we have a family that we could share with a child who doesn't have one. We already had four children, but the reality was that we could make room in our hearts, house, and budget for another.

It wasn't long before God confirmed in our hearts that he wanted us to adopt a child, and as we engaged the long process of adoption, we found God teaching us new things along the way. It all came together for me in a moment on the runway, preparing for takeoff to Ethiopia to finally bring Roba home. Here is a portion of the blog post I wrote later that night about that moment on the plane.

Our plane had just pulled away from the gate when I grabbed the book I was going to start reading, *The Circle Maker* by Mark Batterson. The first two pages share the story of a guy named Honi who was a legend for how he prayed boldly for rain during a drought in Israel and God answered his prayer. The last paragraph of that story says "The prayer that saved a generation was deemed one of the most significant prayers in the history of Israel. The circle he drew in the sand became a sacred symbol. And the legend of Honi the circle maker stands forever as a testament to the power of a single prayer to change the course of history."

As we prepared for takeoff, I sat there amazed at how this brief story connected with our lives at that moment. We were getting ready to fly to the other side of the world to bring our adopted son home. We have been praying for "rain" just like this legendary guy. We've been praying for our son Roba, which means "rain" in his native language of Oromo. We have been praying for two years for God to provide this little boy for us and He has answered our prayers. He gave us Rain . . . He gave us Roba. As we raced down the runway it was one of those moments where you feel like God is kinda speaking to you . . . like he orchestrated that moment to have me read those two pages right when we were heading off to the conclusion of the answer to the prayer we've been sending his way for so long. It reminded me that God answers prayer. He answered this prayer. And this prayer may not change the course of history for a nation like Honi's, but this one will change the course of history for a young boy named Roba. And we're going to remember this. We're going to remember that God loves us, he loves Roba, and he responds to those who trust completely in him. (http://theclydefam. com/2012/03/13/the-legend-of-honi/)

Now I can be a pretty skeptical guy. I could have come up with some good explanations for all that had happened in this process, but instead I chose to believe that God orchestrated each and every step. He was working. He provided Roba for us and us for Roba. I used to not want to bother God with my issues. But now I get that he wants to be bothered. Just as I want my children to share with me so I can help them, God also wants to hear from us and finds joy in coming through for us. So, we are going to keep asking God for help because we're going to need every bit of patience, wisdom, and love that God has to offer over the next several years of our lives. And we're confident he'll come through again.

Roba is amazing and has fit "like a glove" in our family, as I like to say (with a voice like Ace Ventura). However, I find myself wanting for Roba what I want for all my children: to fully trust me. I see doubt in his eyes and in his behavior at times. I wish I could convince him that he is not under the authority of the state or orphanage any more. For him to know without a shadow of a doubt that he's in our family and doesn't have to wonder where he'll be next year. For him to know that we love him and he doesn't have to be afraid.

His feelings make sense, though, because I deal with the same issues. God is my father and all he wants is for me to trust him. I have every reason to, but I usually don't. He just wants me to believe him. To know that he'll always be there. I can imagine it grieves him when I continue to believe what is no longer true. All he wants is for me to grasp how deep and wide his perfect love is for me so I can be free.

I've come to believe that good and consistent communication leads to real relationship. And relationship breeds trust. That trust then becomes a foundation for that relationship to grow. Yet, I've found communicating with a five-year-old to be challenging, especially one that is still learning the language and culture. My children can't fully understand some things because their minds can't yet grasp them, or they may get them initially, but then forget.

In the same way, God is trying to communicate with us, on our level, in our language. He wants us to know him, to get the message that he loves us. But we rarely get it, or we often forget it. I can imagine His loving frustration as we often miss the point. He wants the truth to sink into our hearts to where we are no longer afraid. To where we stop allowing ourselves to be controlled by things that no longer have power over us.

It's hard knowing that I love Roba more than he knows. My flawed ability to communicate, along with his own limitations, compromises the message. I wish I could just open up his chest and place that understanding right in his heart so he would have no doubt. But unless I'm that crazy bald voodoo guy from *The Temple of Doom*, that's just not happening. The reality is that Roba and I have to hang out together. We need to spend time listening, talking, and trying to understand each other for his trust in me to grow.

It blows me away that God created humans imperfect and with the freedom to choose. He created a scenario that he knew would be deeply frustrating. Our humanity limits his communication, yet he doesn't give up on us. He struggles to express his love in one way or another until we finally get it.

So I've decided to keep hanging out with Jesus because he keeps showing up to hang out with me. When we get together he lets me know more about him and his perspective on life. He reminds me of who I am and who he wants me to become. Our relationship grows and I trust him more.

Roba's birth father left when he was ten months old. By God's grace I plan to be a father that Roba knows and trusts. So I'm also going to keep communicating my love to him with my actions and words, hoping it sinks in deeper each time until one day he fully gets it. The reality is that I'm flawed, too, and I will let him down in some ways. But my hope is for him to trust me so I can point him to his perfect Father who loves him even more than I do and will *never* let him down.

Choosing My Religion

by R. Anderson Campbell

R. ANDERSON CAMPBELL is a professor, writer, brewer, and monastic wannabe. He lives near Portland, Oregon with his wife, April, and their two daughters, Sydney and Rylee. He can be found blogging at http://www.thecrookedmouth.com or tweeting at @andycampbell

I think I might be failing as a good, Christian father. I've identified as a Christian for nearly as long as I can remember. I grew up in Georgia, "Bible belt" territory. Our household rhythms revolved around faith in God. We prayed at mealtimes and before bed. We were heavily involved in our Southern Baptist church, in which my father served as a deacon. We attended every Sunday, sometimes twice, and every Wednesday evening.

When I was seven years old, I declared to my mother that I wanted to be a Christian and be baptized. In my particular Baptist tradition of Christianity, one is not considered a Christian until he or she has made a verbal "profession of faith." I remember kneeling at my parents' bedside and praying a prayer that went something like this: *Dear God, I confess that I am a sinner. I believe that Jesus died on the cross for my sins and rose from the dead so that I could have my sins forgiven and go to heaven. Please forgive my sins. Please come to live in my heart,*

Jesus. I accept you as my personal Lord and Savior. Amen. After that prayer, my mother hugged me and we told my dad about it when he got home from work.

I was baptized within a few weeks. I waded into the warm water of the baptismal pool, outfitted in a white baptismal robe that was a bit too big for my scrawny frame. The water came up to my chin, so I stepped up onto the milk crate that was submerged in the pool so that those seated in the sanctuary could see me better. The pastor asked if I'd accepted Jesus Christ as my personal lord and savior. I told him I had. He then placed one arm on my back and raised the other in the air, as if about to be sworn in by a judge, and said, "Then I baptize you, my brother, Andy, in the name of the Father, and of the Son, and of the Holy Ghost. Buried with Christ in baptism, raised to walk in newness of life." The hand he'd held aloft he brought to my chest, placed it on my crossed arms, and dipped me backwards into the water. The whole routine is symbolic of the death, burial, and resurrection of Jesus Christ. When I entered into the baptismal pool, I did so as a sinner, "dead" in my sins. When I was dipped backwards into the water, I was symbolically buried, like Jesus was buried after his crucifixion. When I was raised out of the water, I was "resurrected" to a new life, my sins symbolically washed away by the water.

I'd been instructed to hold my nose, bend my knees, and let the pastor bring me back up from under the water. The whole ordeal would take less than fifteen seconds. All that coaching flew out the window as soon as the water rushed over my face. I'd forgotten to pinch my nose and water poured into my sinuses. I freaked out, thinking I was drowning. My legs locked straight, my feet kicked out of the water, and my hands flailed around, looking for something to grab onto. Then, just as quickly as it started, it was over. I was out of the water, sputtering a bit and trying to get my nose clear. That was my official entry into the faith.

In the years that followed, my brothers and I participated in Sunday School, Royal Ambassadors for Christ (a kind of Christian scouting group), midweek Bible study groups, children's choir, and summer vacation Bible school day camps. When I was older, I was very active in our church's youth group. Every summer I went to a Christian youth camp in Panama City, Florida, and came back with a renewed vigor for my faith and airbrushed t-shirts containing Bible references. I had my doubts and questions about my childhood faith. Was the Bible really "inerrant" and meant to be interpreted literally at all times? Did God really create the world in seven days? How does one measure a day before the earth was created? Would people really burn in hell if they'd never heard about Jesus? How was that their fault? Is sex before marriage really a sin? Where is that in the Bible? While we're on that subject, what counts as "sex" anyway? Yet despite the questions and the lack of satisfying answers I received, I don't ever recall a time in my life where I didn't self-identify as a Christian.

Now, I have children of my own. For the entirety of both of my daughters' lives, I've been involved in some sort of Christian ministry job. My oldest daughter, Sydney, was born during my final year of seminary. Since then, I've been a church planter, a college minister, a staff pastor at a megachurch, and a seminary professor. How could my faith *not* rub off on them? When Sydney was eight, I recalled my baptism and the prayer I'd prayed as a child. It occurred to me that I'd never really talked to Sydney about what *she* believes about God and Jesus. Maybe it was time to have that conversation.

I found Sydney reading a book, tucked into the top bunk of the bed she shared with her younger sister.

"Sydney, I have a question for you," I began.

"Sure, what is it, Daddy?" she said.

"Do you believe in God?" I asked.

"Oh, yes," she said. "I believe in God. I pray to him sometimes, especially when I'm nervous or anxious."

"What about Jesus? What do you think about him?"

"He's God's son. He died on a cross and was resurrected to make things right with God again," she said. Dang. This kid is smart; smarter than I was at her age. Feeling pretty confident about where this conversation was headed, I pressed on.

"So, would you say that you're a Christian like Mommy and Daddy? A follower of Jesus? Because if you do, maybe you want to get baptized. I got baptized when I was about your age," I said.

She paused. She looked up from the book she'd been paging through as we talked, met my eyes, then looked at the ceiling, as if considering her response. "No. Not yet. That's a big decision and I'm not sure I'm ready for that."

I wasn't quite sure what to say. I felt a bit deflated. I heard myself reply, "You're right, honey. That is a big decision, one that only you can make. Maybe someday you will." I kissed her forehead and tucked her in. As I turned out the light and shut the bedroom door behind me I wondered, *Am I doing something wrong as a father? Aren't I supposed to be passing my faith along to my kids?* Wary of being too heavy-handed with my beliefs around my kids and fearful of driving them away from Christianity, perhaps I'd overcorrected and not let them see my faith enough.

Sydney is one of those kids who is a deep thinker. She is sometimes maddeningly slow to make a decision, but once her mind is made up on something, she won't be swayed. Somehow, even at her young age, she understood the gravity of the question I'd asked her, and she wasn't ready to weigh in one way or another quite yet.

I sat down on the couch next to my wife, April, and recounted the conversation I'd just had with Sydney. She listened and nodded in all the appropriate places. When I was finished she said, "Dude, you need to chill out. Give her some space and some time. If, and when, she decides to be a follower of Jesus, she'll do it in her own way and on her own time. And when she does, she won't budge on it."

I knew she was right.

A few weeks later, I was tucking the girls in for bed again and noticed that the book Sydney was reading was a lot bigger than usual. She'd dragged a Bible up into her bed. It wasn't a kids' picture Bible, either. It was a hardback, fully annotated Bible for students. She sat there in her bed, the book taking up her entire lap, carefully reading the tiny text.

"Hey sweet pea. Whatcha reading?" I asked.

"Some stories out of the Bible," she said.

"Yeah? Anything good?" I asked.

"Esther," she said.

Esther? Really? My eight-year-old daughter was reading the Old Testament book of Esther? What kid does that? What adult does that?

The book of Esther is an interesting one. For centuries, a debate has raged about whether or not the book of Esther should be included in the Jewish scriptures or in the Christian Bible. The controversy centers on the fact that God isn't explicitly mentioned anywhere in the book. Not one place. But God is working in the background of the story the whole time.

The book is follows the story of a young woman named Esther and her appointment as the Queen of Persia. Unbeknownst to the king, Esther is a Jew. She was raised by her parents' cousin Mordecai, a Jew from the diaspora created when the Babylonian King Nebuchadnezzar took the Jews captive.

At the same time he chose Esther for his wife, King Xerxes gave a Persian named Haman a big title and a lot of wealth. Haman let all this power and influence go to his head. He wanted to be worshipped like a demigod wherever he went. One day he passed by Mordecai, who refused to bow in his presence. This really pissed off Haman. So he went to King Xerxes to have Mordecai and all the Jews killed. King Xerxes granted Haman his request. The thing is, the good king had no idea that his beloved Queen Esther was a Jew.

Mordecai told Esther the whole sordid tale and how, if she didn't change the King's mind, she would die along with all the rest of the Jews in Persia. Mordecai said to her, "Who knows but that you have come to your royal position for such a time as this?"[1]

In the end, Esther ended up persuading the King not to carry out Haman's genocide. Though never mentioned by name, it is evident that the God of the Jews was very much present in the story of Esther,

---

1. Esther 4:14, New International Version.

knitting circumstances together that led to the protection of the Jews, not their demise.

In my own childhood conversion, God was very much present in the foreground. I expected a similar sort of story to unfold in Sydney's life. When I didn't see that happening, I panicked. But God *is* there in her life. I see evidence of it all the time. When our neighbor died of cancer this year, it was Sydney who asked if we could light a candle and pray for her and her husband. She is quick to forgive others, even when they are in the wrong. Whenever she is in a group of her peers, she seeks out those on the fringes and invites them into whatever activity she's involved in.

Sydney may never have the kind of come-to-Jesus conversion that I had as a kid. She might be one of those people who just grow up believing in God and Jesus without ever being able to point to a specific moment of decision. But that doesn't mean that I've failed as a father or that God isn't present in her life. It just means that God is working in the background instead of the foreground. The best thing I can do is chill out and trust God with her faith.

Fatherhood: Faith and Vulnerability
by Drew G. I. Hart

DREW HART has been married to his wife, Renee, since 2008, he is a father to two sons, Micah (named after the Biblical prophet) and Dietrich (named after the Christian theologian Dietrich Bonhoeffer). The family lives in the East Germantown/Ogontz section of Philadelphia. As an African American with a multiethnic family, Drew is very conscious of racism and injustice, continually calling the Church back to its mission of reconciliation, to joining in solidarity with those on the margins, and to doing justice for oppressed people. This all comes from his commitment and witness to Jesus and his Kingdom.

Drew graduated from Messiah College with a degree in biblical studies and then joined the pastoral team of Harrisburg Brethren in Christ Church (from 2005 to 2008). This church is an urban, multiracial, and Anabaptist Christian community. Drew moved back to Philadelphia in 2008 and enrolled in Biblical Theological Seminary's master of divinity program. He also joined the pastoral team of his home church, Montco Bible Fellowship, while continuing his studies. He currently is a PhD student in theology and ethics at Lutheran Theological Seminary at Philadelphia, studying the intersection of African American theology and Anabaptism. Online you can regularly find him blogging and tweeting. Most importantly though, he loves God and believes that Jesus is a game changer, and is betting his life on it.

I can still remember the feeling I had after my first son was born and our growing family was leaving the hospital all together for the first time. The short drive back to our home was the most paranoid five minutes of my life. I was pulling out of the Einstein Hospital parking lot and onto Broad Street, which is the main north/south traffic artery through Philadelphia. As I cautiously drove, wanting to protect my special cargo in the vehicle, it seemed at that moment as though everyone else was driving especially hazardously. I could sense every car around me, like I was Spiderman with a sort of spider-sense that had me jumpy at the slightest of movements by the cars in front, behind, and beside me on the road. I think it was at this moment in my life, rather than when my son was actually being born, that I realized the deep responsibility I had just taken on. I had become a *Father*.

Now my wife and I have two children, both of them boys, which has been a tremendous experience, despite the normal challenges that are expected for any new parents. However, that isn't to say that I do not have concerns about my role as a father, especially as my boys get older. The two greatest and most constant concerns in my own life have, unsurprisingly, been on my mind as I think about raising my two sons. The first is the conviction that I have to disciple my boys in the way of Jesus, with an authentic faith that walks humbly before God and alongside those on the margins of society. And second, as an African American father in a multiethnic family, I want to teach my boys about their enslaved ancestors and America's greatest and ongoing sin of racial oppression. If I can accomplish those two things I will consider my parenting a success.

I have discipled and worked with adolescents in the Church, in the neighborhoods I have lived in, and for an urban afterschool program. What I have observed over the past decade is the constant temptation many Christian parents are seduced by: to make their kids and families idols and the end goal of their Christian faith, while losing sight of simple Christian practices like discipleship and servanthood. The enticement of providing one's own child with the best of everything that America has to offer (food, clothes, housing, education, vacations, etc.) and the intoxication of making sure our own kids don't miss out on experiencing a typical American childhood (sports, clubs, dances, getting a job, etc.) are very real and constant challenges that we all face. To be clear, I am not suggesting that any of those things are evil, but that they are nonessentials in regard to a life of faithfulness to Christ.

One of the gifts of my college experience was studying under a biblical studies faculty that helped me read scripture faithfully. Within that came the need to take the teachings of Jesus seriously, which I found to be a missing characteristic among many American Christian interpretations of scripture. The expectation that we are to take Jesus at his word without domesticating it to "work" within American sensibilities became an important approach to understanding Jesus in my own life and returning Christ to the center of my faith. This reoriented what I understood Christianity to be. More than merely a onetime confession or prayer that defined your status with God, I believed that to be a child of God demanded that we follow Jesus in our lives and walk as he walked (1 John 2:6). Discipleship meant understanding who Jesus is, as depicted in scripture rather than our own American projections of him, and then committing to following him into the world as we are conformed after his image by the Spirit of God. This means that Jesus' life and character are the standard that God desires to pattern his people after in the world, so that they reflect God's own heart, concern, and perspective in society, especially in relation to his love for people who are poor, marginalized, or oppressed. Fatherhood and discipleship, then, ought to have the same basic goal; I am called to raise my children in an awareness of Jesus' lordship over our family's life, I am to imitate Christ in my own life as a model for my children to follow. Our lives, as a family, collectively should be visibly distinct glimpses into the heart of God. God's people are called to be generous, forgiving, truth-telling, enemy-loving, servants of God who care for our neighbors and confront injustice. However, as I mentioned earlier, this is not what it commonly means to be Christian in America, and so it is easy to get disoriented with the allure of the American way of life.

This tension in my own soul has had me rededicating my kids to God over and over again. While America would love to have my kids (and yours, too, if you are a parent), that is not what I want to be discipling my kids into. My wife and I are trying to raise our kids into a family where Jesus is at the center and where we don't live for ourselves. However, our kids are still very young, and I know there are endless alluring traps awaiting us from now until my children become adults. Until they are old enough to become primarily responsible for their own commitments and values, *I pray for the courage* to raise my children in light of the reality of Christ rather than in the fleeting delusions of American values and materialism.

Right now, our country locks up more African American young men than it sends to college. It seems like every week there is a new story coming out about profiling, police brutality, statistics pointing to systemic racial discrimination, underperforming or closing schools in our city, gun violence, and occasionally even overt hatred for people of African descent. Our country, locked in historical amnesia, refuses to speak truthfully about the origins of these issues and the ongoing legacy of race, which is used as a tool to criminalize black and brown people, or to be apathetic to the unjust systems that distribute resources and educate some in our country while neglecting others.

As I grew up, I slowly had to come to terms with the ongoing racism that continued to plague our society. From very early on I was acutely aware that in my area, if you were black you were most likely poor and urban, but if you were white you were very likely to live in the suburbs, have a big yard, and in comparison were much better off financially. Of course, I knew very little social history in America, so my interpretation of it all most likely was unsophisticated and bloated with misunderstandings. Nonetheless, race was an unavoidable reality that acted as a marker that defined life expectations, identity, relationships, and one's overall place in society. When I was fifteen, my family moved out of our diverse but primarily African American neighborhood and into a predominately white suburban community that was thirty minutes outside of Philly. During my three years attending that suburban school I became very aware of the stereotypes that many kids had of black people. However, I also was the beneficiary of that well-resourced school. Throughout that time my church, comprised mostly of African Americans, became an important community and network for me. They encouraged me, believed in my potential, and affirmed the various God-given gifts they saw in me, like leadership and teaching. And so, when it came time to pick colleges, I confidently followed my emerging sense of being called to ministry by choosing an in-state Christian college. Nothing prepared me for the rude awakening I would have to come to grips with in my young adult life while there.

Unfortunately, my experience at the Christian college was filled with more racial tension than my three years at the suburban public high school. Even though I was there as a biblical studies major, many people interacted with me (or better yet, didn't interact with me) as though I was dangerous, suspicious, or a threat. In general, it seemed like people were very friendly toward one another, but I continually had to prove my friendliness before many would put down their guard around me. While there, I heard some of the most discouraging sentiments directed toward several black students on campus. I left four years later, with my eyes wide open to how people could simultaneously insist they were colorblind and not racist while clearly still having very negative racial instincts that made them look at most black people with a gaze of suspicion.

At the same time, my older brother, while hanging out on a stoop, was randomly grabbed off the street by police who were looking for a suspect that supposedly fit his description. The description he fit was that he was "a black male with blue jeans and a black t-shirt." There was no height description or any other characteristic that offered anything more specific. They also claimed at the time that he had a blood stain on his shirt. After several weeks in county jail before any trial, they eventually dropped all charges when he was finally put in a lineup and cleared. Also, the blood stain turned out to be a food stain when it went through the lab. The truth is that this happens to hundreds of black men everyday in our country and often turns out much worse. But when it touched my own family, it made me especially aware of how vulnerable I was in America, and how I could just as easily "fit a description" and be grabbed and locked up in our society without apology. I've had countless experiences that have shaped my understanding of how race works in America, but

I think what happened to my brother helped me think about racism as a much more active system of discrimination that targeted young black men and made them very vulnerable.

America is a hostile place for me to raise my boys. However, I intend to always remind them of their roots, that they are descendants of enslaved Africans and that those who came before us found Jesus in the midst of slavery and it sustained them. I want them to know about the faith of the African American community that believed Jesus was on the side of the slaves, despite what the slaveholders told them. I want them to learn about how African Americans survived slavery, Jim Crow segregation, the KKK and the White Citizens Council, and the terror of lynching through most of the twentieth century. And I want them to see that Jesus, who also was an oppressed and vulnerable minority living under Roman imperial rule, understands what it is like to be treated wrongly. I believe that this reminder of where we have come from and the God that brought us to where we are now, is the same God that will keep them as they face the challenges of simply being and existing in America. But I can't afford to not let them know explicitly that some people will see them and will immediately, yet unconsciously, interpret their bodies as dangerous or criminal.

If my sons grow up with authentic faith, taking Jesus seriously in their lives; and if they allow their unique African American heritage to provide themselves a lens through which they explore the world as people of God, then I will consider myself as having done my job as a father. But my kids are still very young, and I will need profound courage and deep wisdom from God to do my part in discipling and reorienting my children in Christ and their stories. As I see it, this is my task as a Christian father.

Finding The Father

by Sharad Yadav

Sharad was born to Indian immigrants in Nampa, Idaho. After his conversion in college he pastored in Idaho for fifteen years and is now serving with a church in Portland, Oregon.

Even having heard about the "terrible twos" I sensed that more might be going on in the mind of our youngest son when he started waking us up in the morning by flinging his empty (but surprisingly heavy) Playtex cup at our heads while screaming, repeatedly and hysterically: "MILK!" For Raj, sudden outbursts of intense and unprovoked anger, reminiscent of Joe Pesci in the movie *Goodfellas*, grew at the same rate as his speech and mobility. This was very different than what we had experienced with his siblings; his older sister is as docile as they come and his oldest brother is, if anything, a little *too* good-natured. I'm of Indian descent; we freed a nation with our lack of aggression. But with Raj, conflict seemed to attend practically every interaction; shoes that resisted tying, a gentle admonition reminding him to share, momentary postponement of food or entertainment, minor frustrations of every kind effortlessly escalated into raging tantrums. He frequently responded to family members with unwarranted invective for minor offenses. These encounters seemed to be the norm, punctuated by regular but brief revelations of thoughtfulness, compassion, and charm, reminding us that there was someone we wanted to know buried under all that mystifying anger.

Desperate to bring that person out, we increased disciplinary consistency and assumed that if the heat of our love was sufficient, his heart would melt. We prayed for God's intervention and forgiveness for whatever it was we were doing wrong. Nothing changed. We waited for him to outgrow it. He didn't. And as we continued to fail, the effect of it on me was unnerving. My desire for connection waned. As sickening as it was to admit to myself, my hunger to know and be known by my son began to wither behind this impregnable wall we struggled to understand. With some of his fits he would sometimes scream, "You hate me!"—and I would be crushed under the weight of guilt which came from imagining that someday he might be right.

The failure to connect with my son drew on some pain that went deeper than the immediate circumstances. Growing up as the children of immigrants had been a study in alienation, particularly with my own father. Living on the border of two cultures, trying to bridge the gap created by different languages, different social expectations, and different values complicated an already complex relationship. My father moved to the United States directly out of a PhD program in India, having known his wife only a few weeks in a hastily arranged marriage (in order to avoid the dangers presented by marrying an American). Adjusting to life in diversity-free, rural, small-town American contexts (first in Larned, Kansas, where my older sister was born; then in Nampa, Idaho, where my brother and I were born and we were all raised) proved to be a stress for my father that was magnified to unmanageable proportions by the constant crises he faced in the mental health profession. And all that with a wife he hardly knew, in a foreign culture with virtually no support system.

It wasn't so much his response to that stress that estranged us from one another (a response mostly characterized by quiet despair, closet alcoholism, emotional distance, and periodic bouts of verbal abuse). It was the utter inability to understand one another and his seeming indifference about it. Our internal worlds were, and remain, an untraversable mystery. We didn't have access to one another's motivations or desires in such a way as to translate the other's joys or frustrations. All of my guesses about how he felt about me, what he hoped for, enjoyed about, or expected from me were inferences and theories that he seemed uninterested in confirming or denying. It was that alienation that eventually created the ache to know and be known by God as a Father who didn't just desire to know and be known by me, but Who was (as Saint Augustine put it) nearer to me than I was to myself. It was several months before graduating from high school that the pounding of that ache grew unbearable enough to pick up a Bible that my older sister had discarded before moving to college. Before this time my hunger for relationship had hardened into the predictable, boring nihilism typical of so many teenagers, and my reading of the Bible was attended by withering criticism and uncivil, antagonistic debate with my more religious peers. I was a Nietzsche-adoring, antagonistic atheist when I picked up the Bible and discovered its story mostly through my own study, without the aid of a church or evangelist.

Surprisingly, something about the Bible's story reached through the obstinate fuss I raised in front of it, and grasped me. I was transfixed by the possibility that there might be, at the heart of the universe and hovering over my life, a Person who was actually pursuing me, moving past my disillusionment to embrace me, even (as the story of Jesus goes) at the cost of His dignity in participating in the mess of human existence and ultimately at the cost of His life, given for humanity on the cross. God was someone Who preferred to be defined by a relationship between an eternal, loving Father and devoted, tragically vulnerable Son, conspiring together to bring others into that filial bliss. The yearning fueled by that story reached its climax in a bathroom where I sat with my head in my hands, sobbing after another family meeting failed to resolve the tension and conflict created by my dad's aloofness. In that moment the gears of my estrangement locked, tongue in groove with this story. My dad may have been unable to reach beyond his own pain and disillusionment to find me; but there was a Father who suffered pain and disillusionment for the very purpose of finding me. My attempts to provoke joy and pride and curiosity in my dad may fail; but at the heart of the universe was a love that couldn't fail, because it sought me before I could even attempt to elicit it. All of the assumptions about my unworthiness created by this alienation evaporated in the heated immediacy of God's immanence. The Christian tradition often paradoxically refers to God's immanence (or nearness) as His transcendence—the way in which God is unlike everything in the created order. He doesn't just transcend time and space; His love transcends the laws that govern human relationships, where personal pain predictably and inescapably result in isolation.

Having experienced the love of a transcendent Father in that way galvanized my desire to bridge the distance one day with my own children, to make myself available and near in the same way He had done with me, in the way I'd wished my father had made himself vulnerable. But with Raj, I once again found myself in a position where connection seemed impossible. And once again it seemed to me that this alienation was largely due to the other person's inexplicable resistance to being known. Having resolved to be available to my children in a way my father wasn't, armed with God's own example in my life, it never occurred to me that they might be resolved to be unavailable to me in the same way my father was.

One evening a fairly typical (but no less exhausting) episode with my son prompted some desperate Googling. Some message boards advised that we should seek a pediatric neurologist. The day of his appointment approached with the solemnity of a court date. It felt more like a sentencing than a trial. I expected the doctor to confirm the accusations of my own conscience, that like my own father I was to blame somehow, whether as the cause of the problem or in my botched response to the problem. What I experienced, instead, was another of the great acquittals in my life. The first was that moment in my bathroom, where I was vindicated as someone who was worthy of love. This one came in the form of a diagnosis which assembled all of our struggles with Raj under a single word: Tourette's. As the doctor explained the relative normalcy of our experience my wife and I convulsed with tears and gasps of relief, releasing waves of guilt and the certainty that our relational failure was to blame.

But the real gift came next. After spelling out the physiological details of Raj's condition and the comorbidities surrounding it with miraculous accuracy (ADHD, night terrors, etc.), the doctor wheeled his chair away from us, reclined slightly and rested his hands behind his head in a single motion. His tone warmed from the clinical distance surrounding the diagnosis as he explained what propelled him into his chosen profession. He had Tourette's. He had been diagnosed when he was not much older than Raj. In about twenty minutes, he was able to give me what I had longed for, but what Raj had been unable to provide in the last several years: a rich description of his inner world, a mature account of what his experiences were like from the inside. I learned that his inability to control his inhibitions was a source of deep shame and confusion, an alienation from himself that left him feeling defective. I discovered how difficult it was to for him to find a way back from the anger once the fragile dam of self-control broke. I began to understand how disorienting it was for the world to present itself to him as a television whose channel is changed every few seconds.

What struck me in the eloquence of his account was the truth which bound these two experiences of my father and my son together; the alienation I experienced in my relationships with them had very little to do with my own worthiness or unworthiness. It certainly wasn't because of a willful refusal to be known. They desired connection as badly as I did. My father's emotional distance and my son's oppositional behavior were rooted in an alienation from themselves and a hunger for the same transcendent experience that filled the ache in my own soul. They longed to be understood, to have someone traverse the terrain I had found untraversable, for someone to reach beyond culture and language, beyond their defenses and offenses to know them without translation or mediation, in a way that no human person could ever know them. Just as I was looking for something in my father that he couldn't have ever provided (even if he were a good deal more emotionally healthy than he was), he was hungry for something I was incapable of giving him. And in the same way, I was looking to be something for my son that I could never be, despite the best of my intentions. Up to this point I had been narrating my life as a bewildered father and neglected son. I'm beginning to see that the three of us were really lost sons in search of the same Father.

In the rapture of my experience of God's love there was an imperceptible shift from receiving Him, as a Father who pursues me, to imitating Him as an example, providing the formula for making things as they should be. Gradually this logical (and maybe even virtuous) move began to turn God's love from the unassailable source of strength and comfort that freed me to (fallibly) love others, into an impossible standard of relational performance that crushed my soul. But what it means for God's love to be transcendent is that He always and forever remains *the only One* in the universe Whose pursuit can be thwarted by no barrier of pain or confusion. For His love to be the love of a transcendent Father, rather than a human one, it has to be a love that finds us before we ever plan to seek Him, that yearns not only for us to know and enjoy Him, but for us to feel known and enjoyed by Him. In light of my own experience with my dad, my search for Raj's heart, through the arduous thicket of neurological obstacles, is surely a worthy quest. But it can never replace the most fundamental pursuit in my life—not my pursuit of Raj, not my pursuit of my father, or even my pursuit of The Father, but His pursuit of me.

Raj Yadav, age 8. An apt illustration of connection Raj happened to draw the morning I wrote this essay.

Fatherhood, Reimagined

by Scott Bennett

SCOTT BENNETT has worked in corporate communications at Procter and Gamble for fourteen years. Often described as the most laid back guy you'll ever meet, Scott enjoys long runs and late night baking marathons (in that order), and is a vocal soloist in the P and G Big Band. Scott and his wife, Joy, have been married fifteen years and love to be homebodies with their three living children—Sam, Anna, and Luke—with dog Xena and cat She-Ra ever-present at their feet.

Wednesday, March 1, 2000 was my fourth day of fatherhood. I'll never forget the way our little Elli Renee looked lying there. So innocent. So violated. Stripped down to her diaper, with no swaddling clothes in sight. The top half of her body was yellow; the bottom half ashen. Her fontanel was sunken. She lay completely still except for her chest, which rose and fell exactly thirty times a minute in a mechanized, jerky rhythm.

Instead of a brightly-colored mobile above her head, a heat lamp beamed rays of light down to try to chase the jaundice away. Instead of soft music, a shrill staccato of beeps chirped sour chords when her temperature spiked or her oxygen dropped. Instead of a pacifier, a ribbed blue tube the diameter of my forefinger disappeared between her lips and into her lungs, keeping her alive in measured puffs. Instead of the delicate stub of a navel cord, a tangled cluster of wires and tubes breached her blood-encrusted belly button, feeding life-sustaining fluids and drugs into her. Instead of holding her in our arms, we could only watch her from a distance, wondering if she'd see another day. Or another hour.

Elli's heart had stopped in the night. The unthinkable had happened while we were home for just a few hours, trying to get some much-needed sleep. They had administered CPR for forty minutes, with no success. Finally, a last-ditch hail Mary—a bolus injection of calcium—had brought her back. Had she been home with us when it happened, we would have been making funeral arrangements that day.

Elli had come fast for a first baby, in more ways than one. She arrived two weeks before her due date, and two hours after we arrived at the hospital to deliver. She was born on a Saturday, when the maternity ward seemed to be a bit short-staffed. We noticed a handwritten note the doctor had scrawled in the "other" section of her physical exam form that was troubling—something about a heart murmur. But since it was the weekend, everyone seemed to be in a glass-half-full sort of mood, including us.

They took a chest X-ray and EKG the next morning. But since it was a Sunday, nobody was there to read what we would later discover were chilling results. They said someone would read them on Monday and call us. They reassured us that newborn heart murmurs are common, and typically resolve in a matter of days or weeks. We went home right on schedule, with a ticking time bomb strapped in our back seat.

Looking back, I was such a naïve new father. In all of my eager anticipation during the months leading up to her birth, I had never considered the possibility of complications. My wife and I had no family history of such things. And when it happened, my faith was shaken to its very foundation.

We didn't get a call about the chest X-ray and EKG on Monday, and figured no news was good news. On Tuesday, a nurse came to our house for a routine follow-up visit. By that time, Elli was severely jaundiced and had lost a pound of birth weight. The nurse ordered us to see a doctor that day. Being first-time parents, we didn't know what "normal" looked like. We knew she hadn't been nursing all that well, but figured it would just take time for her to get adjusted.

With much murmuring and complaining, we strapped her in the car seat—again—and drove her to a physician nearby. The doctor heard the murmur, saw the jaundice, calculated the weight loss, and ordered us to the Children's Hospital ER. Had she not called ahead to tell them we were coming, we might not have gone. It seemed absurd to us to be parading a newborn all over town, when all we felt she needed were the comforts of home, and a chance to bond and nurse.

We got lost on our way to the emergency room. By the time we got in to see anyone, it was early evening. A couple of cardiologists took turns roving around on her chest with an ultrasound wand for at least ninety minutes. They spoke indecipherable medical jargon under their breaths to each other. But their furrowed brows and body language were enough to tell us something was terribly wrong. About the only thing I remember them saying directly to us was, "Mr. and Mrs. Bennett, is there any history of congenital heart defects in either of your families?"

"No," we both said, shaking our heads.

Finally, one of the cardiologists took us into a private room. She pulled out a sketch pad and drew two very different hearts, explaining each one in great detail. On the left, a normal heart. On the right, Elli's—the lower chambers breached by a giant hole between them, the valve cuspids severely malformed and inefficient, and some major arteries missing or going to the wrong places. It had taken them all that time to make any sense of her heart anatomy.

The cardiologist's news had no hint of bright spots. No beams of hope. No best case scenarios. No "But the good news is . . ." It has been more than thirteen years, but I can vividly remember her saying, "This is going to be a very long road for you."

Elli had five congenital heart defects: truncus arteriosus, interrupted aortic arch, ventricular septal defect, patent ductus arteriosus and severe truncal valve insufficiency, and stenosis. From that moment, our lives were plunged headlong into a dizzying litany of complicated cardiac jargon, and an epic game of medical whack-a-mole to manage all of the complexities of her condition. We spent the remainder of her life running one step behind the next health crisis that would come along.

Incomprehensibly, Elli lived for another 8 years. She died in her sleep, during the early morning hours on October 19, 2008. We don't know the exact cause of death. Because the heart is a bellwether for other systems, her entire body was rife with complications. In her short lifetime, she underwent four major open heart surgeries, and had many close brushes with death. That cardiac arrest on Day 4 left her with crippling brain damage that handily trumped her heart condition, as serious as it was. Cerebral palsy ended up being the most formidable enemy Elli fought in everyday life. She never learned to walk, talk, sit, or stand. She couldn't dress herself, feed herself, or control her bowels and bladder. She needed so much assistance that I felt more like her doctor than her Daddy on most days.

Standing and sleeping for hours at the bedside of a sick child will test the tenor of untried beliefs like nothing else. Witnessing the intersection of innocence and suffering—like a child clinging to life on a ventilator—will deeply disturb a faith that has in any way been connected to earthly ease, or the power of positive thinking. My faith had grown up that way, in some measure.

This was not the fatherhood I had imagined. This wasn't supposed to happen to me. But I can tell you that much good has come of it. Elli's life and death have shaped my faith—and my fatherhood to my three younger children—like no other experience could have.

For the first time, I was forced to face what I had been taught to believe all my life, but had never experienced firsthand: the belief that God's promises are true. I could still hear the triumphal stanza of the old Baptist Hymn I had grown up singing in church:

Standing on the promises that cannot fail!
When the howling storms of doubt and fear assail!
By the living Word of God I shall prevail!
Standing on the promises of God!

I still believed those words to be true. But from my fourth day of fatherhood, the spiritual wind was knocked out of me. In those moments, *standing* on anything seemed far too ambitious. I was dangling precariously over a cliff. I needed promises. But I wasn't going to be able to *stand* on anything. My lifeline would need to be more like a harness to *hang* from than a rock to stand on.

So I started writing the promises down, like laying out strands of string in neat rows. And I rehearsed them back to God over and over, line by line. This was all I knew to do.

You love me. And all things will work together for good for me,
because I love you.

In Your presence is fullness of joy.
You will never leave me or forsake me.

The sufferings of this life aren't worthy to be compared to the glory
to come.

As the God of all comfort, You give me enough comfort
to comfort others down the road.

If I make my requests known to You, Your unfathomable peace
will guard my heart and mind in Christ Jesus.

This trial is giving me the patience and endurance to persevere to
the end.

As a Christian, I will suffer with You in order that I may be glorified
with You.

You understand my sorrows because You were
the Man of Sorrows, and were acquainted with grief.

With joy set before You, You endured the cross. You went before me,
and will see me through all the way home, no matter what.

I braided these and countless other cords together like rope. I cinched them around myself and lay still, hanging from a cliff face, overlooking the valley of the shadow of death. And they held me.

I could fill a book with stories about Elli's short life, in which she endured more pain and suffering than several long lifetimes. Most of it, for me, is one big exhausting blur. But it was the future promises of God that got me through those days. As I would bathe her, clothe her, change her and spin her around in my arms, I couldn't help thinking that she would probably see the fullness of those promises before I would. So I would rehearse them to her, as if I was preparing her for heaven, letting her in on a secret—almost envious that she would be able to make full sense of it all before I could.

About a year before Elli died, I resolved to treat every bedtime ritual like it was our last. I developed a nightly routine of holding both of her spastic hands still in mine, bending over close to her face and whispering Numbers 6:24-26 in her ear:

The LORD bless you and keep you; the LORD make his face to shine upon you and be gracious to you; the LORD lift up his countenance upon you and give you peace.

She would always look into my eyes and smile, her eyes sparkling. Then I would kiss her on the forehead and stroke her hair. I would tell her I loved her, and that she was precious, about two more times between turning out her light and closing the bedroom door behind me. Her last night on earth was no exception.

I made so many mistakes as Elli's father. I can recall countless bouts of laziness, fits of anger and pathetic pity parties. I credit any success as her earthly father to the grace of a Heavenly Father, whose hope-filled promises held me up and kept me from completely going off the edge in utter despair. I will forever thank Him for His promises—and for moving me toward a simple routine that ended up being a chance to usher her into eternity with a whispered pronouncement of His highest blessing. I wouldn't have wanted our earthly goodbye to be any other way.

No, this is not the fatherhood I had imagined. But *this is my comfort in my affliction, that your promise gives me life.* (Psalm 119:50)

Unaffected Love

by Kurt Ro

KURT is a modern nomad from the cloudy hills of Youngstown, Ohio. He followed the academic buffalo to Chicago and then wandered the Ohio River Valley in search of green pastures. He finally immigrated east to Philadelphia where he lives with his new bride, Katy, and their cat Saber. He is currently working as a credit and housing counselor helping people get out of debt and save their homes from foreclosure. He has described himself as a less fuzzy Fozzie Bear.

One of my earliest memories, or rather the most consistently vivid memory of my childhood, is playing catch with my father while waiting for the school bus. We lived in a suburb of Youngstown, Ohio but out on the edge of our town. I won't try to portray it as something it wasn't. We had running water and electricity—this was Ohio in the 1980s. However, we had a lot more space than most people—including a huge open field that my dad and I would run around in and where we would throw or kick a ball to each other. In the fall, we played catch with a baseball. In the winter, we'd throw the football around, and if the snow got too heavy to run through, we'd make a snowman. When the snow cleared up, we'd kick the soccer ball around. It was a really great memory, and something that always makes me smile whenever I think about it.

Living out toward the edge of town also meant that I was one of the first to get picked up by the bus, which leads to the second part of the memory. As much as I loved doing that with my dad every morning, whenever the bus came, I was relieved not many other kids were on the bus to see it. For one thing, it was weird. When the rest of the kids were getting picked up, I noticed no one else's dad would make them throw a football in twenty degree weather. No one else's dad was making them tromp around in the snow. No one else's dad *made* them give him a hug before they got on the bus. I was so relieved that no one was really on the bus to witness the things my dad made me do before school.

This would be a good time to bring up the fact that no one else's father was a 5-feet 5-inch tall Korean man who owned a flower shop and had a buzzed head like the Sarge from *Gomer Pyle, USMC*. I might have been *slightly* hyperaware in regard to the things that other fathers did or didn't do. One year on my birthday when I was in elementary school, I was told by a helper from the principal's office that my dad was there at school looking for me. When I got out into the hallway to find out what was going on, I spotted my dad in a suit walking down the hallway, carrying balloons with a big smile on his face and looking like a goofball. I was mortified. If other kids' parents did something for their birthday, they brought in pizza or something normal. No one's dad came strolling in with balloons. I thanked him and asked him to get the heck out of there.

When I reached middle school, the time of a young man's life when low self-esteem and hypersensitivity mingle into a blazing inferno of self-doubt, my heightened awareness of my father's differences didn't abate. Surprise! So the times when my dad would come down to the basement to crash my junior high parties, I was ballistic. And he wouldn't just walk down, check in, and leave. No, he would come creeping down the stairs like an awkward ninja mime. He would have a look on his face of feigned amazement that anyone could spot him. My friends would crack up, and I would turn crimson.

Often in those times, he would be bearing pizza, which made his intrusions slightly more tolerable. That is until he pulled out the hot pepper. Yes, we would always order from a certain Padre Johann and there would be the infamous pepper. Why was it infamous? Because my father saw it as another attempt to dig for comedy gold, which again made me cringe at how weird he was. He would, to the delight of my friends, pick up the pepper and in that same deliberate pantomime take a huge bite. His face would scrunch up and he would moan, "Ooooo oooohhh." My friends would die laughing. Laughing at my lunatic father. Laughing at the weirdo. I would typically try to quietly force my father away through clenched teeth.

My painful admission is that when I start to reflect on the emotions that are conjured when I hear the word *dad*, the first thing to surface is shame. Looking back on how I viewed my father growing up, the overriding emotion that colored how I viewed my father was one of embarrassment that made me wish he didn't have to be taken out in public. He just didn't get the norms of what is and what isn't okay to do. The pinnacle of how my father was different from other fathers, the thing that finally brought all of my anger to a head, occurred during my college years.

My father and mother are devout Christians, and they raised me and my three brothers in the Church. As a child I embraced my faith, and it had a huge impact on me during my formative years. As I got older, however, other things in life started looking more appealing, and by the time I reached college I had wandered away from my faith. That statement isn't really honest because I didn't get distracted by a shiny light and wander off. No, I ran. I ran with reckless abandon.

I went to school in Chicago, which is nine or so hours away from where I grew up and my parents lived. It was close enough to go back for the holidays, but far enough that I was pretty much left to my own devices, free of parental oversight. Those were not responsible times. Not a unique story, I know, but it was devastating and terrifying for my parents. To them, it was a slow descent, and they weren't privy to all the things in my life that were causing these troubles. They could tell by a number of symptoms that something was wrong. I was going through serious academic trouble. I was unapologetic about my underage drinking and had become a smoker. However, the most painful for my parents was how hostile I was to Jesus and His Church. Their baby boy was not the bright-eyed young man that they had raised.

So instead of acting like any other regular parent and waiting to chew me out during holiday visits, my father drove out to Chicago during the middle of an academic quarter to try and talk to me. He drove ten hours. Just to talk to me. When I spotted him outside of my fraternity house, I was shocked. It was middle school all over again, and my dad was creeping into the basement. My dad was barely inside the house when I laid into him. What was he doing there?! What did he think he was doing?! I won't relate the rest of what was said because, by some great mercy, I honestly don't remember much of it. I think if I had a clearer memory, I would probably sob from the guilt. What I do remember, though, is chasing him off because I didn't want to see him. I didn't want to face him.

Funny thing about all this reflection on how I've been ashamed of my father over the years has brought to the surface that I've treated my Heavenly Father in a pretty similar fashion. Depending on my surroundings and the company I am in, the level of my commitment to the name of Jesus waxes and wanes. I am so preoccupied by other people's perceptions of me that I find myself hoping that people won't ask me about my time working in ministry. I hope that I don't have to be brought to task about my "backwards" or "narrow-minded" view regarding exclusivity. I silently pray that God won't make me admit that I'm His. I chase Him away because I don't want to be laughed at.

I wish I had a good answer to make everything right. We Christians like things to be tidy and have a hard time admitting when we are failing. Christ made all things right, so how can anything be out of line? And don't worry, gentle reader, there will be some light at the end of the tunnel. However, the sad truth is that as of right now, I'm more concerned with my good name than His. I know this isn't right, but I also know that shame has driven me away from my two fathers in the past. In my shame, I tried to ignore God and chased away my dad. My shame is a mixture of wounded pride and frustration that God is actually just. But Grace is knowing that while God *is* just, my performance isn't what makes Him love me any more or less. I long for the day I can get over my wounded pride; when I will care less about how I look and care more about how God has pursued me far beyond what I deserve. Shame urges me to hide; grace brings me hope.

I can say that it has been another act of grace on God's part to eventually help me see the truth of my crazy father. Through a combination of renewed support from my parents, the guidance of a college dean who saw me as potential and not wasted potential, and a reordered sense of priorities that comes from hitting rock bottom, things turned around for me in college academically, emotionally, and, to a lesser extent, spiritually. I use the phrase "rock bottom" hesitantly because I know my "rock bottom" pales in comparison to the experiences of others. Nevertheless, it was a grueling period in my life, where I had to leave school due to poor academic performance and move back to Ohio with my folks. As humbling as that time back at home was, it allowed me to refocus and find a renewed strength. It was in that period that I first said to God: "I'm sorry." However, I wasn't yet ready to hear Him say back: "You are forgiven."

After about a year, I returned to school, and my father came out to celebrate the end of a good quarter. We went to a Korean restaurant in Chicago and were waiting for some friends of my father's. We sat in the middle of the restaurant at a table that was between two sets of families. As my father and I waited, I started to watch how the men of these different families were making complete idiots out of themselves so that the children they were holding would laugh with pure joy. And it all made sense. Which other father would show his love by waking up to run around in the snow? Which other father would pick up pizzas in order to be around his son as much as possible? Which other father would drive ten hours, uninvited, because he was worried about the direction his son's life was taking? These things that my father has done to express his love for me are huge, but they pale in comparison to the lengths God would go. God has chased after me for longer and farther than my dad ever has or ever could. There is no way to reconcile the abuse I have hurled on my Father in Heaven with the great love He has shown me. No reconciliation outside of Christ.

All of the memories of my father that had once filled me with shame now filled me with awe and gratitude. I turned to my father, leaned in, and said, "I'm glad you and I are Korean."

My parents don't own the flower shop or the property it sat on anymore, but I visited my childhood home in recent years. And that field that we used to play around in? It really isn't that big, but the memory is.

Fudge, Fatherhood, and Faith: Thoughts on a Spirituality of the Baby Bjorn

by A. J. Swoboda

DR. A. J. SWOBODA is a writer, professor, and pastor of the Theophilus community in Portland, Oregon. He teaches theology, biblical studies, and Christian history at George Fox Evangelical Seminary, is the author of *Messy: God Likes It That Way*, *Tongues and Trees: Toward a Pentecostal Ecological Theology*, and with Daniel Brunner and Jennifer Butler is co-author of *Introducing Evangelical Ecotheology: Foundations in Scripture, Theology, History, and Praxis*. You can find his website and blog at www.ajswoboda.com, or follow him on Twitter @mrajswoboda.

"I worship the God of my fathers." –Moses

It haunts me. Because I'm keenly aware that somewhere down the dusty road of time, as a father, I'll hurt my little boy. It's inevitable. That's what fathers seem to do best.

I'm a paid Christian. I pastor a church in secular, cynical, sarcastic, post-Christian Portland, Oregon just down the street from the Church of Elvis and the coffee shop in *Portlandia*. Portland isn't a "churched" city. Not that I'm throwing a pity-party, but it feels at times as if nobody likes me. The Christians—many of them disenfranchised (or "burned" in Christianese)—deeply resent their church and its leaders over how they and their friends have been hurt for this reason or the next. Likewise, the non-Christian natives think the church obnoxious, overly pious and, at times, hateful. The church in Portland exists between a rock and a hard place. It forces me, in a way, to get my loving grace from a secret place: I am a man of my God and my family. I lean on them as an addict leans on their next hit. Without them, I'd go into withdrawal. God's grace is my heroin; my family, the syringe.

Stories of weird families are told in movies, Shakespeare, comics, and the Bible. One might assume that Christian families are supposed to look pristine, but the story of their God reveals a more subtle subplot. Christian homes are fraught with brokenness just like everyone else. Especially the home of a pastor. The expectations for pastors today are ungodly. Pastors are often treated as low-paid babysitters, moral super-stars (and referees) who provide free hospital visits and on-the-dime godly advice. Their spouses are treated worse and their children are expected to be perfect little angels. All of this to keep the contemporary American church, one that is increasingly viewed as a religious market-place where people come to "get" their spiritual goods, afloat.

Because of the unfair expectations put upon the pastoral family, they are *actually* starting to look like the families in the Bible: full of divorce, fraught with unfaithfulness, and full of the practice of po-lygamy. Yes, polygamy. Of course, by calling the pastor polygamous, I am indicting myself. I've cheated on my loving wife many times. Not sexually. Not physically. Emotionally. Most pastors, when they are honest with themselves, have the ability to make love to two: their spouses and their churches. Because of this fragmented fidelity, the family of the pastor is dying.

The hidden costs of the economy of consumerist Christianity are pastor's kids (PKs). Frederick Nietzsche was a PK. The church culture we've established has, in many ways, hurt, alienated, and disenfran-chised the children of clergy. Too often, pastors are better pastors than fathers. So when my adoring wife and I moved toward parenthood, we knew the odds were stacked against us: our kid would probably have heavy spiritual baggage.

It caused me great fear.

The Bible has something to say about this in the stories of the heroes of the Hebrew Bible. Some time ago, I took a well-deserved

Sunday off from preaching at my church. Having preached the previous five weeks, I'd reached what a friend calls "the crispy place," that inevitable space where I couldn't squeeze any more drops of profundity out of my Bible or theology without offending God and all his angels. Preachers call this "preachers block." My soul was just plain tired.

This afforded me an evening with my son Elliot, giving my wife, Quinn, a night free from the constraints of motherhood. I strapped the buddy to my chest in his Baby Bjorn and emceed our Sunday worship gathering. It was my son's first worship service. A worship song began and something struck me about the little kid strapped to my chest: this was his first time he'd watch me sing a song to God in church. At first, I confess, I was overwhelmed with a sense of embarrassment. What did he think? Would he make infantile fun of me for my off-key tone? Would he understand why I was singing into the air? Would the raising of my hands make any sense to him?

In that moment, I understood something about the Bible that had evaded me for some time. The ancients repetitively said, "I worship the God of my Fathers" (e.g., Exodus 3:15). Biblical scholars remind us that this repetitive utterance was actually very practical: in a polytheistic world it was increasingly helpful to differentiate oneself (especially if you believed in One God) from the other religions of the world. But there's a greater point, I think. It seems to indicate that faith and fatherhood are not mutually exclusive.

I became overwhelmed by emotion with the baby in the Bjorn. Worshipping with the boy on my chest, I felt as though I'd come upon a spatial moment of holiness like that of Moses taking his sandals off in front of the burning bush. I understood why the Bible always says that the ancients worshipped the God of their fathers. It was from them that they received the story of God.

American Christianity creates a kind of unintended fatherlessness. For the better part of a century, American Christians have worshipped in their age groups. Elders, teenagers, and children worship separately. We have contemporary services for the hip and traditional services for the older folk. It wasn't always like this. In the good old days of the early church, whole families would worship together, at home. This whole "children's department" thing was a foreign concept. Why? Because church buildings consisted primarily of a living room, some couches, and a table with some food on it. Today, we throw our kids off into other rooms where they learn Sunday school lessons away from their parents' guiding eyes. I think not having our children worship with us can be dangerous. Who else is to teach them why and how we sing? How else are children to learn the ways of worship?

We have our children worship the Father God with their fathers in another room. We literally separate father and son during worship.

Frankly (parents, breathe easy), there are practical reasons for this. There's a certain necessity to putting kids together. They make friends, run around, and get a break from their parents. Kids need different things to chew on than adults. Children's ministers (like my wife) are gifted in the ways of working with children and inspire them to love God. There are important reasons we put kids in the other room. But I worry a bit about what it does. Scholars tell us that the earliest Christians *heard* the biblical letters in house churches around a table. Someone would open a letter that had been written to them, such as in the letter written by Paul to the church in Ephesus. In his exhortation, Paul writes, "Dear children, obey your parents" (Eph. 6:1). For modern readers, this command might be passed by without closer inspection because of its relative simplicity. Note that Paul does not say to the parents to tell their children to obey them; Paul addresses children directly. Why is this profound? Paul addressing children implies that children were sitting around the table and listening with the parents as the text was read. Children were in the first church services. Early churchgoers didn't separate out those who were young so that the old people could have alone time.

In earliest Christianity, children learned faith with their parents in the room. They saw them worship, pray, eat, and argue together. God seems to know that children learn by watching. By seeing. A child psychologist in a class I taught told me that there is a crisis in childhood development in our world: kids rarely ever see their parents argue. Why? Because most parents will argue in the other room. This creates two problems. First, children never learn *how* to argue appropriately. Secondly, children never learn *how* to reconcile. Children, I believe, actually need to see their parents argue *and* reconcile. Because images like that make children who they are. Being a parent is being an iconographer; parenting is painting icons of the good life for their children.

Being a paid Christian but a faithful father means I will need to learn to cheat on the church. I need to put aside my preaching preparation, my counseling, my "holy" jobs to go outside and play ball with my kid. That image will stick with my boy. I want him to have that kind of image. A friend of mine once said he needed counseling because he could never forget the image of walking in on his father watching pornography. The image was burned into his brain. I want Elliot to walk in on me too. But I want him to walk in on me as I'm on my knees praying and eating from the well of Scripture. It will have a lifelong effect. He won't be able to shake it.

If images make children who they are, then I'm fine with my kid looking up at me from inside the Bjorn and thinking his daddy is weird as he sings off-key songs to God. I'd rather he have *that* image than no image at all.

I know I'll hurt my boy. But, for now, Elliot's strapped to my chest. Someday I'll wish he could be back on my chest. Now, I just enjoy his soft breathing upon my bosom. It will end. Until then, I'll stand there singing with him on my chest while he stares at me. I want to teach Elliot to worship the God I know. I don't want the famous worship leaders with the CDs to teach my kid to worship. Or even the worship leader at our church. I want to. Not because I'm selfish, but because I think this sort of stuff is best passed on in relationship. He sees his father love his God and I get to tell him about his God. He looks up at me. He sees me sing to God. I hope he isn't embarrassed, but even if he is, that's fine. I'd rather him be embarrassed *with* me than being embarrassed *at* me.

I remember grandpa's fudge. God would quiver, it was that good. It was one of those family secrets that had been passed down and honed over generations. Grandpa told very few people how to make it. My mom was one of the few. She perfected the ins and outs of this heavenly concoction that could bring peace to the Middle East. She received the recipe directly from him. From watching him, and knowing him, and paying attention to him. And if I wanted, I could get it from her. That's how fudge recipes work.

Worship is like that. Why else would the fathers of old say things like, "I worship Yahweh, the God of my fathers"? Because worship is like my grandfather's fudge recipe. It is passed on.

Worship is for God; but it's learned like a fudge recipe. No one worships in a vacuum. We are *taught* by someone. Scientists call it *echolalia*—that thing kids do when the copy their parents' words, actions, and facial expressions. All worship is a kind of *echolalia*. We all copy someone. Looking up from our Baby Bjorn and seeing someone do what they do with God, we follow. And after all is said and done, I think the greatest ministry I have for my son is to stop being a minister and instead simply to be a dad who loves Jesus. I'll give Elliot my God through my own imperfections. Someday he'll give it to his son, and his son, and his son. And I hope they'll say to people that they worship the God of their fathers and mothers.

Which is why faith, like the best fudge recipe, takes countless generations to perfect.

The Dark Side of the Moon, Absence, and the Suicide of a Father

by C. Wess Daniels

WESS is a papa, a Quaker minister at Camas Friends Church, PhD in intercultural studies, and adjunct professor at George Fox Seminary and Earlham School of Religion. He enjoys a good remix, liberation theology, bourbon, and a wool vest.

"For though absent in body, I am present in spirit. . ."
–1 Corinthians 5:3

THE DARK SIDE OF THE MOON

I was twenty-five when my stepdad, Bernie, committed suicide, but he had started to drift away from us many years before his death. It was not obvious to me back then, but looking back now his growing isolation, depression, and paranoia are far more clear. The last ten years of his life were a road trip toward alterity in which he moved rapidly from presence to an absence like the dark side of the moon. Geographically, the "dark side of the moon" refers to the lunar hemisphere that can never be seen from Earth.[1] The far side of the moon is completely other, absent from our sight from planet Earth and yet,

---

1. Wikipedia contributors, "Far Side of the Moon," *Wikipedia, The Free Encyclopedia*, http://en.wikipedia.org/wiki/Far_side_of_the_Moon (accessed August 12, 2013).

conversely, even in its mystery, we know that it is present. Similarly, Pink Floyd's rock album *The Dark Side of the Moon* is one continuous piece of music that progresses through highs and lows, mirroring the stages of human life from birth to death, probing issues of lunacy and alterity. It is inspired by the degrading mental illness and alleged drug use of the band's lead singer and founding member Syd Barrett, and it mirrors Bernie's life and death as well.

The Dark Side of the Moon was one of Bernie's favorite albums. Many summer evenings you could hear the soaring, psychedelic guitars, the melodic voices, and the now-iconic sound of coins dropping and cash registers opening and closing, jamming through stereo speakers hanging out our living room windows. Sitting around the fire pit in the backyard, Bernie liked to play air guitar on the more guitar-driven songs, and he would get quiet and sentimental during the song "Us and Them." For me the album is both a lens for his life and a reminder of the good times.

US AND THEM

Growing up with Bernie was challenging. This is probably because he liked to be in control. He was like our own personal military sergeant. He believed that a good strict upbringing would not only ensure that my five siblings and I would turn out to be good kids, but that the implementation of strictness was itself a reflection of his love for us. This "spare the rod, spoil the child" philosophy reflected his own strict upbringing, and it reflected an image of God he wrestled with all his life (Prov. 13:24).[2] I remember Bernie once telling us that the word *play* was nowhere in the Bible;[3] "Life isn't about having fun, it

---

2. For Bernie, God was like a strict father, someone who was often distant, someone who was a disciplinarian and operated more from a punitive understanding of justice than a loving or restorative one. From what I remember, Bernie did believe that God loved him and "provided" for him when he was in need, but looking back that seems like the exception to the rule rather than the general nature of who God was to him.

3. It's worth noting, in case you are tempted to say this to your children, *play* actually does appear in many places in the bible—in the English Standard Version, for instance, it appears fifty-five times.

is about working hard and doing the right thing," he'd tell us. Bernie refused to allow us to participate in "Ticking away the moments/ That make up a dull day / Fritter and waste the hours / In an off-hand way"[4] when we were kids because he was refused the same enjoyment when he was a child.

Bernie worked midnights in a family-run business and the hours he worked were long and stressful. By the time I was old enough to really notice, it was obvious that he was, even in his early thirties, burned out. When he would come home he'd mostly zone out in front of the TV or go to bed. He used to tell me about how his dad would wake him up at four o'clock in the morning to work in the shop before he would go off to school. And when he'd get home from school he would go back to work until dinner time. This started when he was young enough to need to stand on a bucket to see over the counter to help the customers!

Due to a serious car accident when I was thirteen, he couldn't work anymore and spent every day, all day, at home. Most often he was in the basement listening to shortwave radio and doing woodwork. If, during his working years, he was largely absent or zoned out, during this period the basement became his hideout. His depression and isolation increasingly took control of his life. As a result of growing paranoia, and an increasing obsession with conspiracy theories he picked up from the shortwave, Bernie began to stockpile weapons. Yes, actual weapons. Like mini-14s and shotguns with folding stocks. Not your usual household .22. This happened in the years leading up to "Y2K," something he was particularly concerned about and very well prepared for. By the time I left for college in 1997, Bernie could have outfitted a small platoon of Ohioans to be ready for the apocalypse. Which was pretty much the idea.

The handguns were hidden in secret compartments in cabinets he used to make, but the bigger guns we buried out back. This was a sure sign that things were getting bad. The day Bernie had me and a couple of my brothers bury a five-gallon bucket filled with firearms and other

4. Pink Floyd, "Time," *The Dark Side of the Moon*. EMI 1973.

weaponry in the backyard, I recall standing over the hole we dug and feeling scared. Not because I was worried about the government coming to get us, or that we would have to "go out in a blaze of glory," but because I felt like he had become so preoccupied with these conspiracies around big government and this "us and them" mentality that I could no longer connect to him at all. What little presence he had left felt as though it was rapidly drifting further and further away.

> Haven't you heard it's a battle of words
> the poster bearer cried
> Listen son, said the man with the gun
> There's room for you inside[5]

THE GREAT GIG IN THE SKY

After college my wife and I decided to move to California. I was going to attend Fuller Theological Seminary in Pasadena and she was going to teach English in the public school system. Shortly before we left for our cross-country road trip we stopped to see Bernie. My mom had since left him and he was living in our old farmhouse alone. I felt sorry for him. I knew he loved and cared for me, despite our tumultuous relationship. And I still loved him in the way you loved someone you've known your whole life, someone who is integral to your story. I have worked hard to learn the truth of these words: "Being over and against is a lot easier than being in love."[6]

On the porch that day, one of the last days we ever spoke face-to-face, he pulled me aside and asked to speak with me privately. "Listen son," said the man with the gun, "I'm worried about you driving all the way to California and I'm worried about your safety when you are out there so I want you to take this."

He produced a black Smith and Wesson nine millimeter and put it in my hands. My heart sank. My tongue was tied. There was another small detail I'd neglected to tell him that now felt like a huge wedge

---

5. Pink Floyd, "Us and Them," *The Dark Side of the Moon*. EMI 1973.
6. Richard Rohr. *Everything Belongs: The Gift of Contemplative Prayer*. New York: Crossroad, 2003. 20.

between us. Since I moved away to college I had become a Quaker. This was in large part because I was drawn to their testimony against war, which felt like a living and loving alternative to what I was brought up around. But that wasn't a conversation I was able to have with him, not with a gun in my hand. The gun symbolized the distance that grew between us, how far apart our paths had become.

I talked to Bernie on the phone a few times after we arrived on the West Coast in August of 2003, but that day on the porch of the farmhouse was really the last day I ever had any kind of deep interaction with him. With each conversation his paranoia and depression became increasingly overwhelming and normal conversation was almost impossible. Then it happened. The week before Thanksgiving, I got the call that Bernie had committed suicide. He started up the gas generator in the basement that he had purchased for Y2K, walked upstairs, and sat down on the couch where his life would come to an end.

> And I am not frightened of dying, anytime will do, I
> Don't mind. Why should I be frightened of dying?
> There's no reason for it, you've gotta go sometime.[7]

ECLIPSE

In the time since this all happened I have had plenty of time to reflect on the absence of a father. For one, there are feelings of guilt, anger, and rejection to work through. And many wonderful things have happened in the last ten years: We now have three children. I have finished school and am pastoring a Quaker meeting in the Pacific Northwest. Bernie's absence means he's missed all this.

In the wake of his suicide, I found it all too easy to let the negative emotions attached to losing him override any of the good memories and emotions I had concerning him. Since he wasn't physically here to shout at, I redirected my anger and hurt toward my memories of him and found solace in thinking about just how terrible he really was. These negative emotions helped to reinforce my own sense of

---

7. Pink Floyd, "The Great Gig in the Sky," *The Dark Side of the Moon*. EMI 1973.

being the victim. Those feelings held me hostage for years.

Then this past spring something began to change. A couple weeks before Bernie's birthday in March, I was at a discussion group where we began talking about issues of death and dying. What I shared in that group revealed to me the negative emotions I was holding onto. It was in this moment of "waking up" to what was going on within myself that God was able to direct me down a new path. I saw that these older, angry memories could be eclipsed by newer "healed" memories and emotions. I can actually choose to remember whatever I want to remember. I get to decide which Bernie "appears" in my conversation and in the stories I share with others. This has freed me in a way that I haven't felt in a very long time.

In fact, I've stopped thinking so much about Bernie's absence and started focusing on his presence. Bernie's whole life, and not just his death, is an integral part of my story. His life has left an indentation on mine; there is a concavity where he once was. Once I woke up to the negativity that entangled me I was able to view this indentation as its own kind of presence. In this way, absence presupposes presence. Absence means that there was first an impact, an indentation. This is similar to the South Pole-Aitken basin, found on the far side of the moon. We cannot see it from Earth but it is the largest known "impact feature" in the solar system.[8]

This is how theologian James Alison describes the incarnation of Jesus. Jesus' life, death, and resurrection are not something we are left to read about in ancient texts, as though our experience of the Risen Lord is meant to be primarily a secondhand experience. Instead, even in his apparent absence, he has created and continues to create a kind of concavity in our world. Our work is not to dwell on the absence but to investigate Jesus' ongoing presence we experience.[9]

In a similar way, Bernie's absence leaves a huge concavity in my life which has inspired and transformed me. His illness and depression

---

8. Wikipedia, "Far Side of the Moon."

9. James Alison, "Undergoing God: Dispatches from the Scene of a Break In," *Bloomsbury Academic*, 1 (2006).

have helped me to understand what others deal with. Even the guns and the paranoia helped me discover the roots of nonviolence. And his work ethic and strong moral stance is a fiber that runs through my own vocation. In accepting his absence as its own kind of presence, I am able to accept all that has happened and move forward with new freedom that has eluded me since the day he died.

> And all that is now
> And all that is gone
> And all that's to come
> And everything under the sun is in tune
> But the sun is eclipsed by the moon.[10]

10. Pink Floyd, "Eclipse," *The Dark Side of the Moon*. EMI 1973.

God the Father is Like Jesus the Christ
by Lawrence Garcia

PASTOR LAWRENCE E. GARCIA is the senior teaching-pastor of Academia Church, a church-plant in Goodyear, Arizona. He is a committed learner of Scripture, a blogger, and is devoted to the educational growth of his congregants and raising up a new generation of disciples who will think, tell, and live out the Christian story.

In what, for me, was to be a shocking show of hands, I asked during my last Father's Day exposition how many congregants had or have fathers who were either abusive, absentee, or authoritarian—shockingly, no less than half, possibly up to two-thirds, raised their hands. This, of course, led me to think: how can I go on to speak of God as heavenly "father" when so many of my listeners have had negative experiences with their natural fathers? And then on to a second thought: I can no longer assume, as Jesus could before his listeners, that to talk about the fatherliness of God is going to sound anything like "good news." Teachers and preachers of the Gospel must in an age of broken homes *demonstrate* by Jesus' sacrificial and loving actions precisely what *this* heavenly Father is truly like.

You see, Jesus' audience were mostly Jewish—people who had been nurtured on the stories of Israel's God as the nation's compassionate and faithful father—who, despite Israel's constant failure to fulfill its national destiny, yearned for deliverance and eventual reconciliation. To speak of God as "Father," then, was to conjure up the great promises of YHWH, the One who painfully longed for the return of the prodigal and exiled nation. Take, for example, this moving passage in Hosea:

When Israel was a child, I loved him, and out of Egypt I called my son. The more I called them, the more they went from me; they kept sacrificing to the Baals, and offering incense to idols. . . How can I give you up, Ephraim? How can I hand you over, O Israel? How can I make you like Admah? How can I treat you like Zeboiim? My heart recoils within me; my compassion grows warm and tender. I will not execute my fierce anger; I will not again destroy Ephraim; for I am God and no mortal, the Holy One in your midst, and I will not come in wrath.[1]

Thus, by styling God as "Father" while perched on the Galilean mount Jesus was both reminding Israel of YHWH's compassionate nature and signaling that this Father's mercy was at last being fulfilled in *his* person and work among them. To assume, however, that the average Father's Day attendee to my parish will understand the sideways reference to the compassionate-father imagery of the Old Testament, may simply be hoping too much.

Without clarification of what *type* of father God is in light of the crucifixion of the Son, it is highly likely that the audience may fill this vacuum with personal content, that is, personal *experience*. Consider, for example, my own life history, which involved not only a biological father, but a stepfather as well. On the one hand, my biological father had very little to do with me; I can only recall seeing him on several occasions in my early childhood and since then he has remained entirely uninvolved. What if God's fatherhood was like this? If so, to hear Jesus refer to God as "Father" might simply mean he is completely detached from life here on Earth, perhaps preoccupied solely with himself somewhere beyond the vast reaches of the cosmos.

If, on the other hand, God were to be like my stepfather, who was a constant authoritarian figure, ready, to punish any infraction

---

1. Hosea 1:1-2, 8-9, NRSV.

of a household rule, we might think God's fatherly nature likewise authoritarian. This, at least for those of us who know we're hopeless sinners, would be stark news upon the lips of Jesus. After all, such a stringent divinity might be more inclined to consign us to eternal torment for failing at his Law than suffering for our sins that we might stand justified before Him in confidence. Thus, in light of my own personal encounter with bad father figures (which actually seems to be more the norm for many in our culture) it is imperative to present a stark *contrast* with the Father's love as revealed in Christ.

This, because, everything *Jesus* does with and on behalf of wayward sons and daughters is precisely what the heavenly *Father* himself is doing. Small wonder Jesus got a tad perturbed when his disciples requested of him that he show them the Father. Jesus' response clearly makes the point that we can in no way drive a wedge between the Father and what Jesus is doing:

"You've been with me all this time, Philip, and you still don't understand? To see me is to see the Father. So how can you ask, 'Where is the Father?' Don't you believe that I am in the Father and the Father is in me? The words that I speak to you aren't mere words. I don't just make them up on my own. The Father who resides in me crafts each word into a divine act. Believe me: I am in my Father and my Father is in me. If you can't believe that, believe what you see—these works."[2]

Is God an absentee father like my biological father just so happened to be? In no way!—the Father in the person of the Son has come to live, eat, and suffer with sinners. This God is "Emmanuel"—God with us—a God who through the incarnation, resurrection, and sending of the Spirit has proven beyond any shadow of a doubt that this God will never leave nor forsake us. The idea of a strict Authoritarian God is likewise subverted when we see Jesus' compassion on sinners—the failing disciples, the adulterous woman, and even, those crucifying Jesus himself. This, then, is the Father we never knew, the One we never knew had until, that is, the bleeding hands and feet of Calvary. N. T. Wright advises:

---

2. John 14:9-10, *The Message.*

Don't come with a set, fixed idea of who God is, and try to fit Jesus into that. Look at Jesus, the Jesus who wept at the tomb of his friend, the Jesus who washed his followers' feet, and you'll see who is the true God. That was Jesus' answer to Philip. It is his answer to the natural questions that arise in people's minds today.[3]

The God that Jesus bids us to call "Father," then, was at work every step of the way on Jesus' long course to the cross. He is also the same God who is now present with us through Christ's sending of the Spirit into our hearts as a seal of our adoption and eventual face-to-face reunion at the end of the age. Moreover, he's the type of Father who has gracefully given us Christ—the priestly Older Brother—as our advocate who makes constant pleading on behalf for our many transgressions. This brings us to the heart of one of Jesus' most famous parables, that of the prodigal son, whose central verses reads:

"I'm going back to my father. I'll say to him, 'Father, I've sinned against God, I've sinned before you; I don't deserve to be called your son. Take me on as a hired hand.' He got right up and went home to his father. When he was still a long way off, his father saw him. His heart pounding, he ran out, embraced him, and kissed him. The son started his speech: 'Father, I've sinned against God, I've sinned before you; I don't deserve to be called your son ever again.' But the father wasn't listening. He was calling to the servants, 'Quick. Bring a clean set of clothes and dress him. Put the family ring on his finger and sandals on his feet.'"[4]

The way *The Message* version of the Bible reads here captures the superficiality of the prodigal's rehearsed "speech," which he assumed would be enough to convince his father to allow him to become a hired servant so that he could pay back every dime he blew among the Gentiles. This was not, strictly speaking, "repentance." It is better understood as what Kenneth Bailey rightly calls a "face-saving plan."

3. N. T. Wright, *John for Everyone, Part 2: Chapters 11-21*. London: Society for Promoting Christian Knowledge, 2004. 60.

4. Luke 15:18–22, *The Message*.

Nevertheless, what is startling about the father portrayed here is that upon seeing his son at the edge of the community he doesn't waste a moment, but *races* out to meet his son in order to reconcile him to himself; and in the honor and shame culture of Jesus, running was considered shameful and unbecoming of a patriarchal figure. Yet despite the public shame it would bring, the father runs, making a shameful fool out of himself in order to restore his son; no doubt, the shame-bearing here of the father points forward in the story to when God would undergo humiliation to restore humanity at the cross of Christ. This, therefore, is the "Father" that Jesus spoke of and that can only be rightly understood and known when viewed through the lens of the crucified Christ. Kenneth Gangel's words are particularly apt here:

> What is God like? I once heard a sermon on this topic. The pastor talked on and on about God being like flowers, sunsets, the cry of a newborn baby, the beauty of a clear blue sky. Certainly, all those are part of God's natural revelation and therefore reflect him. But he never got to the bottom line: God is like Jesus Christ.[5]

The Father, then, is like Jesus Christ. Therefore, preachers and teachers should always speak of Christ's compassion and saving work while speaking of God as "Father." The neglected and abused sons and daughters who are sitting in the pews need to hear that God—the One revealed in Jesus—is truly with and there for them always, even when they make a big mess of things. This way, those with great biological fathers and those without them will all have cause for joy this and every Father's Day.

---

5. Kenneth O. Gangel, *Vol. 4: John, Holman New Testament Commentary.* Nashville: Broadman & Holman Publishers, 2004. 266.

Broken Pieces of Who We Were
by Guy Martin Delcambre

GUY MARTIN DELCAMBRE is a writer, outdoors enthusiast and an ever-learning dad to three amazing little girls. He'd much rather find himself on a wooded trail leading into open sky than a dance studio filled with knowledgeable dance moms, but such is life, the one Guy loves more than anything else. He writes about faith and its resolve in our human condition and the beauty of God's strength in the thinnest, bleakest moments.

My three daughters and I were thrust into life foreign, merely mimicking familiar. The sun rose as before, our faces were still the same but longer, stretched by sadness. Our number reduced by one.

Our hands clinched tighter as we paused for a moment that felt like hours. Our friends and loved ones before us, we moved hand-in-hand together. Their eyes watched us, filled with a tearful mixture of sorrow and pity, and I felt my heart tear from hers as my three little daughters and I approached the casket where her body lay.

Time slowed to a crawl and we, my daughters and I, swayed in the intermediate, tossed back and forth; memory behind, unknown ahead. My youngest daughter clenched me as if not to lose me and my other two daughters sat close by. A look of abandon adorned their faces, rather than their usual happy smiles. Smiles that will forever bear a clear resemblance to their mother, now gone.

One life, all that we knew and had built together and had loved, passed. Resigned neatly now to beautiful history.

Where do we go?

How do we go?

Why, even?

Life was not supposed to be this way, not for me. For my three little daughters, accustomed to the loving arms of their mother, to be severed from that by death's heedless rush into our lives, the cruelty of life and circumstance could not be explained enough.

We broke. Like glass fractured by the brunt force of an object unbelonging, pushing its way through without regard, we lived the days in pieces.

She died unexpectedly, just as life began to stretch out favorably and we, as a young family, were taking strong strides toward all that we dreamed about. One day, all was beautiful and full; the next, all fell into a sea of tossing hurt, confusion, and cold, lonely grief. With one phone call, the tone a damnedest sound, my "good life" began to crack and crumble, leaving a heap of rubble indistinguishable and unwanted; the exact opposite of my prayers. My wife had a history of epilepsy since early in childhood. For the majority of her life, her disease had little effect and caused her little hindrance.

Every so often she would endure a seizure, splitting open our lives; faith would seep through fragile openings. For me, goodness in life served to validate God's love and gave acceptable cause for security. But in each uncontrollable episode, I questioned God's protection and awareness of our fears, of her struggle to understand the absence of healing in her body despite unrelenting prayers. My greatest fear was the worst-case scenario ambiguously hanging in front of us, somehow always a felt future possibility.

Then came that day, slipping in under cover of an ordinary day.

And as feared, that day was different. There was no coming back, no recovery, no day after.

Life shrunk to days, hours, and minutes. No longer stretching out into the happy expanse of all ahead—dreams, hopes, and goals—my grasp on life and God diminished and the days went by blurry and dislodged.

A new journey began.

It had to.

I knew the longer we stood still in awe of such devastating circumstance, the deeper we would sink. We had to move forward beyond the wreckage of life gone wrong. After all, life had just begun. Even though nothing made sense and we could see no further than the calamity and uncertainty death brought into our lives, navigating onward made sense. Life was ahead of us not behind; good laid out in front of us in the continuation of life and a new day. Otherwise, each day would be reduced to me rummaging through memories, frozen in the in-between of yesterday gone and today unchosen. I missed the rhythm of family together, the balance of us all, namely, of my wife and me parenting in conjoined effort. Now that our family consisted of just the four of us, a young widowed dad and three little girls all under the age of eight, we hobbled along through each day broken, dislodged, and foreign.

Slowly, through grief and grace, life re-pressurized. God transcended the death that thieved so much from our family. Rather than betraying me in unanswered prayers, God found me in them. Right in the storm where life raged uncontrollable and waves reached over the top into our boat, He arrived to rescue and revive our flattened lives.

Hope came back.

Into each morning I woke to possibility filling each day. There were three little lives who needed to be shaped and shown and led into tomorrow.

That's how I became a single father to three little girls looking for life, stability and the security they knew before death entered.

Reentering life as a single parent, I no longer had a choice in how much effort I'd give. The girls looked to me for everything.

"Dad, what should I wear?"

"What should I get my friend for her birthday?"

"Can you do my hair?"
"Can we go and get a manicure?"
"Can you meet my friend's mom so she can come over?"
"Dad, I think I need a bra.
"Dad, what is sex?"

The first few months as a single dad swirled like an absolute whirlwind. I was widowed and they were half orphaned. Emotions ran deep and erupted frantically at times. Many of those early days were spent getting through the day and finding balance to each stride we took together. An obvious void rested heavy, them motherless and grieving with an inexperienced single father. Granted, I had enormous support from my mother, who has been nothing short of amazing in her help and stability, but at the end of the day and in the settling dust, I am my daughters' only parent. It is both my privilege and responsibility to show them the way, teach them how, and lead them into tomorrow.

I say to them often, especially in tougher times when they are hurting or frustrated, "God gave you me and me you. And he didn't make a mistake."

As a few months passed us, we struggled to find consistency. Some days were better than others but piled up much smaller than the days when grief rang like a gun blast. I was as lost in parenting as I was in grief and frustrated because as Dad I couldn't hold it all together.

One evening, as the kids were spending time with my mother, I went for a walk under a starlit sky, glowing alive. Memories of our past life flashed through my thoughts like shooting stars leading wonder and wishes across a darkened sky; the smiles, the fun, the laughter, all together as a family. I realized that we needed to reenter life *together*, that I couldn't do it alone.

The stars just made perfect sense in a whole new way that night. The way they hung perfectly, positioned precisely and shining brightly millions of miles away, as if broadcasting a message of hope in the endless panoramic expanse of the night sky, whispering order and security and future, raptured me from living as a victim in a day I felt I didn't belong to. I felt closer to God that night, standing under the stars, his stars, and asked simply of him to just help me build the family that we, my wife and I, had started together.

I lost the part of me diseased and crippled by her death and came back a different man. Grace forged a new resolve in my heart and identity.

I wasn't just a dad and I wasn't only widowed. Life didn't take from me; it gave to me a beautiful opportunity to lead my daughters through a precarious time and plant a seed of God's magnificent strength in the fragility of one life ending in death and another unknown one ahead. I was, and would be from then forward, a parent, openhearted to life with my three beautiful daughters through the pain, the hurting, the confusion, and the loneliness.

After that night, slowly over the next few weeks, we began to grow again. I wasn't as concerned with how to raise three little girls, however little girls should be. I resolved to raise them in the exact context we newly lived in, one maimed by death and loss but alive to, and dependent on, God's grace in each new step.

I introduced them to adventure, in order to keep their hearts curious and growing. We attacked our weaknesses together. I learned how to make a ponytail, and they learned how to fish. They taught me how to paint nails, and I showed them how to scout a hiking trail. Our life together will always be my most beautiful treasure. I absolutely adore it.

My goal as a parent has largely simplified. I'm not immediately concerned about getting things just right or always making the correct decision. For me, parenting well lies in the ability to simply not lose them along the way.

There's so much that can go wrong in parenting, so many pitfalls and mistakes, so much that can seep through the cracks. One can't possibly always know exactly how to be, what to say, and the correct way to go at every fork and bend. But I do believe the key to parenting and getting those little hearts nipping at your heels one moment, and running from you the next, is to show, display, and guide; to live life out in front of them giving them a pattern and context to mimic and to own.

To that end, most Wednesday evenings have been set aside for one of our favorite new family traditions: family cook night. It's quite a simple tradition. We cook, together.

For us, the kitchen is definitely an adventure. Our measurements are generous, and each of us thinks we really know what we're doing. Emily's a pro at cutting anything; Elizabeth expertly dabbles in everything; and Chloe can stir like a boss. Honestly, it's crazy stressful watching it all happen, but the payoff is magic. Our hearts are open, conversation flows freely, music typically plays in the background and we just go at it celebrating our togetherness in a new family way.

When the kitchen lights are turned off and the sink is full, half the dishes dirty and the other half clean, as a single dad often insecure in being a full parent to my three little daughters, I'm reminded that we are indeed all okay.

Courage and Change in Southern Christian Fatherhood

by M. Bryan Blaise

BRYAN BLAISE is a New York City boy with deep Southern roots who thrives on diversity and daily discovering the power of unconditional love. The son of two loving parents living in a red and religious Central Florida community, he sees his life journey of understanding God, the Father's love, and himself as a gay man, as one entirely of blessing despite the bruises and bullying along the way. Bryan is currently a national Point Scholar getting his MBA at Columbia Business School in organizational strategy, with a keen interest in building efficient systems of equality and inclusiveness in global corporations. In his spare time, he continues his work of building bridges between the LGBTQ and faith communities, and thanks The Marin Foundation and Urban Village Chicago for their exemplary role modeling in these areas.

"I honestly did not see it working, Bryan. You have always had this vision and drive to do something bigger than just for yourself. And the person you spend the rest of your life with has to share that desire for changing the world."

I sat in the passenger seat next to my father during a recent trip home to Florida as he offered perspective on my freshly ended relationship. As we drove on, I sat in silence and thought about my alleged desire to change the world. It sat in stark contrast to my humble beginnings in Central Florida, the small town where my parents grew up and my brother, sister-in-law, and extended family still remain. A refugee to the metropolitan confines of Chicago and now in the organizational change management courses of Columbia Business School in New

York, I wondered where this passion for transformation came from.

Where did this desire to make a difference for others originate? How did my fixation on change develop amidst a family and town so comfortable with the status quo? I looked back at my dad to contend his last statement, and that's when it hit me.

Southern Christian fathers, those strong stalwarts of household order, authoritarian respect, and above all, patriarchal religious traditions. As heads of houses, theirs is a moral legacy of establishing and maintaining a family unit which instills a fearful commitment to God, family, and country—through the same methods and constructs their own fathers taught them.

It is a model of fatherhood that undoubtedly has largely served our country and faith communities well. Good Southern Christian men raising the next generation of masculine, rational Promise Keepers[1] of the faith. But for all the intrinsic value of tradition and ritual in our homes and houses of worship, is fatherhood an institution beyond improvement?

To understand my perceptions of fatherhood and my dad, you first must know his father. My grandfather was born and raised as deep and poor in the South as one can go—rural Mississippi. His dogmatic adherence to traditional gender roles was only exceeded by his commitment to the teachings of Church of Christ's[2] conservative doctrine. These beliefs and experiences served as the foundation and architecture for the home in which my dad grew up.

My father was not the firstborn of his family, but was the eldest male. Thus, he assumed the most scrutiny and responsibility for eighteen years, given my grandfather's traditional valuation of gender

---

1. Popular in the 1990s, Promise Keepers is a nonprofit faith-based organization focused on developing men's relationships with Jesus Christ, as well as their family, church, and community. For more information, visit www.promisekeepers.org.

2. One of several predominantly conservative protestant Christian denominations, this faith community is generally known for its belief that the Bible is the literal immaculate and inerrant word of God, its a capella worship style, and its practice of full body immersion as the only acceptable form of baptism.

and ability. And at age ten, he traveled with his two younger brothers, older sister, and parents to equally rural and largely conservative Central Florida, where I would spend the first eighteen years of my life.

The respect for elders deeply permeated every aspect of my dad's early instruction, from church to home. So it is no surprise that he deeply valued the crocheted creations of his grandmother and recognized that her creations were a simple generation from extinction. My dad took upon himself to learn the trade from my great-grandmother, just as he would later do with favorite family recipes as the rest of us were too busy with our own lives to appreciate the treasures of our predecessors. One day in his tweens, after weeks of proudly practicing enough stitches to design a dress for his mother, my dad looked up from his handiwork to find my grandfather's disappointed stares. The moral of that day was clearly stated: Men do traditionally male things, which does not include making dresses, regardless of my dad's larger objectives. This experience would be replayed in various ways throughout my dad's teenage years and told to me several times.

When the time came to carry on the tradition of Southern Christian fatherhood, and become a father himself on February 4, 1985, my dad decided to buck tradition. Though devout and still attending the many weekly gatherings at Church of Christ in our hometown, my father set his mind to do things differently than his father. He had both the scars and strengths of traditional Christian fatherhood. However, he felt the commitment to those historical practices should evolve to improve upon outdated perceptions of appropriate behaviors, interests, and emotions. To make such a change took courage, a masculine bravery seemingly admired by the criteria of his upbringing. Quietly and diplomatic, he directly questioned the men of the Word that preceded him on the possible improvements in raising men.

As I grew up, my father set a standard of full support and unconditional interest in my pursuits, which I quickly challenged as a toddler, turning aside outdoor activities and most sports after a seasonal try, in favor of literature and artistic endeavors. He followed through with his commitment to offer a change from his experience, even through high school when boys my age sought spots on the football team or Future Farmers of America. I simply asked for a pair of ballet slippers and tights. He came, regardless of his schedule or the ridicule from our community, to every performance and recital, always beaming with pride.

My coming out after college as a gay Christian man was still a shock to my father and mother. It most likely, too, challenged my father's conviction in his change efforts over the past twenty-two years to support my interests, no matter how nontraditional and gender nonconforming. This change in his understanding of my intrinsic constitution led to a year of questions and conversations that strained the bonds between father and son.

How did I justify this by the Scriptures? Where was my relationship with my Holy Father? What did I mean I still planned to be a father?

My Christian father, with his years of unwavering support of my passions and professional pursuit of corporate communications, seemed to be drifting away. This change in his perception of me was perhaps too much, I thought. Suddenly, my own faith—in him and God—shook. In the months ahead, prayer, reading the Bible, and work with Andrew Marin and The Marin Foundation in Chicago presented several opportunities to share thoughts and readings with my dad, things I had never before been able to share. I waited in Chicago, anxious that my dad would be there at the end of this trying time, still beaming and still proud now that he knew me as fully as my father who created me.

Later that same year, I stepped up to lead a new business proposal for my firm's LGBTQ communications practice. Given the small budget of the potential project, I was the sole creator of our firm's bid. The night before the file was to be sent to Taiwan, I sent the full bid, which included programs about international homophobia, to my parents with a desperate plea for their edits to the grammar and a blind eye to the content.

I arrived at the office early the following morning to make any adjustments my parents had noted and swiftly send the file off to the client. In my inbox was the following note from my father:

Son,

As a recovering homophobe, I want you to know how proud I am of the important work that you do and the people's whose lives you will ultimately change. I love you very much.

Your Dad

We did not win the business, but for me personally I received so much more. While I still did not recognize it in the moment, my father—much like my Heavenly Father—fully validated the person that I am and the call on my life. Though different from me in many ways, including sexual orientation, my father had made the tough decision to deviate from his personal and cultural upbringing, which enabled me to thrive as a closeted gay kid. He also modeled the effective power of change in such a way that he helped set the course of my life.

It was during that same recent trip home that discussions of differing political and theological ideologies with my brother peeled back old scars of growing up closeted in a religious conservative home and community. Heated words were exchanged, emotions flew, tears streamed. Staring into the faces of the three people who knew me the longest, I struggled to capture the mix of anger, resentment, fear, and shame I felt when going to bed at night after discussions like these.

"You all can close your eyes and fall asleep, but I lie there and wonder, wonder if how God made me will truly take me to the condemnation of hell—the direction I know you think I'm headed despite your love of me," was all I could muster.

My dad—recovering homophobe and change agent—said softly, as he always does when what he has to say is heartfelt and heart-changing, "I do not go to bed thinking you or any of us are going to hell or heaven. None of us are worthy to get into heaven by our acts. And we all have sin, particularly right now as we are trying to judge and parse out worse sins from others. The truth is, the message of Jesus is to love. Love yourself for who you are and how God made you. Love others for who they are and how God made them—perceived flaws and all. You and your life as a gay Christian man have taught me this. You changed my perspective. Now please, I hope we can change yours to know that we truly go to bed every night with only one thought of you. How much we love you."

He bucked tradition and his own upbringing to show an even greater love and acceptance, one that truly imitates the unconditional love of our Heavenly Father through Jesus Christ. It has strengthened my faith, my relationship with him, and given me the resolve to withstand the pain the world and those I have trusted deeply can inflict.

He showed me the power of change, when done with empathy and love, for improving lives of the marginalized and the meek. His strength of character is one I daily hope to uphold, and one day plan to teach to my own son with my future partner.

He shaped my destiny by rewriting the one he was originally conditioned to direct, and I am entirely thankful to both God and him that he did.

From One PK to Another

by D. Kyle Canty

KYLE and his wife, Pam, have been married for nearly fifteen years and have three children, Micah, Karis, and Shiloh Elyse. Kyle is a graduate of Cairn University (Philadelphia Biblical University) with a bachelor of science in Bible/Pre-Seminary and a master of science in Christian counseling. He also has a master of divinity degree from Biblical Theological Seminary. Kyle is currently pursuing a doctorate in urban missiology at Biblical Theological Seminary and is an assistant pastor at Great Commission Church in Philadelphia. Kyle's aspirations are to write on the topics that will bring about the reconciliation of the fractured church in North America. He hopes to one day teach at a seminary or Bible/Christian university. His heart is missions because he believes missions are close to God's heart.

I had a vivid childhood. My parents were great and many of the experiences that I relish now took place as a child inside the walls of a church building. I was the fourth of five children, the youngest boy. The picture that always comes to mind as I think of growing up as the son of a pastor/preacher is "fishbowl." It best describes a life that seems to be on display for amusement or critique. I was the son of a pastor, or a PK, a preacher's kid. There is the stigma that PKs have mastered the ability to shed their Christian upbringing. Yet, contrary to popular belief, PKs are not all drug dealers or pimps. It's so easy to characterize all by the extreme cases. I also think it's important to say up front that we are not all socially awkward and relationally inept. God has been gracious. Being young and black can be a hazardous endeavor in itself, but I was brought up by parents who loved God and loved their children.

My relationship with my father is a unique. Our personalities differ; he has an entrepreneurial spirit, whereas I tend to lean toward the analytical administrative type. Growing up, I remember spending a lot of time at my father's side. He was a bi-vocational pastor, which seemed to me to suggest working twice as hard but remaining just as poor. He owned an auto-repair business for a while before pastoring full time. My brothers and I spent most of our summers in that rotisserie oven called J. C. Auto Repair. These summers were filled with frequent how-to lessons and other nuggets of wisdom from a man who lived a tough life, but a life surrendered to Christ. I can remember on many occasions holding a mechanic's droplight so that my dad could see properly while he worked under the hood of a vehicle. I can't help but think that God was shaping character in my life through these mundane experiences. My father was a giving man who would drop everything to help a friend, whether it was by repairing their vehicle without cost or fixing a leak even if it took all night.

My father's other calling included pastoring a small church in South Philly. One of the things that I remember most about my childhood was my father taking me with him almost everywhere he went. I can recall on a few occasions being with him experiencing a discussion he had with a friend that lasted hours. I can distinctly remember a frightening chill coming over me at the realization that the conversation might go on forever. My dad's conversations were long, colorful, and engaging. He was from a generation that enjoyed face-to-face discussion over a vast range of topics. I found myself frequently in the company of older men, pastors and businessmen who had experienced a lot, so every conversation was a rhetorician's dream. These discussions touched on race, politics, business, and religion. *Entertaining* doesn't quite describe what I was allowed to observe in these formative years.

I grew up in North Philly and my household was an anomaly. Two-parent households stood out like an orchid among weeds. North Philadelphia was a poor Black community where residents struggled with issues of poverty and violence. Many of the homes in my neighborhood did not have a strong male presence, so my father stood out. At one point my presence around my father became a point of conflict with friends growing up—not sure why, but childhood friends questioned why I was with him instead of being out in the streets with them. I look back and know that growing up in the home of a pastor was God's grace; the streets claimed so many young lives. My parents' prayers were a hedge against the tragedy that visited so many urban households in the 1980s and 90s.

My experience as a pastor's kid was filled with expectations. Many of the expectations were the creation of observers who tried to use my siblings and me to get to my father. If church members disagreed with my father's decisions they would often take out their frustrations on my sister and me through comments and condescending stares meant to "even the score." Needless to say, my impressions of the pastorate turned sour. I didn't like church folk, especially those I went to church with. I still loved God, but I couldn't wait to get away from the fishbowl. As a young man I would contemplate, "Who would ever want to be a pastor?" I was not a rebel, but I simply had it, the calling, in part because of what I saw my father go through. In many cases during his ministry there was betrayal as well as extreme sacrifice, poverty, and the anguish of shepherding people within oppressed communities.

My plans did not include the pulpit; instead I planned to become a high school history teacher. I would change the world through a classroom, outside of the church and away from church folk. I resisted, bad-mouthed, and at times flat out rejected the notion of being a pastor. I didn't consider my father culpable for where I was—the sheep, not the shepherd, were at fault. One of the things I respected most about my father, especially during this time of personal exploration, was that he did not pressure me about the ministry.

It seems that the Lord has a sense of humor because as soon as I declared, "I would never," God responded with what seemed like a very personal question: "Who will go for us?" (Isaiah 6:8). That plan involved the pastorate and I sensed the Lord's calling on my life, but for a while I must admit that I attempted to sabotage His plans. In the midst of my struggle I thought about the pastorate and how I would deal with my children as a shepherd of God's people. Would I be a good father? Would I be able to avoid the mistakes of others who served in this office? Would I apply undue pressure on them to fulfill outlandish expectations, or would they be allowed to express their own personalities and follow God's will for their life?

The "Isaiah call" stayed with me. I remember accepting my call. It was during undergrad studies, I was doing research over the weekend in the library. It was a period of wrestling with what I had experienced secondhand. The wrestling that weekend culminated with my cry for mercy. I liken my response to Isaiah's, "Here am I send me." I finally came to embrace God's call on my life—husband, father, and pastor. I am now an assistant pastor at a church in Northwest Philadelphia. This is a community struggling with a nagging sense of hopelessness. God calls individuals to unique places and uses our lives to display the gospel in word and deed—this gives hope in these dry, destitute places.

I've been married to my wife, Pam (a missionary kid), for thirteen years and we have three children. I excel as a father through my wife's support. Strange as it seems, I have learned a lot about being a father by watching my wife as a mother. My wife has been used by God to help me navigate my role as a husband and pastor. There are times when the imbalance shows up and it is usually on the side of ministry receiving an inordinate amount of time and energy. She reminds me of priorities among priorities.

My kids are all unique individuals. My son, Micah, is a young man with big dreams and a mind that never quits. He loves Jesus and his heart is tender. My prayer for my son is that he be comfortable with who he is in Christ. As a young black man, I struggled to gain the approval of others only to go through a long period of low esteem and lack of confidence. As a father, the task of equipping my son for a very difficult world is vitally important. He will grow up in a land still dealing with strained race relations and forms of systemic op-pression. When I think of my boy, I go back to the times when my father would engage me in a theological debate to test my doctrinal fortitude. Preparing him for life's challenges requires quality time. I want my son to know that my love is unconditional and like the father in Jesus' parable there is nothing that he could do to stop my love. I hope that he understands his responsibility to love God and others.

My daughter Karis is the apple of my eye. She invades your heart and will never leave—her smile and eyes are infectious. To know her is to love her. Those who take the time to remain in her presence know exactly what I'm talking about. She does not have conversations like other girls her age, nor does she interact emotionally like kids her age. However, she hears every word, observes every little gesture, and has a unique affinity for music. As the father of a girl diagnosed with Autism Spectrum Disorder, I am always inspired by her achievements; whether big or small. My daughter has transformed my wife and me into activists for a cause that was once an issue for "others." To have a child with special needs requires a unique blend of patience and a bullish aggressiveness.

My parents were instrumental in demonstrating what it took to care for a child with disability. They raised my late sister, who at the age of twenty-four lost a painful battle with Sickle Cell Anemia. I can remember them pushing doctors who didn't understand the disease and refused to go the extra mile. Fathers will attempt to remove insurmountable obstacles for their children. Fatherhood is the process of stewarding my children into adulthood and beyond. There is no universal model for how to raise children, but good examples are hard to ignore.

Most recently, my wife gave birth to our second daughter, Shiloh Elyse. With her birth God has again given us an opportunity to bring Him glory as we provide an influencing presence in her life. As I write this, we celebrate Shiloh turning a month old. As a father I look fondly into her soft eyes and well up with an almost overwhelming need to protect her from the world around. Her needs at this tender age are so basic; to sleep, to eating, and to receive love. Whether she is one month old or twenty-one years old I hope to be the kind of father who will comfort when she feels pain, challenge when she's ambivalent, and rejoice when she has stepped out on faith and taken a risk no matter what the result.

As a father and pastor now, I can't help but wonder about my youthful chagrin at the fishbowl. Now that I am finally here, I am at peace. Yes, there is no way around carrying the cross that Christ has for those who call Him Lord. Actually, I must admit that there is a tremendous sense of fulfillment in what I'm doing. It's taken years, but God has healed many of the wounds and has used many of the lessons of my father's pastorate to help me in my duties as a bi-vocational pastor in West Oak Lane. Perhaps God brought me to the very place that I dreaded in order to heal past hurts and repair my perception of the ministry. My hope is that with a renewed perspective on pastoral ministry, I can raise my children to know that PKs are also loved by an awesome God who tenaciously goes after those He loves. I flinch sometimes to think of what preacher's kids go through under the microscope of some church cultures. Hopefully, my journey will help someone.

Immanuel: Dad is Here

by Marty Troyer

Marty Troyer is a husband and daddy, pastor and writer. He's been living his dream life in Houston, Texas since 2008. He and his wife Hannah have three children: proud big brother Malakai, little sister Clara, and baby Ruby. Throughout their marriage Marty and Hannah have struggled with infertility and the loss of two children from miscarriage.

Marty is the pastor of Houston Mennonite Church: The Church of the Sermon on the Mount. He also blogs as "The Peace Pastor" for *The Houston Chronicle* at blog.chron.com/thepeacepastor/. He loves preaching, encouraging people to become what they were created to be, and dreaming about what Houston could look like if we truly worked to make God's "kingdom come on earth as it is in heaven." Marty is a Wheaton College graduate, attended George Fox Evangelical Seminary, and graduated from Anabaptist Mennonite Seminary with a master of divinity.

"It's time to stop babying him!" would have made more sense if the son I was angry with wasn't six weeks old. The previous day, I was studying in our seminary apartment alone with our son, who would not stop crying. Nothing I did calmed him in the least; the longer this went on the hotter my anger burned. At one point I picked up a remote control and threw it at the door my wife was not coming through to save us.

Her retort, when I shouted, buried any self-righteousness I may have retained: "Who's the baby you're talking about?"

We laugh now, but those early months were hard. I was an angry dad. Mostly at myself, if I'm honest. I loathed that I couldn't help him, couldn't soothe his crying or fix whatever was happening in body or soul that needed tending. The character I was playing in my dad-script was that of Savior Dad, sent to rescue his son from that which he couldn't do for himself. Only I wasn't any good at it. I'm not making that up; he would cry if you changed him, fed him, burped him, or snuggled him. And nothing I would do changed that.

Dads are supposed to save you when you need it. Or, at least, that was the dad-script I inherited. My own father was a savior many times in my life, always available to swoop in and rescue me when needed. I grew up a classic white middle-class youngest child. I was never without a safety net.

My screwed up dad-script was underwritten by an equally screwed up god-script. This Savior business is, after all, what Super Dad in the sky is all about, isn't it? The divine wand-waver who answers prayers, forgives sins, and gets us all out of the cosmic mess we're in. According to this script, god doesn't need our help. We are, after all, only passive recipients!

But here's the thing I had to own up to: this "you will walk through the fire and not get burned" kind of thing didn't work. I'd been burned—bad. And worse yet, I felt like god was the one who'd led me right into the heart of the fire.

Forget for a second how poorly my dad-script was working. My *god-script* was shit. It made no sense anymore and didn't function. Locked in place since I was thirteen, it was forcing me to act like a, well, thirteen-year-old. As Walter Brueggemann says, "We are indeed made in the image of some God. And perhaps we have no more important theological investigation than to discern in whose image we have been made."[1] I had fashioned myself in the image of my thirteen-year-old god. An image that deteriorated the more impotent I felt.

At one point I literally had to shut Malakai's door, walk away while he screamed, and talk myself down from hurting him. My mind had settled on dropping him. It was going to be a well-crafted and carefully arranged drop from two feet above his mattress. He needed to learn

---

1. Walter Brueggeman, *The Prophetic Imagination*. Minneapolis: Augsburg Fortress Press, 2001. 8.

a lesson. He needed to stop crying. And if I couldn't help him stop, I'd teach him to stop. Salvation offered and not accepted requires . . . punishment. It's important to note that I didn't *agree* with anything I just wrote, I just *felt* it, and it fit the dad-script. I was treating my son precisely how my script said I should treat him. The script just didn't play out well.

That little Golem-like negotiation with myself forced me to choose: I could lose faith entirely and betray my conscience (a very live, vital option for me at that time). Or, I could change the script.

It's a hard thing to do, let your god die. I grieved, I cried, I felt depressed, alone, and scared shitless. But I let it happen.

And as it turns out, it was only hard on me. God didn't seem to mind at all. In fact, it suited God even better to free him from the bit part my thirteen-year-old self had assigned. Let your puny god die and all kinds of goodness will grow up into your soul. Seeds of healing, work you actually care about, humility, freedom to not be the smartest guy in the room, an entirely different kind of sex life, better parenting.

And a new script. One whose integrity (i.e., workability) matched the meaning my life deserves. To hell with the old script and its cheap knockoff savior complex that left me feeling emasculated. My kids don't need saving.

But one night, late, after many long minutes of crying, it finally dawned on me what my son Malakai needs. What we all need. He needs someone to be with him while he fights it out. He needs me. Not super me, answer me, hero me: just me. And he doesn't need me to fight it out for him, as if that were even possible. He just needs someone to hold him, someone who will never ever leave.

And a word, charged with energy like a replacement battery in a dead power tool, jolted me into a new script: *Immanuel.*

Immanuel, that ancient word meaning "God-with-us."

This was like a second birth, equally messy, what with both of us crying now. I can't even tell you who needed it more, Malakai or me, but when that new script appeared it made perfect sense. Life is about presence, being together, actually together in such a way as to know each other, and know you're in it through hell or high water.

This Immanuel God is the kind of god you might even want to have a beer with. He's certainly open to it. Immanuel, God with me in the midst of *my* life. Not here to take the bad or add the good, but to simply be, non-judgmentally, present. What I wouldn't give to have someone see my junk and not make me feel like shit at the same time. Someone who sees me at my worst and leans over to offer me, "Another?"

This new script, a script that rippled from my theology into my parenting, drained my anxiety and anger and opened me to become a different functioning dad. The goal changed. My script no longer asked me to produce, it asked me to commit to never leaving my kids alone while they work it out for themselves. To parent without agenda, with nowhere you'd rather be, nothing better you'd rather be doing.

Immanuel, dad is with us.

This seems so basic, so impossibly obvious you wonder how I could miss it. Until you look around and realize how many dads aren't actually there with their kids. They're out climbing the corporate ladder, working their tails off for a future payoff, a blessing they swear is for the kids. It's all too easy to be physically present with the kids but completely zone out in round four of Candy Land while typing that extra email in your head.

We say to ourselves so flippantly, *I know I'm gone a lot, and that I work many hours. But I'm providing for them long term.* I pull that "but" out like some magical incantation that eradicates the missing relationship. Or maybe it's more practical, *In my career the company prospers on the backs of the new guys. I don't have a choice! But one day it will get better.* Isn't not having a choice a choice?

I've always fancied myself as a well-known leader when I grow up, maybe even one with a bit of a legacy. I use to say I'd love to see my face on a bobble-head, that's when I'd know I had arrived! Or at least give me a byline. Now all of a sudden, I've got a family. And family changes everything.

I'm becoming ever more suspicious of the idea that long-term is more valuable than short-term. Show me where this has worked. Find me a young adult glad his dad traded genuine relationship for college tuition. Or better yet, find me an incredibly successful church man who is known for his incredible love of his family. Billy Graham? James Dobson? Isn't our society and youth culture in particular a screaming testament to the terrible myth of long-term payoff? By then, for far too many families, it's too late.

So I've carried this image of God as Immanuel forward as my children have grown. And continued to embrace the reality that my own spirituality, theology, and personal baggage deeply effects my capacity and presence as a dad, and therefore also my children's development.

My script change happened nearly five years ago now; but I'm still working it out, sometimes in some pretty pathetic ways. Recently it dawned on me I pray differently for my two children. My prayers for my oldest are flat and perfunctory, bland and distant. I don't connect well with his life or speak freely as if God really were present in the room with us. But in my prayers for my daughter I'm deeply personal, remarkably patient, observant of her gifts, always connecting those to what's happening in our world and my hopes for her to connect with what's really going on out there.

It wasn't by choice, my prayers were simply locked into the script I was living *at the time of their infancy.* When my oldest was born I was in a bad script with an untrustworthy god who was seldom around. It was my thirteen-year-old god, and I was still praying like I was thirteen. Only problem was that I knew *that* god had died. And so when I prayed for him, it was because that's what good dads do, not because I felt it. But I want my son to grow up to be a man of prayer. And changing my god-script has helped me unpack my baggage and start over from today, which has breathed new life into my prayers with my son.

When my daughter was born my script was much more spacious. God was like the old college buddy who would notice but never care you were wearing the same outfit for the eighth day in a row. But he also was up to some pretty crazy stuff in the world, the kind of stuff you want your daughter to join: unmasking injustice, subverting our bloated empire, defending pretty much everyone. So I keep seeing Clara actively addressing the world's biggest problems, and it absolutely energizes me.

You think you have things figured out, or at least covered up, and your fragility oozes out sideways to betray you! What a mess. I hate that our personal junk can hinder our parenting. But it's never too late. Learn from it, drag it onto the couch and force it to teach you everything it knows. Then set it free.

It's what it will take. Otherwise we'll still be that pimply thirteen-year-old, wishing everyone would just shut up and getting pissed when they don't. I didn't even like being thirteen when I was thirteen. It's pathetic now, though. I'm committed to growing into my new god- and dad-scripts. It's giving me the plot I need to be fully present with my kids.

Immanuel, Dad is here.

Lessons from Infertility

by Andrew Marin

ANDREW MARIN is President and Founder of The Marin Foundation (www.themarinfoundation.org). He is author of the award winning book *Love Is an Orientation* (2009) and its interactive DVD curriculum (2011), as well as a forthcoming ebook on civic engagement. Andrew is a regular contributor to a variety of media outlets and frequently lectures at universities around the world. Since 2010 Andrew has been asked by the United Nations to advise their various agencies on issues of bridging opposing worldviews, civic engagement and theological aspects of reconciliation. He blogs at www.patheos.com/blogs/loveisanorientation, is married to Brenda, and splits his time between the LGBT Boystown neighborhood of Chicago and St. Andrews, Scotland, where he is earning his PhD in cultural theology.

As my wife, Brenda, and I walk into a side conference room I can't help but notice the two huge pictures hanging on the wall. The one on the left is a collage of every ethnic child that comes to mind. *African*, check. *Asian*, check. *Latin*, check. *Indian*, check. *Middle Eastern*, check. I think I even see a blonde-haired, blue-eyed white child toward the bottom third. Is that child American, Canadian, Nordic, British, Russian? I can't be certain, but the possibilities are endless.

My eyes then move to the oversized picture hanging to its right. Neatly positioned in the middle of a fully grown field of wheat stocks sits a suburban-looking American husband and wife. Her diamond ring glimmering from the reflection of the sun. His dark hair cropped in a faux-hawk. Both are wearing untucked button-down dress shirts, khakis, and sandals. And each is holding a black baby.

Immediately my brain begins processing all that is right and horribly wrong with those still images; communicating too many cliché stereotypes than two pictures should ever put forth. With that as our first impression, Brenda and I sit down at a shiny conference table. I get comfortable in a large, black leather chair, anticipating the people about to walk in the door. I soon realize that this chair is fully adjustable to any and all of my height, swivel, lumbar, and reclining needs. I partake.

The pictures. The chairs. The hundreds of pamphlets neatly aligned in dozens of individual categories—all clearly labeled to elicit a singularly efficient, or hey, a multitude of efficient choices. The subconscious reality of this room oozes Options. Choices. Wants. Needs. Exactitude. Just pick. It's right there.

You can see it; it's at your eyes. You can touch it; it's at your fingertips. But most important, you can *feel* it; because your heart is bleeding your greatest desire to one day be a parent.

And thus, the epic beginning of adoption.

TRUTH

The door gently opens and our heads turn to greet two warm-spirited women approaching the table. They sit right across from us, adjusting their own chairs to optimal choice and comfort level. Each has a bright white folder, which they elegantly slide across the table. We snatch them up and open them right away. But, do it cool, you know, like we've been-there-done-that.

Inside the folders are even more options. Despite the inundation of daily options for choice and maximum comfort, I never thought it applicable to buying children. I also never thought I'd utter the phrase *buying children.*

But that is what I quickly learn is the truth of the matter. Staring at the options in the folders while sitting in these seats with those large pictures looming over my consciousness, sure makes me feel like my choices are endless. What do I want? Whom do I want to father? It can be provided.

For a cost. For a varying cost, that is.

And all of a sudden I get very, very uncomfortable.

The more *white* in the biological pigment the more expensive the child. The more *black* in the pigment the cheaper. An *older* kid? Even cheaper still. A *disabled* child? The cheapest. A *newborn white* baby? You can guess . . .

In one moment I became acutely aware that the economy of supply and demand is again dictating a sub-population of human life. Sounds eerily familiar to me: the metric of a life is financially marked and valued from the threefold combination of a human's, in this case a baby's, age, skin color, and measurable health. We escaped from this type of vile commodification almost one hundred fifty years ago in a darker period in America's history, only to have a similar bureaucratic structure appear again in a new form—adoption.

Please understand that in no way am I suggesting these children don't need homes, or that adoption isn't a worthwhile endeavor for couples to commit themselves to! The corruption stems from a system that promotes selling humans as commodities whose worth is inherently attained through birth, yet clearly ranked on arbitrary social factors defined by purchaser(s). Explain to me the dignity in this situation?

Many talk about adoption as a justice issue. I see no systemic justice in something that forces couples to participate in a system of economic whoremongering clouded in "choice," to one day love a child as each child deserves. Love should never be based on age, color, health; or gender or orientation, for that matter. Love must always be based on one's inherent worth as an equal part of humanity.

Our journey toward adoption started four years previous, when my wife and I decided to try and get pregnant. After a year and a half of "trying," we ended up going to an infertility specialist. There was some obvious confusion, frustration, and even some sadness at not being able to conceive a baby naturally. At this point though, Brenda and I still believed having a baby was a done deal.

All of the traditional factors were in our favor: We were young enough at twenty-nine years old; both of us were physically, emotionally, and spiritually in good standing; neither of us had any past or lingering health issues that might complicate the process; and we had great insurance that covered up to three full in vitro fertilization (IVF) treatments.

Brenda's OBGYN studied under Edmond Confino, one of the original pioneers of IVF, and they circumvented the three-year waiting list to see Confino, getting us an appointment in one week. From that point forward Confino became our infertility doctor. Such trusted hands brought us immense reassurance.

If nothing else, Brenda is thorough in everything she does. We understood that even IVF only works 38 percent of the time. There are a lot of shots, and a woman's body, emotions, and stability can be affected in a number of different ways. Be warned all you want, but one never knows what will happen until it actually happens. An obvious oversimplification on my part, but with an implantation, some shots, and some prayers, nine months later we expected to have a baby of our own DNA.

FAILURE

Our three failed IVF treatments took a year and a half. I don't remember much about that time. I remember some themes—awkwardness, helplessness, frustration, annoyance. From the day of the implantation to the day of the results two weeks later, I had to stick Brenda twice-daily with inappropriately long needles filled with intense chemicals attempting to artificially trick her natural reproductive process—the one that doesn't work naturally for us—into thinking she was pregnant.

Each day, two pricks into Brenda's stomach prior to the harvesting of eggs and implementation procedure, and two each day in her butt afterwards. Over the course of the daily shots I could see physical proof of my torture, a trail of bruises, none of which had time to heal with the unceasing barrage of shot after shot; day after day. The doctors told us that during the two week in-between stage the mother has to *believe* she is pregnant. Odd, isn't it? Believing she's pregnant when every time she looks at her naked body she sees dozens of discolored reminders saying exactly the opposite.

With each failed IVF attempt, Brenda was feeling *failure* enough for the both of us. I was horrified and scared of the trauma I saw in her, and couldn't bear to let myself go there. I literally didn't think I had the strength to keep any amount of sustained stability for the both of us if I allowed my emotions to match hers.

Brenda felt each prick of the needle: the pain of the progesterone-laced olive oil that I forcefully injected into her body. The extra hormones, changing body chemistry, emotions, and closeted fears encompassing her uterus, soul, and psyche, knowing the weight of *a normal family,* within this foreign experience, falls upon all of it. I closed all this off to the fullest extent I could.

Between the two of us, I'm always the one that *feels* everything more deeply. In this case, not only were the roles reversed, but I had unforeseen consequences as well. I was pissed all the time. I was pissed because I couldn't allow myself to feel what Brenda felt. I was pissed at Brenda for feeling so much. I was pissed her body changed with the daily injections of Follistim and Lupron. I was pissed that she made me force this pain upon her to one day potentially see a product of her and my DNA—for the benefit of both of us.

My heart broke the most when I heard her cry out, "I can't even do what God created women to do."

As a husband, how do you handle that? I was helpless. I couldn't fix, or even ease any of it. Not the emotions, the pain, the fact that I was the one having to inflict it upon her, or the constant realization that with each failed attempt we were doing all of this for *nothing.* The one thing I learned is how over-spiritualizing *confusion* is helpful to no one. So instead I'm going to ask you to sit in reality with me.

REALITY

I'm finishing writing this on Sunday May 12, 2013—Mother's Day. In honor of Brenda, her sacrifice, and journey, I share here something that she wrote in the middle of her grieving process over three failed

IVFs:

Things I will miss, that I have to heal from:

I will never know the excitement and uneasiness of a positive pee stick.

I will never make the call to my partner to tell him the results.

I will never utter the words "I am pregnant and having a baby."

I will never feel the growth of life inside of me.

I will never hear my baby's first heart beat.

I will never experience the excitement of seeing the life growing inside me on an ultrasound.

I will never see the joy and fear on my partner's face when he views the baby for the first time.

I will never have my partner put his hand on my stomach to feel the baby.

I will never pray over the baby in my tummy.

I will never go through the hospital visits and birthing classes.

I will never feel the pains of labor.

I will never witness the fear on my husband's face as he races me to the hospital.

I will never give birth.

I will never hold my baby (or any baby) right after they are born and experience the skin to skin touch.

I will never have the connection of breast feeding.

I will never be able to see the baby that Andrew and I could make.

Copying this list still makes me want to throw up. I am no more healed today than I was when she first wrote it. I know God is in it all. But reality doesn't mean comfort, no matter how much I believe in God's peace. I no longer care for answers. I only want for Brenda to know she is loved more than anything in this world—just as she, and I, together, have been created. Baby or not.

I've heard fathers say that one doesn't know love until one loves their own child. Does that make Brenda and my love for each other unknown, or less than that of a father and his child? I've learned through this journey that being a father must stem from a place much deeper than a child entering this world. It must stem from the inherent understanding of what it means to live into *love* throughout life, just as full as a father might feel for his own flesh and blood child. This, is what makes a true father.

Much love.

To Be a Father Like My Mother

by Brian Bantum

BRIAN BANTUM has been assistant professor of theology at Seattle Pacific University and Seminary for five years. Before Seattle he completed his PhD in theology at Duke University. His teaching and writing asks questions like, "Who are we?" and "Who is God?" and "Why do our bodies matter?" His first book was *Redeeming Mulatto: A Theology of Race and Christian Hybridity* (Baylor, 2010). He is currently working on a book that explores the theological significance of embodied life, as well as an "illuminated" theology that expresses theological claims through word and image. Brian lives in Seattle, Washington with his wife, Rev. Gail Song Bantum, and their three amazing sons.

My world was new. Holding my firstborn son in the hospital, eyes just like mine staring back at me under a mop of straight black hair. I had become a father. But even with Caleb in my arms "father" was just a name, a role, until I ventured into the world without him for the first time a few days later.

Out-of-my-mind-tired and walking through the mall to pick up some film, I would hear a baby crying and find myself moving toward the sound. "That is not my child. Caleb is at home," I would tell myself. I was a father now and there now existed someone who was *from* me. My life drawn to his cries and his laughter. But who was I? Fatherhood, for me, would be disorientation. It would not be drawing on the steady memories of my own father's presence in my life.

Fatherhood would be a life of perpetual questions. What was it to be a father? How would I love in the midst of my father's absence? What would I be to him? Would I be absence and uncertainty? Now with three sons, my life is still full of questions. But even more, it is finding the way my life as a father is about becoming more like my mother, about how a life of discipleship, crying *"Abba,* Father"[1] is not about living into an abstract role of father, but displaying the manifold manifestations of love that constitute my life, my manhood. Would I be sacrifice? love? presence? courage? Would I be like my mother for my sons?

My father was a complicated presence in my life. Arriving two hours late for his allotted Saturday outing, but sending me flying into a mound of blankets in a fit of laughter. The smell of alcohol on his breath at my thirteenth birthday party and a present handed to me in a paper bag with the receipt falling out. Comforting me while I sat at the base of the toilet with the flu. My mother left crying in the bedroom after his phone calls. But most of all, thoughts of my father bring to mind thoughts of his absence.

It was my mother whose life permeated my childhood, whose love was the center of my life. She was the one who had "the talk" with me, who taught me to shave and tie a tie, who listened to my declarations of devotion when I thought I was in love for the first time. Sitting in an empty living room when no one showed up for my tenth birthday party, she took me to the toy store and brought me home to an impromptu family party, complete with streamers, balloons, and the tangible reminder that I was loved. She listened to my adolescent pining late into the night and embraced me in all my imperfections. She was not a perfect woman, but she filled my life with love and the perpetual sense that I was seen and loved and remembered.

From the presence of my mother, and despite the ambivalence of my father, the hope of becoming a father remained throughout my young life. I am sure some of this was a desire born from this sense of

---

1. *Abba* (αββα) is the Greek transliteration of the Aramaic word meaning "father." It carries with it the idea of a personal, close relationship with one's father. Some scholars suggest the word is the English equivalent of "daddy," though this correlation is not universally accepted. The author's reference here is to Mark 14:36, in which Jesus is recorded as praying, *"Abba,* Father, . . . everything is possible for you." In using this word, Jesus was expressing a personal, close relationship with God, his Father.

lack, a vain hope to fill in the hole my father never filled. Fatherhood seemed to be a job to attain, a function to perform, something I wanted to live into, to fill the gaps I felt so deeply in my own life. But in the midst of this absence being a father was not just about not being like my father. Being a father was the substance of what I would offer my children. To be a father was to be present in the life of another the way my mother had been present for me.

With the sounds of my own sons' lives filling my home, and looking back on the father I have tried to be, I have come to see that fatherhood, for me, was never about my father's presence or absence, not at the marrow. When I now imagine what it means to be a father, I see my mother's tenderness and laughter, I feel her sorrow at the sight of my pain. As I grew and learned more of her story and the tragedy that filled her life, I came to see fatherhood as her courage to love even when her own life was filled with betrayal and terror. Racked with arthritis and constant back pain, wrestling with mental illness and depression, my mother strained everyday to love me in such a way that that the pattern of pain and violence would not define my life as it had hers.

When I was fifteen, I became a Christian and waded slowly into the waters of discipleship. In my particular pond, a small suburban Southern Baptist congregation, what it meant to be a father and what it meant to call God "Father" flowed in and out of one another, knitting together into the figure of "tender warrior." These were men who embodied the "Father" in the leadership of their home and in their communities. Wanting to be a faithful Christian man and being told this is what it meant to have a biblical worldview, I did the best I could to shape my life into that form. I read my Bible, imagined myself as the spiritual and financial provider of my home. The "promise keeper" father was one who honored his wife and his children, but the wife was always at home. She was sensitive and emotional while the father was steady and certain. But in the face of this image I could only see my tendencies toward nurture and my proclivity to sensitivity as weakness, as contrary to what it meant to be a father.

And I wanted strength and certainty to be right. I wanted that to be me. In this image there was compassion and courage and strength. And most of all there was certainty about what I needed to be. I did my best to find those things in my own father, who had eventually become sober and Christian, fought cancer, and became a new man in the process. Through his witness in that moment I began to follow Christ. During his illness and even in his death, I etched and scraped and tore, imagining him into that man I hoped I should become.

But the pasted man would not hold together for long and the dark absence that was at the bottom of his presence in my life would seep in again, reminding me of who he was in all his good and broken ways. Only in the burning embers of his life did he find the time to sit with me, to hear me, to see me. His body, his life, even at it succumbed to cancer, could not fill in the absence that had been carved out over so many years. He was a gentle and loving man who could see little beyond his own needs and life, even despite his desire to be something different to his sons and his wife. The cancer would finally overtake my father when I was seventeen. He left me with glimpses of reconciliation and the possibility of transformation, but also a profound reminder that his life, or any one life for that matter, was an insufficient image of fatherhood.

Becoming a father has not been a matter of fulfilling biological imperatives or prerequisites of manhood. Fatherhood has been wrestling with my own imperfections, my fear of becoming like my father to my sons, of fleeing from my own selfish tendencies, seeing the limitations of my life as well as coming to see the fullness of what I have to offer my children. Fatherhood was not a role to fill my own gaps or a preordained image of "father." Fatherhood has become, for me, an offering. My fatherhood is an offering—to God, to my children, to my wife—of my mother's and father's lives manifest in my body. It is the peculiarity of my manhood, the reservoir of many streams that flow into and gather in my life and are poured out in this male body. What I offer my sons is not a model of fatherhood that somehow gives them an image of who God the Father is. I offer them a community of faith, the gathering of my wife and my mother and my father, that have merged in my life in the multiplicity of ways God has pieced me together. I offer my sons the love and courage of my mother and the stillness of my father knit together. At times this looks like building a catapult with my nine-year-old or teaching my thirteen-year-old my mother's secret spaghetti recipe. Sometimes it's being the one who wakes up at three in the morning to clean up vomit or just being there to listen to my sons in their moments of not knowing what to say or do. I inhabit fatherhood in this way not because of roles I feel I need to fulfill, but because I am the son of a father who is a carpenter, the son of a mother who is a nurse. My childhood was filled with presences of comfort and patient listening and this is what I have to give my sons.

So when I am pressed in my most desperate moments to think about who God is, about who the one is to whom Jesus cried, "*Abba*, Father," while pain tore through his body, the image that comes to mind is not the faint presence surrounded by absence that was my own father. The image that comes to mind, the visceral body that communicates to me what "father" looks like when it loves and mourns, is my mother. It has been a life of living into a reality that the world is new when a child is born of you. *Abba*, Father. Jesus' cry of dependence and God-forsakenness, a cry of fear and courage and hope that he is heard, a cry of pain and sacrifice and love. When I hear the "father" of this cry I see my mother. When I hear this cry, I am pressed to ask if my being a father exhibits her love and sacrifice and strength. Does my life press into the lives of those I love in the way my mother's pressed into me?

Eight years after my father died, my mother joined him with God. She too was overcome by cancer, after eighteen months of fighting and struggle to make sure she saw her second grandchild born. The reality of her absence ebbs and flows in my life, oftentimes in overwhelming ways. But her life remains an image of God's love, an image of what I mean when I cry out with Jesus, "*Abba*, Father."

In my best moments, I hope my fatherhood participates with God's life, not in its likeness of the name "father" and some imaginary, fixed image of what this must look like. Rather, I hope my life offers the fullness of those who have loved me, who have sown their lives into me. Prayerfully, my life does not image the fullness of the name "father," but rather declares the impossibility of anyone fulfilling this image without a community of women and men knitting themselves into the children they love.

A Letter to My Unborn Daughter
by Shane Blackshear

SHANE BLACKSHEAR is a blogger and host of the podcast Seminary Dropout. Shane has served in numerous roles in the past including college ministry and founding pastor of a small church. Shane lives in Austin, Texas with his wife Kate and their daughter Margot.

As I write this it is exactly two days after I've learned that I am going to be a father for the first time. So many thoughts, and one worry: Will the baby be healthy, and if not, will it be because of something I've done? What if I've eaten too much mercury-rich tuna? What if there are real consequences for that time I wore a swimsuit as underwear?!

But mostly there is joy, excitement, and a fluttery stomach; the kind you have when standing on the edge of a tall cliff or when you strap yourself into your seat on a giant rollercoaster.

For two days I've known.

The baby's arrival is several months away and already I feel that I need to begin explaining myself to this soul that I will meet face-to-face in the coming year. If I start writing now maybe I'll have something of substance by the time he or she is born or at least able to read.

Dear Baby of Mine,

I am your father. It's good to meet you. So . . . what are you into? Sports? Music? Throwing up and pooping? That's cool.

I'm writing to explain some things to you. At some point you may start to do the math and wonder why your mom and I waited relatively late in life (I'm thirty) to have our first child. I suppose there are a lot of reasons, not the least of which is that I feel as though there are many parts of life that I haven't figured out yet.

There was a point at which I thought I knew everything, or at least almost everything. I would say that at nineteen I pretty much had everything figured out. Everything from God and life to less important things. For instance, if your shirt has brown in it you should wear a brown belt and brown shoes; the same is true of a shirt with black and a black belt and shoes. Then I spent my twenties realizing that I didn't have anything figured out. For example, if my shirt has black *and* brown, what then, *what*? Why is life so hard!?

During my twenties I realized that I didn't have God and life completely figured out either. How do I help *you* navigate life if I haven't figured it out yet either!? So many questions: What does real manhood/womanhood look like? How is it possible to teach you about who God is, while allowing it to be your faith and not just mine? Am I able to model for you God-given manhood that doesn't conform to the culture's idea of what that is? How do I raise you to not love money, to care for the poor, the oppressed, and the marginalized?

And what about the problems of contemporary society? There are *so* many messes for a child to step in these days: eating disorders, drugs, alcohol, underground fight clubs. How can I protect you adequately without being overprotective? How can your mother and I love you in such a way that you do not seek fulfillment from the wrong things?

This problem is further complicated by the fact that I'm told parenting is not easy for *anyone*. I have *no* problem believing this. I've seen wonderful people, people that I love and look up to, people who are wise beyond their years, raise complete jerk-wads. Along that note, I had an excellent father, and what did that produce? A guy who knew it all by nineteen and spent the next ten years unlearning it.

So you can see that this is a little terrifying for me. The only thing that brings me solace is this: Part of what I spent my twenties learning and unlearning is that I had been telling God who he was. I then realized that there was a mystery to God, that I would never have him totally figured out on this side of eternity, and that is a good thing. I embraced the mystery and found a God more exciting and wild than the one I had figured out. As for the things that I do not know, God's grace fills in the gap.

There are many things that are *not* a mystery, that I know firmly. Chiefly, Jesus is who he says he is, and he loves us.

Your mother and I took time a few days before this new year to sit down and write out some goals for the new year. It is the first time I've done such a thing, but I hope to do it every year from here on out. I think it helps us to be purposeful about our lives, and that is what I want to do for you. Without being overbearing or manipulative, I want to be purposeful about your life. So I promise to you that I will:

- Show you Jesus, his love, grace, and mercy.

- Help you find out who God has made you to be.

- Teach you to love justice and mercy.

- Put you in proximity to the poor, and those who do not look like you.

- Remind you daily how much I love you.

- Try not to be super-dad, and be transparent and vulnerable with you.

Why I have been afraid of inviting you into the same wonderful mystery I have found, I do not know. Perhaps it's because I have heard that children need security and consistency, but maybe just knowing that Jesus is who he says is, that he loves you, and I do too, is the most secure and consistent feeling in which you could peacefully rest.

As for the rest of it, the wonderful sea of mystery; I've decided that we can explore it together, you, me, your mother, and the family that God has given us.

By the time you are able to read this you will have learned that doing things in a timely fashion is not your father's forte, so you will understand that even this short letter has taken me over a month to write. In that time your mother and I have learned that you are a girl. You are my precious baby Margot, and we have seen your sweet face for the first time thanks to the miracle of three-dimensional sonograms. We're so excited for your arrival. You are teaching me about Jesus even now because I am already enamored and in love with you even though you have completed no tasks to earn my favor other than existing and belonging to me.

Your mom and I are still preparing as much as we can, but we do know that you will have a home with a crib to sleep in, a mom and a dad, and a wonderful, mysterious Savior for us all to explore together.

Sincerely,
Dad

Broken, Missing, Waiting

by Jason Boyett

JASON BOYETT is a writer, speaker, entrepreneur, and dad from Amarillo, Texas. He has written or contributed to more than a dozen books, including *O Me of Little Faith* (Zondervan) and the Pocket Guide series (*Pocket Guide to the Apocalypse*, *Pocket Guide to the Afterlife*, etc.). A designer and former creative director in the advertising industry, he spends his days ghost-tweeting for celebrities, hosting the 9 Thumbs podcast (9thumbs.com), and holding forth on Facebook and Twitter (@jasonboyett).

Jason and his wife, Aimee, have known each other since they were pre-schoolers and are the parents of Ellie, Owen, a Yorkie named Daisy, and a hamster named Josh. Find him online at jasonboyett.com.

Spend enough time in and around evangelical Christianity and you'll hear some version of this truism: *How you relate to your earthly father deeply influences how you relate to God.*

From childhood until now, I've enjoyed a healthy relationship with my own father. It is as strong as it has ever been.

Now, at the age of forty, my belief in God is weaker than ever before.

And yet, as much as I want to dismiss that earthly father/heavenly Father correlation as a tired cliché, it has proven accurate in a way I never expected.

Taos, New Mexico, 1994. On the flattest, easiest slope at the bottom of a legendary ski mountain known for its expert terrain, my relationship with my dad changed forever.

He became human.

It happened on a church ski trip for my brother's senior class. I was twenty and tasked with leading worship. My parents attended as sponsors, along with my new fiancée (now my wife) and her parents. It was a family ski vacation disguised as a church retreat.

At three-thirty p.m., the end of a long day on the slopes, I glided down a low-grade, let's-head-back-to-the-lodge ski run. As I rounded a curve, I slowed to avoid two ski patrol personnel securing a tightly wrapped body onto an emergency toboggan—the kind designed to tow injured skiers behind a snowmobile. It's never a good sign, the skier's coffin. The injury looked bad. I slowed out of respect and caution.

That's when I recognized the ghost-white face bundled into the toboggan.

My dad. My God. My dad.

He'd been on the same boring slope and had turned around to ski backward. It was an old skiing trick, one I'd admired since he first introduced me to the sport when I was ten. But this time, in one of those random half-seconds that divide a life into Before and After, he lost his balance. He fell. On the way down he twisted to catch himself. He hit the icy slope in that contorted position and the ball-shaped head of his femur snapped in two.

My strong, happy, healthy forty-six-year-old dad broke his hip.

I skidded to a stop. "Dad?" I asked. I felt like a cannonball hung in my stomach. "What happened?"

His face was pale as the winter afternoon sunlight. "I hurt myself," he said.

My mom, sister, and fiancée were sixty miles away at a retreat center near Santa Fe. My brother was elsewhere on the mountain. None of us had cell phones back then. Alone, I followed the snowmobile to the emergency room at the base of the mountain.

Thus began the longest and loneliest seven hours of my life. I heard my dad scream in agony as the medics tried to x-ray his hip on a steel medical table. I heard him whimper as they finally gave it up and lifted him back onto a bed. I sat beside him in an ambulance as it screamed down the mountain to a hospital twenty miles away.

I listened as the orthopedist pronounced his need for emergency surgery as soon as possible. I made dozens of phone calls attempting to locate my mom. I filled out paperwork. I tried to comfort him. I shuddered at the fear in his eyes. I clutched his hand as they wheeled him away for the first major surgery of his life. I prayed and prayed.

Meanwhile, a snowstorm rolled over the mountains and dumped on Taos. I had no idea where my mom was, or when she would arrive. That snowy night in the dark, empty hospital, I'd never felt more alone. Never.

That weekend preceded multiple surgeries, a year of crutches and canes, months of therapy, and eventually, a hip replacement. Two decades later, my father still walks with a significant limp.

In healthy family situations such as mine, a boy trusts and admires his dad at a level just below superheroes or Jesus. My dad could build and fix things. He took me backpacking. He drove a sports car. He taught Sunday school to high school girls, which meant that all the older girls I had crushes on at church thought my dad was awesome. He was no Batman, but he was strong and cool and might as well have been indestructible.

Then, in the snow, I saw him broken. When a child observes fear or pain in his dad's eyes, even as a young adult, it changes the relationship. It exposes the father's weakness, his limitations, his fragility. It makes him fully human. This sudden humanity transformed our simple father-son relationship into something more complex.

That same year, coincidentally or not, my relationship with God also began to change. The new-found depth between Dad and me found its parallel in my spiritual life. Most Christians categorize a more mature relationship with their heavenly Father as a good thing. But just as my dad's accident opened my eyes to his vulnerability, the path I began over the next few months uncovered weaknesses in my view of God.

I can't help but wonder if they're related.

How do you wedge a spiritual autobiography into a few sentences? I grew up a Southern Baptist in one of the most morally and politically conservative cities in Texas. Though our church leaders would have bristled at the "fundamentalist" label, I was taught fundamentalist staples like biblical inerrancy (the belief that the original manuscripts of the Bible are without error), a dispensational eschatology (the *Left Behind*-style rapture[1] and end-of-the-world scenarios) , and a God who punished and judged my sins. I was also taught a passion for Jesus and a commitment to sharing the Gospel message with the world around me. Our church was *evangelical* both in "capital-E" categorization and also in its emphasis on proselytizing and conversions. We attended multiple times a week.

Church was family. I still love that church and recognize how much of the good things in my life are due to its influence on me. I met my wife and her family there, and I learned to love the Bible there, along with music, community, and service. But I also spent my teenage years doubting my salvation, fearing hell, and bound by legalism.[2] I felt uncomfortable around anyone who drank, smoke, cussed, and watched R-rated movies, which is to say I felt uncomfortable around most of my friends.

Though rich and loving, my childhood faith tradition was also narrow. In my early twenties, I set out from that base camp to explore the religious world beyond it. My interest in the musician Rich Mullins introduced me to the contemplative Catholicism of Brennan Manning. Manning's writing on grace, so helpful to undo the restrictive legalism of my youth, brought me to writers like Henri Nouwen and Frederick Buechner. From there, I found my way to

---

1. The conservative evangelical belief that faithful Christians will be physically "lifted up" to heaven prior to the Second Coming of Christ, based on a contemporary interpretation of 1 Thess. 4:16-17. This controversial but widespread perspective is on prominent display in the bestselling Christian fiction series, *Left Behind*, by Tim LaHaye and Jerry Jenkins.

2. Legalism, in Christian theology, is an overemphasis on religious rules or behavioral ideals, as opposed to reliance on God's acceptance, love, and grace. Legalists are said to pursue salvation by adherence to the law, otherwise known as "works-based salvation.")

John Polkinghorne, N. T. Wright, and Robert Farrar Capon, and then Marcus Borg, Jaroslav Pelikan, and Bart Ehrman. It's a lengthy list.

The weight of this new knowledge began to press against my beliefs. Small imperfections grew into larger flaws. Cracks spread through the foundation, one after another until I looked down, years later, and saw that my faith was mostly rubble. My bedrock devotion to a literal understanding of the Bible crumbled into a more contextualized reading of Scripture. I love the Bible, but I read it as an ancient collection of documents that owe more to their human authors than the Holy Spirit's dictation. I spent the first two decades of my life fearing hell, and have spent the last two decades wondering if I believe in it at all. I no longer doubt my salvation; today I doubt whether God exists.

If anything, I live today as an external Christian, still attending church and still committed to the teachings of Jesus Christ, while feeling like an agnostic on the inside. I have lost the strong, intimate God of my childhood. He has been replaced by a distant God dirtied by too many human fingerprints. I'm struggling to identify with a religious system characterized by too much superstition, too much fallibility, too much dissonance between the Christ-embodied Servant of the New Testament and the jealous, capricious deity of the Old.

My dad's skiing accident brought us closer by making my father more human. My adult spiritual journey has also humanized God, but the result has been less desirable. I have matured spiritually, I have learned more about Christian history and theology. But I've lost my simple childhood faith.

The God of my conservative evangelical upbringing has been broken, or worse, has gone missing. Again, I think of my dad.

My dad gave me my first fly rod when I was thirteen. Fly fishing is still one of the things we most like to do together. We live four hours away from the pristine trout streams of northwest New Mexico, and a few times each summer we load up before daylight for a quick trip to the Cimarron River. Fly fishing is a solitary activity. Though we fish the same stretch of stream, we never really fish *together*. We park the car and head in different directions, arranging to meet back up at a particular time for lunch or to travel elsewhere along the river.

Punctuality is a low priority for my father when he's on the water. Despite his limp, he thrives on finding the least accessible, and therefore most potentially successful, stretch of trout water. He allows the promise of an unfished pool or a productive riffle to hijack any previous commitment he might have to our mandatory check-in. Time means nothing at the end of a trout line. Often, Dad leaves me waiting for him at the car.

When he's ten minutes late, I become mildly annoyed. *I brought in my line. I stepped out of the river in time to walk back. Why can't he?*

After fifteen minutes of waiting, I worry. Dad's in his sixties and easily thrown off-balance due to his limp. He could fall prey to heart problems, head injuries, slippery rocks, or rogue bears. Or he could just fall. The wilderness can be a dangerous place for a stubborn fisherman with a bum leg.

So I wait. And when my father doesn't show up on time, I feel nothing more intensely than his absence. I forget the quiet beauty of the Cimarron Valley, the towering Palisades above me, the smell of pine. Incomplete and unsettled, my vision narrows to the furthest spot on the trail alongside the river. Like the Prodigal's father[3] keeping watch from the front porch, I await that first glimpse of my dad's slow walk. Only then do I relax.

Dad has always returned, unscathed. Always.

I'm still standing, perhaps, alongside the same stream as God. But we parted ways too long ago. Regular check-in times have come and gone. God's absence is real. It is devastating. I feel it more powerfully than I ever felt his presence.

In *Secrets in the Dark,* Frederick Buechner writes: "Faith is a way of waiting—never quite knowing, never quite hearing or seeing, because

---

3. Jesus' well-known parable of the prodigal son is told in Luke 15:11-32. While awaiting the return of his son—who left home and squandered his inheritance on "wild living" (v. 13)—the passage describes the father as having seen his son returning "while he was still a long way off" (v. 20), at which point the father runs to meet him.

in the darkness we are all but a little lost. There is doubt hard on the heels of every hope, and many holy things lie in ruins because the world has ruined them and we have ruined them. But faith waits even so, delivered at least from that final despair which gives up waiting altogether because it sees nothing left worth waiting for."[4]

I wait.

Ask a Christian to define "faith" and he or she will likely equate it to "belief." They will say it is an intellectual acceptance of a list of doctrines or a confidence in God based on the characteristics implied in those doctrines. It is a steadfast trust in something unseen and unproven.

I don't have that kind of certainty. All I have is the stubborn, doubt-hardened hope that remains when God goes missing. Abraham clung to that hope after God promised him a nation but left him barren in the desert. Mother Teresa embraced it when God called her to serve the poor in Calcutta and then went dark for the next few decades. She pressed on, broken, incomplete, and doggedly pursuing love.

Abraham waited. Teresa waited.

I am waiting, too. Spiritual maturity has damaged the loving Father of my childhood. Years ago, God became too human. Now he has gone missing. For some of us, it seems, God breaks and disappears. Faith is the waiting for what comes next.

So I stand here near the river, checking my watch and waiting on the Lord. I wait for his healing. I wait for his return. I learned this from my father.

---

4. Frederick Buechner. *Secrets in the Dark: A Life in Sermons.* New York: HarperCollins, 2006. 108.

Fatherhood Has Changed You

by Tim Ghali

TIM is the Pastor of Community Life at Grace Chapel in Lexington, Massachusetts and serves in the areas of small groups, adult discipleship, student ministry and our alternative Sunday night service. Tim and his wife, Susan, have been married for thirteen years and have three little children, Nathan, Dylan, and Janelle. He loves his faith and family and truly believes adding milk and sugar to good coffee is sinful and that sarcasm is a spiritual gift.

"Fatherhood has changed you," my seminary friend said to me.

I replied with a somewhat startled voice, "Yeah, maybe, probably. Yes, I think so."

I hoped it was true but had no idea how she came to this conclusion. As far as I knew, I was still terribly sarcastic, slightly less cynical, and I smiled a bit more. But in fact she was right; fatherhood had changed me.

That thought pinballed around my head on the drive home. At that point, we had two children. Our oldest had just turned two years old and our second was just six months old. Our home was filled with two noisy baby boys, plenty of gifts and hand-me-downs, and our little family looked incredible on Facebook. But on that long drive home from school, I couldn't help but think of all the pain and confusion we carried just a few years prior.

Susan and I were one of those couples who got married shortly after graduating from college. We took our time in our family planning, and settled into our careers in vocational church ministry and in sign language interpreting. We traveled, volunteered, bought a townhouse, and decided it was time to begin our family. We generally made wise and prudent decisions, we had good credit, and we were pretty fun at a party. But things were not going as planned as we tried to begin our family. The short story is that after a couple years of trying, we decided it was time to see a fertility specialist.

Our lives were soon filled with statistics, percentages, testing, consults, and hormonal treatments, and every day on the calendar meant something. If you or someone you know has ever gone through fertility treatments, you know how the days are filled with anxiety, and the process can make you feel as though you have lost your chance at having children. After three years of fertility treatments, a miscarriage, a motorcycle accident that took the life of Susan's brother, and a promising first pastorate that turned dysfunctional, we were doing our best to avoid the conclusion that we were cursed.

My personal theology did not actually suggest that our benevolent God was going out of His way to bring such great pain into our lives. But if you could have eavesdropped on my prayers (which were more angry accusations and confessions of doubt), then you might have wondered what I actually believed. It's somewhere in your mid-twenties when you receive the interrupting news that you are not in control of your circumstances. It's in your mid-twenties that you find yourself sitting on the "wrong" side of the desk, whether that is across from your supervisor, your fertility doctor, or the funeral director. I could not help but recall these painful scenes as I drove down the highway toward our home which in all likelihood would have too many lights on, crying children, and an exhausted wife. Fatherhood has taught me to see the goodness of this as you learn that quiet, dark homes are not necessarily good ones. There is a feeling of satisfaction in seeing the woman you love and married expending her energy caring for these precious, needy little ones and your meager budget covering formula, diapers, and a little extra electricity.

Just a few years prior to this night, happiness, fulfillment in the ministry, and peace all seemed like very distant concepts. Then there was the idea of fatherhood, which at that time meant we were grateful to still have our fathers with us. Both Susan and I enjoyed great relationships with our fathers. My father, Amir, was born and raised in Egypt but was sensitive enough not to succumb to some of the middle-eastern patriarchal stereotypes. Susan's father, Dave spent most of his life in Florida, loving his family, working hard, and enjoying Southern culture. But for me, the mention of fatherhood during this time was more a "third-person" perspective as the pain of infertility was limiting my ability to ever see myself as a father. Our few comforts included the strength of our families, a marriage growing through perseverance, support, communication, and our belief that God was still listening.

We entered into our thirties deciding not to pursue fertility treatments any further and channeling our energies to adoption. I was serving full-time in my second pastorate, studying in a full-time accelerated masters of divinity program at Biblical Seminary, and confronting my entitlement and deconstructing my cynicism. It was during this season that selfish expectations and a posture bent in distrust were trumped by humility and hope. We were exiting the gray cloud that had hung over us and were now dreaming again.

Then in the beginning of April of 2008, we received a phone call that changed our lives. "Would you adopt my baby daughter? She's going to be born in three weeks and I am not in a position to raise her."

"YES!!" [Regain composure.] "We're just going to think and pray about this for the night but we'll call you back tomorrow. But we're probably going to say 'Yes, absolutely.' Is this a good number to reach you at?"

It felt completely out the blue as at that moment, we did not know who this young woman was, nor were we aware how she got our number. It turned out she was a receptionist at Susan's uncle's office in Florida. She had shared with Susan's uncle her concerns of being young, single, and not ready for motherhood, and he prayed. Within a few days, they had a conversation that led to him giving her our numbers. Looking back on it, there were a lot of prayers asking for wisdom, courage, and strength.

We agreed immediately, found an adoption agency and legal counsel in Florida, packed up a suitcase of pink and purple baby clothes, debated names, and didn't tell anyone outside of our family and a couple of friends. Hope was peeking in, but if this adoption fell through, we wanted to avoid the complexity of a Facebook wall and a church-full of sympathy.

We learn in our twenties that nothing goes as planned, and why should our thirties be much different? The birth mother, still in her teens, invited us to go to her final doctor visits with her. My wife stood right next to her during the sonogram while I found a seat in the farthest corner of the room to avoid any awkwardness. It was the day before the due date that the doctor informed us that we were actually having a boy! Sure why not? We can get new clothes and deliberate over a new boy name. By then, we knew how to adapt.

On April 26, 2008, Nathan was born. He was a beautiful healthy big boy. He ate a lot, slept poorly, and cried with fury. He may not have had any of my genes but he was going to fit in well with my Middle-Eastern side . . . or would he?

I enjoyed my upbringing and loved my parents but our contexts were so different. My parents were living the American dream and have always thanked God for their immigration. Fireworks on the Fourth of July mean a great deal to them and among their most prized personal truths are that their children's upbringings were different than their own.

Then there was Susan's personality and Southern upbringing. She is a tender soul who knows how to punch back and knows all the Southern sayings that border on cute and crazy. She is part Irish, part Welsh, and as family legend has it, part American Indian. We knew we would be loving parents, but three weeks' notice was barely enough to have a full parental game plan.

I had always assumed that I would be the strict parent and Susan would be nonchalant and appeasing. I could not have been more wrong. The day that best illustrates this dynamic was when Susan threw all of Nathan's pacifiers away and calmly explained that he could not use them anymore. Mother and son moved on quite well but I admit to still being a little traumatized. It's amazing the surprises and new discoveries that a marriage enjoys after having children

Nine months after bringing Nathan home, my wife showed me a pregnancy test and said, "Umm, you're not going to believe this but I'm pregnant!" Nine months later, we welcomed Dylan into our home. He looked like Susan's side of the family, slept peacefully, ate little, and seemed to cry only after exploring all other options. It was what my side of the family always wanted to be like.

On this long drive home from seminary, I started wondering how my friend arrived at the conclusion that fatherhood changed me. Indeed, fatherhood has taught me to take responsibility for the things we cannot control. Few things go as planned and fatherhood has shown me the need to adapt from a different perspective—one that remembers suffering, one that's been awakened by hope. I have found this to be essential and life-shaping as I expect pain and beauty to be recurring themes in the days to come.

Fatherhood has drastically changed my tears, pains, and joys, and my prayers have never been the same since. Fatherhood has also shown me that even a once-infertile couple may need to use proper contraception because some seven months after this conversation with my friend at seminary, my wife told me she was pregnant *again* and she was really hoping this time it was going to be a girl.

We now have three children five and under. The youngest is our gorgeous little daughter, Janelle. She looks like my wife, eats like my wife, sleeps like my wife, cries like my wife, and I assume will have great taste in men (like my wife). But until then, our house is loud, littered with toys, and we are praying we create a truly loving and emotionally healthy culture in our home. We are praying we have a home that truly honors the calling of being a Christian. We are hoping our family serves the common good while following Jesus.

Fatherhood now feels a little more natural. There is no glamour but there is a calling being fulfilled. A crying child in the middle of a winter night? Well the truth is I do not remember ever gleefully hopping out of my bed and skipping down the hall to whisper and sing lullabies to the little one. But such nighttime interruptions sure beat those painful sleepless nights of longing. When compared to that, give me the beautiful inconsolable infant. Prior to our infertility, I doubt I would have been able to see the beauty of such a moment.

Perhaps the greatest gift fatherhood has given is to show me that we inhabit a world where anything is possible. This is a world that allows the possibility of both unspeakable tragedy and immeasurable joy. Infertility may or may not be temporary. Adoptions may or may not fall through. Children may or may not grow healthy, strong, and always be with you. As grateful as I am, I'm trying to avoid living my life with blinders but with the beauty of living a life marked by hope, humble before God, and caring toward others. I hope Susan and I can pass this along to our children.

In the meantime, part of the love we have for parenthood is in the backdrop of those painful years. We've prayed, reflected, celebrated, and have come out on the other side of the grief as grateful and joyful people. It is not simply about being relieved that we can have a family, but more about experiencing the complicated and beautiful meaning that can be found in this life while sensing the nearness of God along the way.

"Fatherhood has changed you," my seminary friend said to me. "Yeah, maybe, probably. Yes, I think so."

Epilepsy and Autism in the Church Family: A Case Study in Difficult

by Chris Morris

CHRIS MORRIS loves telling stories to inspire and encourage people, because life is hard some days. He is a CPA by day, but a creative at heart. He loves telling stories to inspire and encourage others, even when life seems busted. Because his daughter Cynthia is epileptic and he suffers from seizures himself, these stories are sometimes focused on seizures. Helping others find hope, strategies, and encouragement in the face of seemingly insurmountable circumstances is his focus.

His writing centers on five core beliefs:

We need a community of people to life us up when we are weary.
We need practical steps to take when we feel lost.
We need to be reminded of God's character in the darkness.
We need to know we are not alone.
We need to be reminded that belly laughs are always welcome in life.

Several years ago, I took my now-eleven-year old daughter up for prayer at the end of a church service, in response to a call for healing of chronic conditions. I was filled with hope. Maybe this will be the time God heals her! I feel some anticipation, I wonder if that's just me, or maybe the Holy Spirit? Oh God, let this be the time my daughter is healed.

We patiently waited for someone to pray for my daughter. There were a lot of people with chronic illness, ranging from lower back pain to migraines and arthritis. When it was our turn, I explained my daughter had epilepsy. The person praying looked at Cynthia, sighed, and apologized. She said, "We can't pray for demonized today, only for healing."

Then the non-praying prayer team member walked away. I wasn't even sure what to do. I've never been rejected for prayer before, and I thought the healing of God was available every day. We stood there awkwardly for a few more moments, and then walked down the aisles.

I hoped nobody noticed we were never prayed for, because then more questions would come. Questions I was not ready to answer. As we walked back to our seat my daughter asked me, "Dad, what does demonized mean?"

There are no words to explain the way my heart shattered in that moment. How can I tell this precious young lady that somebody she has never met believes she has an evil spirit residing in her? I mumbled something lame to her and gave her a hug as we walked out.

I wish this was an isolated experience, but that is not the case. Because I have heard this more times than I can count, I stiffen my heart and prepare for a fresh wound each time I choose to open up and share. I never know when I will have a well-meaning person say something ridiculous and painful.

I understand now my daughter's epilepsy is a blight against the lie of Christian happiness. Today's pulpits are full of five steps to a better life, or seven ways to improve your prayer life, but not much on how to survive a pain that never leaves. It is easier to leave life black and white, rather than delve into the grey we live in Monday through Saturday night.

Many followers of Christ then are not prepared to cope with the apparent contradictions of a God who created the world but cannot seem to keep it perfect. We like to pretend that because we are Christians we live in a happy shiny world with no blemishes or scars. That somehow the blood of Jesus not only gives us access to the Father and a future in heaven, but protects us from the pain and sorrow of life.

What are the results of this type of incomplete understanding of pain in the life of faith for my family? For us, the result is pain: About twice a year, a person with a robust theology and poor people skills comes to me and says, "Your daughter is demonic." Often without knowing me or my family, without spending any time with my daughter, without even taking the time to see the image of God in her.

In addition to being epileptic, Cindy is high-functioning autistic. Her autism is also an affront of sorts to this shiny happy Christian life, but subtler than the epilepsy. It is subtle because my daughter doesn't "look retarded."

I hate that word. I think the word retard should be removed from the English dictionary. But that is the word people think, so that's the word I will use here. Because she doesn't "look retarded," people think she is okay. Then my eleven-year-old five-foot-one-inch daughter who looks fourteen walks up smiling and says, "Hi I'm Cindy, and I can hop on one foot."

People give us strange looks that ask, "Why is your daughter doing that?" Except the question never comes, because they are too afraid to ask. They don't know what we are going to say, and they don't really want to hear it. Because it's unhappy. Because it's not wonderful. Because it's not, "Praise the Lord!" Because it's difficult.

Now we really get to the crux of the challenge. There is an assumption people have once they see our daughter being her quirky self. "Oh, you've got one of *those* kids," they think to themselves. They assess their lives, their time, their priorities, and they quickly decide, "I don't have time to have another difficult family in my life." So they pull away from a future friendship, and we are left lonely.

It continues to surprise me how quickly people walk away from relationship with us, in large part because of my daughter. I understand, in a sense. It is difficult some days to be in a public place. There are days where she doesn't want to be out, and it's obvious when she feels that way. She doesn't completely understand social and societal expectations, so her actions in these moments are embarrassing.

She doesn't have the emotional control she should have all the time, so she acts out. I am not excusing her, but it is her autism in large part that prevents her from being able to process the emotions or interpersonal situations and respond in the socially expected manner.

So things like this happen: my good-hearted, kind daughter was suspended from school for two days for spitting in her aide's face. Granted, this event was the result of a poor medication reaction, and she does not understand the full implications of her choice. But her actions were still inappropriate, so she was suspended. This is my daughter, sweet some days, spitting other days. It is hard, and because most people decide they don't want difficult relationships in their lives, they slink away.

It's important to note that I am simply speaking out of the experiences we have had as a family, not anger or frustration. I imagine other special needs parents experience similar things. Even from those in the church, or perhaps especially from Christians.

I used to expect more from church members when it came to these circumstances, but I have realized people are people. When I discovered my faith, everything changed—my heart grew more tender toward others and I looked for opportunities to show kindness to the difficult. I assumed everyone at church would have the same experience, but I now know just because someone claims to follow Jesus doesn't automatically make them better, or kinder, or less busy. Sometimes it doesn't mean anything except Sunday morning is for church.

Nevertheless, I find myself saddened. So many potentially wonderful friends miss out on the joy my daughter brings to this world. Her smile lights up a room, her laughter is infectious. But they are afraid, because she is difficult.

Yet I praise God we are not alone. There are three families who are as committed to Cynthia as I am. Families who love her because of her quirkiness and envelop her in their unconditional love. The difficulties we find as a family stir a deeper gratitude in our hearts for those who stand by our side. I thank God almost every day for these solid companions on the tough road we walk.

My daughter's lack of healing also stirs spiritual challenges in my parenting. I believe I serve a healing God, and as a family, we have seen God move in ways that can only be described as miraculous. I once prayed for a man with a herniated disc and felt the bones in his back move as God answered my prayers the instant I spoke them. My wife prayed for a coworker who had literally just been told to have her family travel cross-country to say good-bye because her liver failed and she was dying. Two days later, this woman walked out of the hospital with a perfectly healthy liver and doctors proclaiming a miracle. I believe in the deepest core of my being that God is actively involved in our lives, taking pain away in this world.

I understand the biblical concept of the Kingdom of God. Jesus did what he did by the power of the Holy Spirit, the same Holy Spirit within us. We have the authority and ability to demonstrate the same miraculous things as Jesus because we have the same Spirit he did. We live in an in-between time, where God is king, but the devil is on the throne. Sometimes good things don't happen.

Kingdom of God theology is very meaningful when prayers are answered with a "yes," but more difficult to accept when prayers come back with a "no." I am left to explain to my kids why God does not heal their sister, no matter how often they pray. I have to answer questions like:

Are we praying wrong? Does God not love Cindy? Does He like boys better than girls? Why won't God heal Cindy? Is he busy? Does He not care? Should we pray more? Do we bother God by praying so much?

There are no easy answers to any of those questions. This is the life I live. This is the challenge God has placed before me and my wife.

So what do I do as a father in these moments? There are a few things I focus on to help my kids cope with the social brokenness and emotional pain that comes from having a sister with chronic conditions.

I always answer questions honestly. I refuse to give the pat Jesus-loves-you-this-I-know answer to the sincere, heartfelt, and difficult questions they ask. *At the same time, I don't always answer what they are asking.* The question in their heart is often different than the question on their lips. The question they are really asking in this:

Where is God? If He loves us, where is He?

So, we talk about what means to say we are loved by God. We talk about God's ultimate desire for us, which is *not fundamentally* to be happy and whole, but rather to reflect the heart and lifestyle of Jesus. We look at the hard things in Scripture, where people don't get what they prayed for. We talk about what it must have felt like to be Job,[1] a man whose life was destroyed on a bet between God and the devil; a man who eventually had his fortunes restored, but nevertheless saw his children perish.

I also keep praying. Almost every day, I pray God will heal my daughter. Some days I believe it more than others, and some days I feel like I am going through the motions. I am not giving up just because I don't feel zeal in the moment; it doesn't mean I shouldn't pray just because I feel grumpy.

But I don't pray alone, or pray only about my daughter. We pray as a family. I make sure to communicate to my kids that my daughters' seizures are not more important than their insecurities about acting, or their struggles with their grades, or the girl teasing them, or false rumors about them. I never want my boys to feel somehow less in my eyes or God's because they are "normal." So we pray.

Beyond that, we prioritize being silly together. The power of laughter to lighten heavy loads is profound, because we all speak the language of joy. So we have tickle fights. We watch comedies. We read silly stories. We play games. Together. Because we will always have the support of each other.

It is difficult to answer to have these issues in our life every day. My hope for myself and my family is that we will be able to grab tight and never let go of God's character, even when His actions and our expectations do not mesh.

---

1. Job is a book of poetry in the Old Testament, in which Satan states to God that the man Job only serves God because he is wealthy and happy. To prove Job's faithfulness, God grants Satan permission to bring tragedy into Job's life. His children are killed, his wealth is taken, and he contracts a painful skin disease. After lengthy discussions between Job and his friends about why this happened, God arrives in a whirlwind. God speaks of his power and might, but does not answer Job's questions. God restores Job's wealth and gives him more children.

Raising Dreamers
by Ethan D. Bryan

ETHAN D. BRYAN is an author, musician, and storyteller. He has completed century rides on bicycles, under-par rounds of golf, and is a world-record holder. He dreams of one day playing baseball with the Kansas City Royals. He and his wife, Jamie, live in Springfield, Missouri, with their two daughters.

"The creative adult is the child who has survived."
–Ursula K. LeGuin

Mom and Dad said, "You can do it," so I tried out for the school baseball team and got cut on the second day of tryouts. Even though I knew there was "no crying in baseball," I shed a few tears in the backseat on the drive home. No one ever wants to get cut.

Mom and Dad said, "It's okay; don't give up. Try again." The following year, I tried out again and made the team. I was the best benchwarmer that school has ever seen.

Dad said, "This is a great essay," so I submitted it to a scholarship contest. I won first place. When I went to the ceremony to receive my award, I was notified of an editing error and was immediately disqualified from the contest. Dad took me to get ice cream on the way home.

Mom and Dad said, "Your most important job is to learn, to think, to spend these years being a kid. Soon enough, you'll grow up and move away. You'll have other responsibilities—family, job, bills, taxes—don't waste your teenage years working for a car payment."

Mom regularly bought me books from the local bookstore and the school book fairs, whether I asked for them or not. I loved all of her literary suggestions. Dad took me and my sister to movies and to see new places on mini-vacations. And most importantly, more evenings than not, my whole family ate dinner together at home.

A dreamer was born.

I was a student at Truett Seminary the first time I took the Myers-Briggs Personality Inventory. I remember how hard it was for me to wait an entire week to see the results. The professor distributed folders to each student and slowly talked through all the personality descriptions, asking students to raise their hands when their personality type was read. The last personality type was "INFJ."[1] Only two of us raised our hands. The professor rolled his eyes and said, "I had a suspicion of you two. INFJ's are the dreamers who actually believe their dreams matter, make a difference in the world, and will come true." In front of my friends and classmates, I had been publicly diagnosed as a dreamer.

Pablo Picasso once said, "Every child is an artist. The problem is how to remain an artist once we grow up."[2] John Lennon sang the invitation to dream, "You may say I'm a dreamer. But I'm not the only one. I hope someday you will join us. And the world will live as one."[3]

---

1. The Myers-Briggs Type Indicator (MBTI) is a personality assessment tool with results based on an extensive questionnaire. It measures sixteen different personality types, psychological preferences in how people perceive and interact with the world, and the basis for their decisions. INFJ stands for Introversion, Intuition, Feeling, and Judging, and is the rarest of types: http://www.personalitypage.com/INFJ.html, accessed May 2013.

2. http://scienceblogs.com/cortex/2010/03/25/childish-creativity/, accessed May 2013.

3. Lennon, John. *Imagine*. Capitol Records, September, 1971.

I am now a father, a dad to two amazingly creative and compassionate girls. It is my desire to do everything I can to raise two dreamers—young women who refuse to accept the status quo, who live by courageous faith instead of by suspicious fear, who are learning to trust the whispers of their hearts. And it all centers on the dream.

Jesus lived and proclaimed God's Great Dream—God's kingdom come on earth as it is in heaven. Jesus first announced this dream at his inauguration speech (Luke 4:16–19, NIV). When God's kingdom comes on earth, all things will be made new, all things will be set to rights, all things will be made whole. Oppressed freed. Blind healed. Debts forgiven. And the best part of the good news is that God's coming kingdom is for all people. Throughout his life and ministry, we see how Jesus makes God's Great Dream a reality.

He invited those from the margins of culture to taste and experience the new life of God's kingdom. His creative word calmed seas and cultivated the kingdom-come party. He shattered the expectations of religious rituals and ushered in the new covenant of God's grace and love. Even as the crucifixion neared, Jesus continued to teach about God's Dream and how we, too, can live in such a way to make God's Dream an earthly reality.

Because God's Dream has come true in Christ on earth, I am learning to live out that Dream with my daughters in the here and now. We are learning that as we love our neighbors, regardless of where they call home, God's Dream becomes a reality.

We laugh at the advertisements that try to hijack our dreams. If our dreams can be reduced to what we consume, we have bought into the unattainable-status-quo-chasing-bootstrap-pulling-self-sufficient-newer-faster-more-and-better American Dream. Chasing the American Dream will only leave us and the world longing for something more. Our imaginations must be stirred by God's Great Dream instead of creative copy or flashy images.

Raising dreamers begins by redefining success. True success is not measured by wealth gathered or accolades accrued. For people of faith, success is simply the lifelong journey of growing in love for all people. As I learn to consider the perspective of others, "climbing inside of their skin and walking around in it" as Harper Lee wrote,[4] I grow in love. When we learn to see success relationally instead of materially, we are open to hear the amazing stories of others and freed from the rat race of pleasing others and accumulating more useless stuff. Raising dreamers is rooted in love. Of course I am proud of my daughters when they bring home good grades or awards of excellence. But I also celebrate when they take the time to work through disagreements with their friends or go out of their way to make a new friend.

Raising dreamers is not for the faint of heart. When a dreamer risks, creates, and engages the world, she opens herself up to criticism from and rejection by others. Some people will laugh and mock the creation, often quite loudly. Even in the face of criticism, however, it is important to encourage patient and bold perseverance, trusting that the visions and intuitions of their hearts will point to the in-breaking of God's kingdom today.

Raising dreamers means encouraging the gift of questions. Most of the questions my daughters ask come after they have spent time internally processing events or something they've read, and I don't have any idea how to answer them. Questions connect the worlds of imagination and reality, even if answers aren't readily available.

Every morning, I drive my oldest daughter, Kaylea, to middle school. One morning, her brain whirred as she processed her dreams from the previous night. She started asking me questions that were nowhere near my areas of expertise. Instead of trying to answer her questions, I responded, "Great question! Ask a harder one!" And she did, again and again and again. When we pulled up beside her school, Kaylea said, "Thanks, Dad! That was a lot of fun!" I didn't provide one single answer, just simple encouragement for her to push herself to keep asking harder questions. Kaylea did all the real work.

Raising dreamers also means a willingness to endure messes. I dare you to enter the bedroom of my youngest daughter, Sophie,

---

4. Harper Lee. *To Kill a Mockingbird*. New York: Grand Central Publishing, Hachette Book Group USA, 1960. 39.

when she's in the middle of a project, and not twist your ankle or get overwhelmed. About once a month, my wife summons the courage and strength to attempt to help Sophie straighten out her messes. She almost always comes out showing me some new creation that amazes both of us. I refuse to obsess over the "godliness of cleanliness" and want to see what new things my daughters can create, even if it means a multitude of messes.

Raising dreamers means learning to live by imagination, not just by what we see (see 2 Corinthians 5:7). Think of the stories and adventures of Spaceman Spiff in the *Calvin and Hobbes* comics or the worlds created in Narnia and Hogwarts. Exercising imaginations requires engaging in stories where our perception of "reality" is temporarily suspended. George Bernard Shaw concurred: "You see things; and you say 'Why?' But I dream **thi**ngs that never were; and I say 'Why not?'"[5] It is imperative that people of faith engage and live by their imaginations, refusing to believe that the seemingly overwhelming darkness can overcome the power of God's love.

I love to watch movies and read books with my daughters, engaging them in conversation about the stories afterwards. We have longed to walk the halls of Hogwarts as well as spend some time playing Quidditch. We have wanted to hear the roar of Aslan and play baseball in the Field of Dreams. We have even imagined which actors and actresses we'd prefer portray us if our lives were the story of a movie.

Raising dreamers means teaching children to hear God's whispers on their own. There are some parents who try to live vicariously through their children—burdening their children with their own dreams. We are familiar with the stories of Tiger Woods and other athletes who were pushed into the world of competitive sports as soon as they were able to walk. Raising dreamers is not making my children live out my dream, but helping my daughters recognize God's whisper in their lives as they find ways to live out God's Dream through their gifts. This happens best by modeling.

5. Bernard Shaw. *Back to Methuselah. A Metabiological Pentateuch*. New York: Brentano's, 1921. 6.

Kaylea has asked me on multiple occasions how to hear God's voice. I balk every time I try to answer her question. God's whisper is felt in gut-level intuitions and dreams that keep us awake at night. God's whisper sounds a lot like our own voices, our own internal dialogues, and rarely makes sense when placed on a list of pros and cons. I love the burning bush scene in the animated movie *The Prince of Egypt*. I thought it was a brilliant directorial move to have Val Kilmer, the voice of Moses, also voice God in the scene. God's whisper challenges our constructs, reorients our relationships, and helps us see truth and beauty in the broken and ignored people and places of creation.

My wife created a chore chart where the girls can initial the chores they have completed, earning their allowance. One of the chores is "playing catch with Dad," as I hope to one day fulfill my dream of being a baseball player. The best way I know how to encourage my daughters to embrace and chase the whispers they hear is by inviting them to help me live out mine.

Too many times, parents see their child's "lucky fins" and echo Marlin's words, "No, you can't! You think you can do these things, but you can't, Nemo!" But in Christ we learn to say yes, to encourage the faith of the leap, to chase whispers and take risks in order to catch a glimpse of God's Dream on earth.

The most important thing I can do as a father is to help my daughters know with the entirety of their beings that Love is the most powerful force in all of creation. When they know that they are loved for who God whispered them to be, they won't be easily distracted by persuasive marketing techniques. When they define success as growing in love for all people and making new friends, they will engage their imaginations to use their gifts for the good of the world. When they catch a glimpse of the greatness of God's all-pervasive, all-creative Love, they will help make God's Great Dream a reality on earth, just as it is in heaven.

In the Mold of My Father

by Jonathan A. Carroll

DR. JONATHAN A. CARROLL is the oldest of three children born to educators John and Emily Carroll. The Philadelphia native grew up to follow the legacy of his parents and become a teacher. In addition to being a leader in the classroom, Jonathan has also concurrently been a leader on the pool deck, continuing a lifelong love affair with swimming and sports. Dr. Carroll is also an emerging scholar who seeks to document the experience of students and teachers of color within the current educational landscape. He is currently the head of aquatics at Harvard-Westlake School, where he oversees both the middle school and high school programs.

When I would get in trouble with my father as a young man, which was often, I would inevitably have to endure one of his lectures about how he wanted me to grow up to be a mature, responsible man, and how my latest silly act did not measure up to that plan. There was also a spiritual component to all of these lectures because he would always work it into his speeches that he lived by the credo "There, but for the grace of God go I." As he explained it to me, it meant that he understood that all his blessings flow from God's grace and mercy. It was therefore his job to be an obedient servant. He fulfilled this belief by serving as a deacon in our church and a member of the choir. He would rise early on Sundays and get to church before my siblings and me; we arrived with my mother just after the start of service. When the pastor would take a moment in the service for members to greet one another, I would walk up to the pew where my father sat with the deacons to give him a handshake or hug. My father's role-modeling set the foundation for how I am raising my own sons. My father now serves as an eager counselor and guide as I continue to make discoveries in my walk in faith.

Despite my strong foundation as a Baptist Christian who participated in all Sunday school activities as well as the children's choir, when I went off to college my attendance and participation in the church dwindled and my behavior was noticeably less faith-based. I had premarital sex with multiple partners, I experimented with marijuana, and I was not as diligent in my studies as I had been previously. Throughout this time, my father never chastised me about my poor attendance on Sundays, even though I lived only fifteen minutes away. He simply continued to love me, and pray for me much like the father of the Prodigal Son (Luke 15:11-31).[1] When I did make sporadic appearances in church during my college years, my father welcomed me with open arms, as did the rest of the congregation. It was a reminder that God's love is everlasting, and that because of Jesus' sacrifice, my sins would be forgiven as long as I repented. While this was a valuable lesson to learn, I still struggled with being a consistent church attendee through my early adult years after college, and even after I got married.

My wife Nkechi and I moved away from the East Coast in 2004 after being married for two years, to pursue our passions in Los Angeles. As we got settled in our career pursuits and started talking more seriously about starting a family, it became increasingly important to find a church home. This was a struggle for us in LA, as we were not enamored with the large "megachurches" in our area that our friends recommended. My father was quick with encouragement during his biannual visits and would subtly remind me to keep praying and we would be shown the way. When we did settle on and join a church, I quickly felt that the more I studied and was obedient to God's word and his movement in my life, the more that my family was blessed.

---

1. In the parable of the Prodigal Son, the younger of two sons asks for his inheritance from his father, and squanders it recklessly. When he is destitute and starving he realizes his sin, and returns to his father's home where his father celebrates the return of his son who was "dead, and is alive again."

Our first son, Isaiah, was born in 2006 and both my family and my wife's family made sure to be present when he was christened into the church in the summer of 2007. We adopted our second son, Elijah, in March of 2012, after going through the process of becoming foster-to-adopt parents through the local Department of Child and Family Services. Elijah was a particular blessing because our foster-to-adopt training prepared us for the idea that we would not get a newborn, and that we would have to learn how to build and maintain connections with the birth parents. That was not the case with Elijah. We brought him home from the hospital only two days after his birth and we have been free to raise him as our own, with no contact from his biological parents. We have felt particularly favored by the way Elijah came to us and for me it has only strengthened my resolve to conduct myself as the best Christian I can so that my family unit remains strong. As the boys have gotten older, there are a number of lessons that I have begun to teach them through both action and verbal communication.

It fills my heart with joy when other parents remark to Nkechi and me that Isaiah is both polite and kind. We try very hard to have him understand that he should be kind to his peers and respectful of adults. When we get positive feedback that this is how he is behaving, it is an affirmation that he understands what we are trying to teach him. It was one of the biggest lessons my father taught me. He knew that it would not always be easy for me to maintain my composure and remember his teachings as a Black male. He also knew that there would be many who would expect the complete opposite when they saw me, but that I could shatter those perceptions with my personality. My father based his lessons in the biblical message that we should love one another as Christ loved the church (Ephesians 5:25). I do the same for my boys because I have seen firsthand how it affects people when you approach situations with kindness and not hostility. Even when I get frustrated at something the boys have done, I try to make sure I explain why I am frustrated, help them understand why a certain thing they have done was a mistake, and reassure them that I love them. Equally important as what I say to them are the behaviors that I try to model, which they will hopefully pick up on as they grow older.

My father was never an abuser of alcohol or drugs when I was growing up and I make sure that my boys never see me in a compromised state where I am not in control of my actions. My father also made sure to control his tongue around my siblings and me when we were young because as a Christian he knew that one of the best ways to worship God was to control the tongue. As Psalm 34:13 states, "Guard your tongue from profanity" (MSG). I try to do the same for my boys so that they understand that there is power in control and that they don't have to witness the destruction that a loose tongue can cause. I also try to set a tone for worship by listening to gospel music often so that the faith-inspired messages wash over my children. Soon they will not just see it as "Church music," but just "good music." I cannot lift up my voice to the heavens like my father did singing in the choir, but I can certainly sing along with Donald Lawrence and Marvin Sapp with the best of them.

Ultimately what my father's Christian role modeling showed me is that it is okay to be a man of God. There is no shame in it. It is not something that should be done in secret. People will still respect you and you will find a discipline that helps enrich your life. I have embraced this lesson as a father, and try to embody that for my sons by being a more emotional worshipper during church. Many times men in church are content to just sit back and digest the sermon with no outward expression of agreement. But we should, if we are really excited about the possibility of God directing our lives. Ironically this was a lesson that was made even clearer to me in a book that my father recommended titled *Dare to be a Man: The Truth Every Man Must Know and Every Woman Needs*. Pastor David G. Evans devotes a whole chapter to the impact that it had for his church when he was able to help men understand that it was okay for them to unleash their emotions in church in the same way that they would at their favorite sporting event. If I can get my sons to see that I get excited by understanding the teaching of the Word, then they will be more likely to keep seeking knowledge themselves and less likely to seek it in unsavory places. The message to them will always be, *I love you like the Lord loves me, and I am happy about that.* I am proud to say that my father has seen me trying to teach these lessons to my sons and has shared that he could not be more proud.

I Saw Fear and Wonder in His Eyes

by Jamie R. Johnson

JAMIE JOHNSON was raised in the Pacific Northwest, the place he now calls home. He is married to Erin, an assistant professor of social work at George Fox University, and they are joyfully outnumbered by their three children, who consistently run circles around them while chanting, "Kids rule!" He is an associate pastor and director of the Friends Leadership Program at George Fox University, his alma mater. In his spare time he enjoys running, reading, playing guitar and watching the Boston Red Sox and New England Patriots.

I used to think I was a good parent . . . and then I became one.

You see, for my entire life I have suffered from the (particularly) male syndrome known as overconfidence. There is only one symptom of this disease, and that is the overwhelming belief that I can do anything if given the chance to do it. There is no task too great and no fear too overwhelming that can convince me to give up.

Could I build a house if I wanted to? I believe I could, though if you came and looked at the fence I built in my front yard you would never set foot inside any house I might build.

Might I be able to replace the handle on a broken toilet? Absolutely, but not before I crack the water reservoir, requiring the purchase of an entirely new toilet. Plus, replacing entire toilets is way more enjoyable than merely replacing a measly handle.

And so, before I had ever celebrated the creation of an embryo, I had convinced myself that I was going to be an excellent dad.

The seminary I attended owned apartment buildings for married couples who were students. And though my wife and I were not parents at the time, it seemed like every other family living in the apartment building had at least one child.

The Barneses lived across the hall and had two boys under the age of six. This family was from the South and exuded a southern charm that immediately drew my wife and me into their lives. We often found ourselves seated at their dinner table eating grits (is it really food?) and learning what it meant to be a family.

Occasionally I even offered up my own parenting advice.

One time I told their two-year-old that the tiny green orbs he was supposed to eat were better utilized as nose plugs. Because I was already such a good father and an excellent communicator, he listened. Of course, I was not invited to be a part of retrieval process, in which tweezers were used to extract the pea from his nose. Perhaps his real parents thought I might try to convince him to instead use the tweezers for pinching his brother. The peas would come out eventually with a hard sneeze, right?

I was also convinced of my awesome parenting techniques by how many children would come to our apartment door to play with me. I would often study at home, and many afternoons the intellectual aura of my living room would be interrupted by a small knock on the door. The door would barely open before a two-and-a-half-foot tall blur would dash between my legs, ready for another epic afternoon of playing with the coolest dad-who-is-not-really-a-dad in the apartment complex.

Yet, by the time I turned back into my apartment, the small child would often dash back out into the hallway, multicolored drool emanating from both corners of his mouth, hands filled with melting candy pilfered from our candy bowl, which was always kept full and approximately a foot and a half off of the ground. You know, because I was going to be an awesome parent.

Often, our interactions with the Barnes children were in the hallway adjoining our apartments. If the snow outside was piled too high, or the mosquitoes were too hungry, we would play soccer games, race hot wheels, and wrestle on the well-trodden carpet.

It was nearly two years later that, while at work, I was surprised by a visit from my wife, who uttered one of the greatest two-word sentences I've ever heard: "I'm pregnant!" All my years of playing dad were finally going to be put to use, for now I was to become the real dad of a real child. If a snapshot of my face existed from that day, I imagine you would see an overwhelming sense of wonder cascading from my wrinkled forehead to my mouth, open wide in excitement. And if you looked deep into my eyes, I'm certain you would also see fear.

I was not only incredibly excited for this new adventure—I was also terrified.

As my wife's pregnancy reached its conclusion, fear and wonder became regular feelings for me, companions that I neither invited nor wished would leave. They had found their way deep into my psyche by the day my first child was born. Even after every type of preparation an expectant father could possibly partake in, I was still surprised as I stared into the eyes of my son. I saw his lungs breathe their first breath, a gulp of oxygen that must have felt unlike any other sensation a human body can experience.

Fear and wonder. How could such a tiny being have been knit together so perfectly inside my wife's womb? His fingers were so spindly, his head so beautifully bald, and his limbs flailing to their fullest extent after months of being squished together in a space the size of a basketball.

The two days we had spent in the hospital after his birth were amazing. The hospital staff cared for my wife in ways that lulled me into a false belief that made me hope they would let us stay there until our son's second birthday. So, when I arrived at the hospital on day two and saw my wife dressed, bags packed, looking like she was ready to go outside, I panicked.

I tried to think of every reason we would be allowed to stay longer: *Doesn't the baby look jaundiced? I don't think he is latching on very well! Can't you see the blood on his fingers from where we tried to clip his fingernails? I don't hear any women screaming in labor, surely you don't need this room, do you?*

The nursing staff just smiled and continued with their preparations for us to leave.

And as I placed my two-day-old son in his fire-department approved car seat, buckled him in so tightly he must have felt like he was back in the womb, and made sure his bald head was covered with the cutest little crocheted hat, I looked at my wife, my eyes wide with fear and wonder and uttered, "What the hell were we thinking?"

It was in that moment of having to leave the comfortable safety of the hospital with its wonderful staff that my self-confidence exploded into tiny slivers, like the thousands of fragments from a shattered Pyrex dish.

Though the birth certificate said I was a real parent, I realized I previously had no idea what I was doing. Overnight I developed a parental sense that did not exist twenty-four hours prior. I knew, instinctively, that shoving peas up my child's nose was gross and unsophisticated. I learned that candy bowls were meant to be stored up high. And I realized that kids are so good at imaginatively creating their own scary stories that they don't need my help making things scary.

I've also learned using a vacuum to clean up vomit from a carpet is a horrible solution, unless you want a perfectly good reason to replace a vacuum that is not technically broken. And that the last thing a child needs is extra distraction at the dinner table.

Most importantly, what I have learned is that I am, by myself, not the greatest parent—because parenting is not a solitary endeavor. The old saying is absolutely true—it takes a village to raise a child, and any false notion I have that I am pretty good on my own is not only ludicrous, but harmful to my children. I've come to realize my overconfidence was, in fact, the band-aid I was using to hide my fear.

Though I taught the Barnes children all manner of inappropriate behaviors, they allowed me into their lives because they, too, knew the truth of parenting. They never articulated it to me, but I learned from them that parenting cannot be done alone.

As I have grown more in my understanding of who God is, I have come to see that God is a relational being. And God has created humans to be relational in all things. Wherever you see people living into the life they have been given by God, they are doing so in community. Community is a thread that originates in God and weaves its way through every person who chooses to live in relationship with God. As we allow ourselves to be sewn into the tapestry God is weaving, we realize we are not alone, nor are we asked to live our lives alone. We are a communion of saints, our feet resting on someone's shoulders, and another's feet upon our shoulders, creating a living witness of our dependence upon one another and, ultimately, upon God.

Society has increasingly taught us that what happens in our homes, behind our fences, or even out in public is the business of no one else. But in my experience this only creates alienation and hardship.

At one time or another, I think most moms and dads have experienced how alienating parenting can be. If it were not for the people who have come alongside my wife and me, we would have given up a long time ago.

Nestled within the Christian Bible are over one hundred songs and prayers that followers of God have used for millennia to express the joys and sorrows of life. I can't imagine a better way to articulate this grand adventure we call parenting than the words found in one of these psalms:

> For you created my inmost being;
> you knit me together in my mother's womb.
> I praise you because I am fearfully and wonderfully made;
> your works are wonderful,
> I know that full well. (Psalm 139:14)

Fear and wonder. I saw it in my son's eyes. I see it in mine. And the Psalmist saw it in how God created each one of us. It is what will either draw us together or tear us apart. And I've learned enough to know that by myself I am not that great of a father. I need others to come alongside me, to share in this fear and wonder.

A few years ago we moved back to my hometown. When I had first moved to Newberg, I was five years old. Now I was thirty.

As a five-year-old, I had ridden the last leg of the journey in my grandparents' motor home, laying down in the bed that was directly above the driver's head. As we came over Rex Hill and made the final descent into this small town, I stared through the window at this new place of trees and hills, and felt afraid.

What we found in this small college town was what I would come to later recognize as community. I did not have a word for it when I was a child, but I knew what it felt like. It felt like people at the university where my father worked knowing my name. It felt like a church family that taught me the Bible, introduced me to friends, and gave me opportunities to serve in ministry, even though I was just a child.

Even though this place was familiar, I was afraid.

But what we found upon our arrival years later is what I had found so long ago. Though I had changed, the community's capacity to invite us into meaningful relationships had not changed. The village here has helped me see, once again, that I am not alone. My parents, our church, the places we work, all have played an important role in the parent I am today.

I am still frequently visited by my old nemesis, overconfidence. But I am trying to no longer hide behind it so that others won't see my fear. Because parenting is difficult, and I need help.

Feelings of Inadequacy: Learning How to Be a Single Dad

by Steve Knight

STEVE KNIGHT is cofounder and community architect of TransFORM Network, a missional community formation network. In addition, Steve is cofounder and co-CEO of Sogo Media, a new kind of Christian television network on YouTube. Steve is the former manager of the Internet division for the Billy Graham Evangelistic Association and international communication coordinator for SIM (Serving In Mission). His work has taken him all over the world over the past two decades, but he's proud to have put down roots in the Gastonia, North Carolina community with his three kids Olyvia, Hayden, and Elliot.

It was probably the first time I went to the grocery store after my wife had moved out of the house. As I walked down each aisle, unsure where to begin, backtracking to collect things I'd missed on my first time past, I began to realize I didn't know what the hell I was doing. I was hopeless. I had no strategy, no coupons, and very little real-world grocery shopping experience, to be honest. I had little more than a short list of the items I thought we needed. Of course, when I got home, I discovered there was a whole other list of things that we were fresh out of, and so I had to go back. And I would go back, again and again, at least twice a week (if not more) in those first few weeks of separation, just to get everything my kids required for their school lunches and the dinners I would be preparing for them, and even to feed myself, although I didn't seem to eat a whole lot during the start of that painful season.

I lost some weight as a result, but I still didn't know how to be a single dad. I was just beginning to figure it out. A lot of the responsibilities I thought had been shared were really things my partner had carried the lion's share of, even after she reentered the workplace. As progressive as we'd become, we had still continued those "traditional" gender roles, it seemed. And we hadn't handled our finances particularly well, either. Getting a grip on my own finances was a challenge. How much money did I even have to spend on things like groceries? I knew how to make money, just not how to manage it very well.

One of the questions I quickly learned to answer was, "How are your kids doing?" My first few attempts at responding to this were pretty lame. "I think they're doing pretty well. Umm, I guess."

During any kind of separation or divorce where kids are involved, people are naturally concerned about the children. I appreciated that concern, but there also came a point where I just wanted to say, "We've talked with our kids. They know what's going on. They know they can talk to us at anytime about how they're feeling and what they're going through. But, honestly? I don't know exactly how they're doing. They seem to be handling everything as well as can be expected. I hope they're doing okay, anyway."

Sometimes people just don't know how to respond when they learn you're separated or getting divorced, and so it's "safe" to talk about the kids. I get that. By talking about them, it's a nonpartisan conversation. Friends would rather not feel like they are picking sides in a domestic disagreement.

The consistency of that recurring question led me to talk with my ex about investigating counseling options for our kids. Maybe if they don't feel comfortable talking with us about their feelings, they would feel comfortable speaking with a counselor? There were some wonderful options out there for that, for which I was grateful. (Heck, if I was seeing a therapist through all of this, why shouldn't my kids?) We let our kids know what was available to them if they couldn't, or didn't, want to talk to Mom and Dad. So far, none of our kids has taken us up on that offer, but it's there. It is on the table. Our kids know they are not alone, and they don't have to go through this alone. They know I have a therapist (and a pastor and a spiritual director and a personal trainer and a tattoo artist, a whole support team!) and whatever they need, they can have that also.

Okay, maybe not the tattoo artist. But what about the pastor? Or the spiritual director? It seems that very few people ask about how it's going with our kids' souls. But that's one of my biggest concerns, as a father and as a spiritual leader: How am I nurturing faith and values in my kids, especially in the midst of this season of pain and confusion and turmoil?

At this point, my daughter would tell you she's agnostic. (Heck, I'm agnostic about a lot of things, too, these days.) I have to admit that there are a lot of things that I just don't know, but, unlike my daughter, I haven't given up on faith. She, on the other hand, is not really interested in things of faith at all, even though many of her friends come from religious homes and participate in church activities regularly. My kids feel left out of the conversation, even at public school, when the primary assumption is that everyone here in the Bible Belt goes to some kind of Christian church on Sunday morning. Heck, I'm a paid religious professional (as much as it makes me throw up a little in mouth to admit that), but our faith community is very nontraditional and intentionally interfaith. (We meet every other Saturday night in my living room, not in a church building.)

The exclusive evangelical faith of my childhood has given way to a much more expansive, inclusive theology and practice. I no longer fear for my children's eternal destiny (or destination), but I still put my hope and trust in Jesus. As hard as it is sometimes to have faith, I still believe Jesus is who he said he was. And I still want my children to be followers of Jesus. So I continue to share with them the stories, and I often share the wisdom and the truths I find in Scripture as things come to my mind throughout the day. Sometimes I have to remind my daughter that to respect me as her father means to respect my faith in following Jesus. You don't have to love Jesus like I do, just don't diss Jesus!

Without counselors to guide my kids at this stage, I'm actually strangely comforted by the fact that half of all marriages end in divorce. Practically speaking, this meant that each of my kids had at least one close school friend whose parents were going through separation or divorce at the same time, or had in the recent past. As long as that was the case, I knew, and assumed they felt, they weren't "the only one" experiencing this kind of upheaval. They had peers they could talk to about it. They could exchange notes about the process and where things were at with each of them.

Despite the cultural climate of suspicion, I'm grateful for the parents of my kids' friends who would allow their children to have sleepovers at our house. I would've completely understood if any of them had said, "You know, we're not comfortable with our child staying at your house, since you're a single dad." I have the same hesitations about my kids staying at someone else's house. Who's going to be there? Who's in charge?

But I think I've actually gotten pretty good at hosting a sleepover, whether it's for my daughter or one of my sons, complete with making pancakes on the electric griddle for breakfast in the morning! I put on some streaming music, loud enough to rouse the sleepy late-night crowd, and look forward to them stumbling down the stairs to the kitchen table and pulling up a chair. Half the pancakes will be plain, and half will have chocolate chips in them.

Come to think of it, it all comes back to food and table.

After we watched the documentary *Food, Inc.* together, my daughter decided to become a vegetarian. And three years later, she's still going strong, although technically she's a pescetarian, since she eats fish and other seafood occasionally. So, buying food and preparing meals that accommodate my daughter has been very important. Sharing meal times together, even though it's just the four of us now, has continued to be an important ritual. The challenge now is getting everyone around the table, including myself, to put away all electronic devices for the duration of the meal!

I guess we stopped doing a traditional mealtime prayer around the same time many of my other evangelical habits began to fall away. In lieu of a prayer, I've recently begun reading blessings from a collection excerpted from the writings of the Irish poet and spiritual teacher John O'Donohue. A friend had gifted me with these blessings, and it was a gift for me to be able to pass them along to my kids. I know the deep meanings of many of the blessings often sail right over their heads, but it's just so fun to let the beautiful language that O'Donohue uses wash over us. I know something meaningful is sinking in.

I want my kids to appreciate beauty and poetry and art and music: good, thoughtful, significant music (okay, and the kind that just makes you want to dance too!). I want to give my kids the gift of new experiences, expose them to new ideas, to creativity, and to possibility. I'm grateful for an ex-spouse who is a fantastic co-parent. I realize so many of my divorced friends don't have that and I see how much harder life is without that ongoing support. Although I'm a single parent now, I'm still not parenting alone. And, for this past year, I really never was. Every friend and family member who has reached out or come alongside has helped me through. I'm so grateful for a faith community that is helping to raise my kids as well. Maybe their faith will get passed on to my kids, even if mine is shaken by doubt and uncertainty for a season, or longer. I hope so. I'm not letting go of that hope.

The Boy with the Train Set

By Juan Carlos Lopez

JUAN LOPEZ is a youth pastor at Casa de Dios Assemblies of God Church in Bell Gardens, California. and also manages a paper store in Hollywood. He met his wife, Anabel, in their tenth grade algebra class. They've been married for three years. He spends his spare time chasing his two-year-old son Joshua around their apartment, blogging, tweeting, Instagramming, and Facebook updating most of the random thoughts that pop in his head. He is an avid runner and competed in his first marathon in 2014. He longs for the day when the unscripted freedom of Pentecostal theology will hold hands with the beauty of sacramental liturgy.

We are born into our families. Unable to break free on our own from the blessings and curses passed down by the choices our parents made, and their parents, all the way back to Adam and Eve. We make our own choices based on the faulty information we are given, unknowingly digging our own graves with shovels passed down by our parents. Yet I've learned that when all hope is lost, Jesus reaches down and pulls us out of those graves.

I was born in East Los Angeles but when I was two years old we moved to Mexico to live with my grandfather in Guadalajara, where I was raised until I was eight. My earliest childhood memories are of getting train sets from my grandfather on Christmas, breaking piñatas on my birthday, and a steady diet of Gansitos, soda in a bag, and Chocomilk. I remember playing with our nine dogs in our backyard. I remember my teenage babysitters kissing me on the lips for "practice," my seven-year-old mind unable to make sense of anything that was happening. It was a simple time for me. I was just a boy with a train set. I knew I was loved and had no insecurities about that. I was unaware that I didn't have a father to play with me.

After my grandfather passed away we moved back to Los Angeles. It was here that the boy with the train set was buried alive. I experienced relentless bullying because I didn't speak English, then because I had good grades, and because I wasn't very good at sports. We lived in El Paso, Texas for two years, then found our way back to California. We moved around from apartment to apartment until finally settling in a converted garage that my godmother rented to us.

The first time I met my father I was in ninth grade. I was watching Spiderman when my mom came in the house.

"Mijo, vamos a ver a tu Papa."

Son, we're going to see your father. This was such an odd phrase for me because up until that moment I had never met the man. We took a short bus trip to where my father was waiting for us. Growing up, my mom had told me he drove a huge, red eighteen-wheeler. I imagined he drove all around the country in a truck that looked like Optimus Prime, getting in adventures and such. I knew he was married and that I had older half-siblings.

You might think it would be an emotional experience to meet your father for the first time, but there weren't any tears. It wasn't anything like the reunions I'd seen on *Sabado Gigante.* I don't remember much of what was said. We ate shrimp cocktails at a nearby seafood restaurant and he had a Scientology book with him. He was overweight and didn't drive. He took the Metro to his job in the fashion district. He worked at what seemed like a typical L.A. sweatshop and my mom had run into him at a bus stop. Needless to say there was no big rig. I didn't even bring it up to my mom because I was unsure of what to make of it all. One thing I knew for sure: *I did not want to grow up to be like this man.*

A few weeks after our first meeting he told me there might be a bus worker strike and since he couldn't drive because of back problems, he would lose his job because he had no other way of getting there. The strike happened and I never saw him again.

Several years after this chance meeting, the *mi papa* conversation came up while talking with my mom. It turns out they met at a shoe factory where they had both worked. He was thirty-seven years old and married while my mom was twenty-seven and just arrived from Mexico. I still don't know the entire story, only that I was born out of an affair. He never actually drove a big rig; it was just my mom's way of making me feel proud.

After our conversation all I was left with was the fact that my father had cheated on his wife with my mom. He had worked in the clothing industry for most of his life. He propositioned my mom the day I first met him to go get a hotel room just "for old time's sake." It seemed to me he was still trying to make sense of his life; he was reading *Dianetics* by L. Ron Hubbard, after all.

It wasn't until I came to Christ that I realized the importance of a father in a child's life. The Bible tells us that fathers are to bring up a child in *discipline and instruction*. There are some things that only a father can teach. Don't get me wrong, mothers are equally important. My mom did her best as she raised two children on her own. She loves us with all her heart. My younger brother and I are twelve years apart. We never missed a meal. We always had clothes to wear. We moved around a lot. Mexico, Los Angeles, El Paso, False Pass, Alaska. We never settled anywhere for more than two years, but we didn't care. Something was always missing though. The love of a father.

Learning how to love is vital in raising a child who will make wise decisions in life. Without the love, instruction, and discipline of a father, I grew up lazy and complacent. I had no one to correct me or lead me by example. I had no one close to me to teach me about sex. I learned that from 2Pac, Biggie, and pornography. I had goals and dreams that changed depending on who I followed. I gave up on anything difficult. Somehow I believed that all I had to do was be in the right place at the right time and I would catch my big break. Instead of focusing on college, I spent the first three years of high school focused on finding a girlfriend. It was in high school that I met my best friend and future wife. I told her all the "guy secrets" and she helped me with my many insecurities. She was one of the few girls I spoke to without ulterior motives, probably because she had a way of seeing right through me.

I regularly attended Catholic mass, for the girls of course, and I remember that the re-creation of the crucified Christ scared me. I understood none of the liturgy but I remember pounding our chests with closed fists and saying "My fault, my fault, my fault" in unison: I remember confessing to the priest that I couldn't stop looking at girls the *wrong* way. I tried. I promised him that I tried. But I just couldn't stop. I forget the amount of Hail Mary's and Our Father's he told me to pray.

From the time I was a senior until I was twenty-six I went from one manic-depressive, codependent, and unfaithful relationship to another. I believed my best friend was "the one" but didn't have the guts to become the man I needed to be to date her. So I slept around and cheated on whoever I was with at the time. I was too much of a coward to ever break up with anyone. Unknowingly, I had become my father.

All these choices led to one of the worst days of my life. Just like the day I met my father, I still remember it clearly. I was twenty-six years old and recently single for the first time in a long time. I had just parked my car and I was walking to my apartment with a bag of groceries. My cell phone rang and I picked it up with my free hand. It was a number I did not recognize.

"Hello?"

It was the nurse from my doctor's office calling me with my test results. After a bit of small talk she finally gave me my results:

"You tested positive for herpes."

I went through an emotional rollercoaster for the next couple of months: denial, depression, anger, and disgust. I felt lost and alone. Everything came crashing down around me. How did I get to this?

All of my choices had led me to that moment. This is what I had planted and this was the harvest that I had reaped. I had nowhere to turn. There was no magic pill to make it go away. It was when I was at my lowest point that I actually began to consider Jesus as the answer to my problem. Don't get me wrong, I always believed in God. But I lived my life as if he couldn't see anything.

After a few lonely and depressing months, I finally reached out to my best friend. I couldn't think of anyone else to talk to. I hadn't seen her in years but we spoke every few months. She had become a Christian the year before, and when I reached out to her, she invited me to her next church service. I remember walking into church feeling like I had come home. The pastor greeted me with a hug and it was exactly what I needed. The church loved me and comforted me. As time went by I began to see that God wasn't punishing me, but had been in fact pursuing me. I had decided to follow Jesus and there was no turning back. I began to read what else Jesus had done for me by dying on the Cross. What it means to all who believe in his name.

A few months after I became a Christian, I went to another doctor for a checkup. All this time, I was trusting God for my healing. I prayed and claimed all his promises. The tests came back negative. My blood showed no signs of any STD. I had a choice to make: Do I go back to the life I lived?

I was convinced I would never marry, that I had cursed myself and I deserved every bit of punishment I got. Yet, by God's grace Jesus is redeeming my life. Which is why I cried on the day I married my best friend and it's why I cried tears of joy when I found out I would be a father for the first time. It's why I cried tears of sorrow when we buried our second son, who lived for only five hours. It was a painful time for us. Early on we were told there would be complications and that our baby wouldn't be able to survive outside the womb. For eight months we prayed for a miracle for our son. We learned that miracles come in different forms and I finally realized God was right there suffering with me. He's a Father who knows the pain of losing a Son.

There are days that I wonder about looking for my father again. It's usually when I learn something new about God the Father and his love for us. I was never really tempted by drugs or alcohol, but I couldn't manage to stay out of bad relationships. It's ironic that I became my father without him directly influencing my life. Yet God's mercy found me and I found my identity as a beloved child of God. He is a father to the fatherless and I found what I longed for all my life. I have a father who feels my pain and suffers with me. I can now give my son the father he deserves. I was able to break free because of God's mercy. Not because of my own efforts but because of Christ's sacrifice and resurrection. It hasn't been easy, but now I have a heavenly father to guide me along.

Stay-at-Home Dad: Joy and an Unintentional Twelve-Step Program

by Brian Shope

BRIAN is a thankful husband (he married up), a proud daddy and part-time #sahd, a fair-weather bike commuter (let's be honest, winter in Pittsburgh is not kind), student of culture, and part-time geek. French Press Powered.

Brian is trying to figure out—with others—how people make the journey of life around justice and spirituality, given the ability to talk to an infinite amount of people online. How people culturally engage, behave, gather, and exercise their authority is of great interest and enjoyment to him. He has turned these passions of culture, tech, and his experience to help churches and organizations broker their practices and voice with individuals via social media. The French Press part makes all this possible.

My late-morning breakfast was an amalgamation of last night's leftovers crafted into a quesadilla. The boys climbed up onto the stool on either side of me, requesting a try. As we shared rice, cheese, and corn-avocado salsa bites, Owen and Elias (four and three years old) became increasingly excited about eating it. They lavished love and hugs on daddy. The impromptu meal was a moment of bonding. Owen then moved to my seat and initiated the most beautiful moment of the morning:

> Owen[leaning over toward his brother, Elias]: I love you. [Wraps his arms around him and gives him a big hug.]
>
> Elias [leaning in, turning and reciprocating the hug]: I love you.
>
> [Owen gives his brother a kiss on the head.]
>
> Elias [pauses, looks at brother]: Did you hear me purr?

It is moments like these that keep me going as a stay-at-home dad (SAHD). However, it has its ups and downs and the staying at home was not part of my parenting aspirations as a young adult.

SAHD BEGINNINGS

My wife, Megan, and I were pregnant when we moved to Pasadena, California. Actually, she was the one doing the pregnant part. I'd been accepted into Fuller Theological Seminary's School of Intercultural Studies for graduate work, and we were about one-third of the way into the last forty weeks of our couple-only life. Southern California is one of the most expensive places in the country to live, and my loans alone couldn't keep us in the black. So, Megan got a full-time job offer just three months before Owen's due date.

We could only afford about eight weeks of having Megan on maternity leave, so starting on week nine, I became a SAHD. It was something that we had discussed at length, and we asked ourselves all the questions new parents face: Can we afford to put our little one in daycare or is it financially better for one of us to be home? Do we even *want* to put an eight-week-old in daycare? How can we offer a flourishing life to each other and our children? We felt strongly about caring for our little ones directly, and decided that staying at home with them nearly full-time was what was best for us and our kids. We felt a peace about it, although I had great fear trembling below the surface.

A significant portion of this fear was, and remains, my proclivity toward impatience, anger, and codependence. I grew up in a family of addiction where relational boundaries were poor at best, criticism was rampant, and it wasn't "safe" to be a kid. On the cusp of becoming a parent myself, I'd lived enough life to begin to recognize unhealthy patterns and characteristics from my childhood, but had not yet put in enough work or discipline to feel I'd shape a healthy child. I was excited for Owen's arrival, and scared shitless. How was this going to work? And really, is the best option for me to stay at home with him, *by myself* for eight to ten hours a day?

My search in the local community around Pasadena for stay-at-home dads came up empty. No one else I knew was doing it, nor did they have any SAHD friends, either. Somehow I stumbled across a Twitter community under the hashtag "#sahd". Although I knew none of these other men, they became a lifeline for me. We connected over the struggles of messy diapers, potty training, nursing infants, teaching our children, and other parenting stuff. Though we may not have always tweeted each other directly about these things, the regular feed of information through tweets was often enough to keep me sane. I was not alone.

RECOVERY FROM VIOLENCE

In my own experience at home as a child, the manner with which our addictive family environment was lived out made violence a regular part of life. With one parent alcoholic and the other codependent, I didn't learn to care well for myself, or for those around me. I was selfish, often practicing coping mechanisms that only appeared to be healthy self-care or care for others around me. Addiction was a neglectful parent, and the codependent baggage that comes along with it was traumatic. Addiction is often carried forward from previous generations, slipping into each subsequent generation with, as Anne Lamott once described, "ninjitsu stealth."[1] It communicates through passive aggression, silence, and fear, and is also impatient, critical, explosive, and appears without warning. There is often no peace, no solace.

I can't think about my role as a SAHD without also thinking about my own brokenness. The depth of my work and feelings about being a dad are wrapped up in my history and healing. Given that I was with my boys for up to ten hours a day at times, how I parent is very much wrapped up in my recovery.

As a Mennonite, pacifism and nonviolence are a significant part of my faith narrative. One of my ethics professors and friends at Fuller attended Pasadena Mennonite Church along with our family. As she was lecturing in one class, we discussed the violent tendencies we

---

1. Anne Lamott, *Bird By Bird*. New York: Anchor Books, 1995. 139.

share as humans, whether manifested as murder in the first degree or in passive aggression. She confessed, "I am a recovering violent person." That resonated deep within. It described me too closely: I don't know how to be patient; I've got a hair trigger for stress, for being in control, for anger; my posture toward others can be quite selfish. I'm recovering too, and I'm not alone. I can't fix myself, but as a follower of Jesus, I look to the one who not only showed us who God is, but who we are. Jesus chose peace over violence, honesty over lying, openness instead of passive aggression.

Violence is the conditional acceptance or rejection of the other. This is true in my default parenting style as well: My love for my children is conditional upon their behavior. My default reaction is to withdraw attention or love during times of undesired behavior, and to lavish more attention or love on them during times of desired behavior.

Every day I struggle with patience and maintaining a posture of empathy toward my boys. Addressing their emotions and trying to figure out how to facilitate growth from that vantage point is tiresome. Imagine how this is compounded for a recovering violent person who is impatient! But it allows me the chance to be a parent of peace, one who is recovering from a violent orientation.

The walk of recovery is always most poignant when it is incarnated with loved ones and in loving surroundings. My role as a parent is one of the hardest things I've ever done: bottle feeding a newborn with breast milk, which I had to thaw; learning how to help him sleep well (rocking, gently bouncing, swaying?); remembering that he wasn't trying make things difficult, that his life and behavior wasn't about me; understanding that crying is how babies communicate their needs. These things don't jibe well with a recovering violent person. I don't know how many times I visited my wife at work with a hungry, exhausted, or sleeping newborn, and said, "I don't know if I can do this another day." Megan cried and I felt inadequate, ashamed, incompetent, frustrated, and sad.

Some days the pendulum between my broken self and my recovering self is maddening. My hair trigger stress response fires, highlighting my character defects of impatience and anger. I respond to my boys from those places, squashing their little hearts or desires. I've learned that, at the very least, I must ask forgiveness of them often. At times, I can see my parenting working, because *they* will call *me* out: "Dad, you're being mean!"

There are other times when I've got to choose between "allowing" them a request or desire while fighting my default posture of saying "no," or offering instead a relaxed "yes" that creates a flourishing life. My mind reels back and forth about my need to make a healthy decision, one that loves and cares for them, yet somehow my broken self has identified these two little beautiful people as adversaries who I must tame, to the point of breaking their spirit. The pull for consistency is strong, yet I've found that just being loving, limping along at nurturing, is what I'm most capable of.

THERE IS ALWAYS LIGHT

The joys I've experienced as a stay-at-home dad are ones not many men can share. One of my favorite memories of Owen was his first time using sign language. Megan was at a conference, and during Owen's late dinner of clementines I asked him, "Do you want more?" He answered by touching the closed fingertips of both hands together, the American Sign Language sign for "more." He stabbed his seven-month old index finger to his right palm in a common infant rendition of the sign. I erupted with jubilation; breaking the clementine into as many individual wedges as possible, I kept prompting and signing, "More? More?"

Owen and I discovered that we share a love of music; the Beastie Boys' song "Intergalactic" is all drums and rhyme, a simple and metered piece. Sublime in its infant perfection. Owen loved to be held and whirled around our living room while MC Mike sang of their celestial renown. That first day, he wouldn't let me put him down, and Megan returned home to the "Look at this!" joy of daddy and son jumping around the room. Daddy was exhausted.

The result is a close connection between me, Owen, and Elias.

They often run straight to me when they fall down. They share their treasures with me, trusting that I'll keep the acorn safe in my pocket. They ask for me to do their bedtime and stay for "one book" if not more. When my wife comes home from work after I've been with them all day, they still want to hang out with me, and request I keep my word on whatever activity we were to do before her return home. It's not that they aren't connected to her—rather, my connection with them, although different in nature, is similar to that of many stay-at-home moms.

I never dreamt that I would be a SAHD. I didn't want it; I'm too selfish. I have trouble taking care of myself, much less a wife and two little people. But after finding some foundation for healing from my own trauma, I've acquired tools to do it differently, with peace. Violence is still present, but Jesus, Prince of Peace, has wrought something different for me, my wife, and my boys. It's a work of repentance, constantly turning away from the impatient, stressed out, angry boy I still am. But change is slowly happening, one day at a time, and the health that my children will have, health I never had as a child, makes the work worthwhile. I go forth with the grace of YHWH[2] and his son, Jesus, my wife, and the widening love and resilience of two small boys. They show me Jesus.

---

2. YHWH is the name the Old Testament Hebrews used for God. The believed pronunciation is "Yahweh," but the first ancient Hebrew scribes left out the consonants, leaving some interpretation until later scribes added them in. I favor the use this name over "God" because it is uniquely rooted in my own faith story, and articulates which "God" I'm referring to. The name is translated "I am that I am."

Growing Up
by Aaron J. Smith

AARON is a husband and a father living in Portland, Oregon. He grew up in Utah, lives with a bipolar mood disorder, and drinks too much coffee. Currently, he is writing a book about theology and a memoir, working in customer service, and recovering from insomnia.

I have a shitty relationship with fatherhood.

Growing up, I had two father figures. There was my actual dad and my papa. Being raised by my dad's parents was an odd experience. You can't really expect "normal" to happen when your mom dies before your third birthday. So, I grew up with two men defining fatherhood for me.

I still have only a vague concept of what it means to be a father.

I don't really feel like anyone failed me. I mean, I had more of a father than plenty of other kids. I had a father figure at the head of the table every night at dinner. I had someone there to pin on the scouting badges I earned. Someone was there to help me play baseball. My papa even coached my team the one season of little league football I played. Papa taught me to depend on myself. He put me in martial arts when I was bullied. He made sure I went to private schools, that I had clothes, food, a home, toys, and books. I never wanted for anything because he provided. He was always there when I needed him; he never failed to bail me out when I needed it.

There was never the absence of the father figure in my childhood, even if it wasn't my dad most of the time. Don't get me wrong, my dad was there too. My dad would take me to the arcade and let me waste his money playing "Gauntlet II," TMNT," and "The Simpsons." We would get lunch from Chick-fil-A, and maybe head to his girlfriend's house for the weekend. He made sure to physically be there for my birthdays, Christmas, and lots of weekends. I know he loved me, and he will always be my dad. His own broken heart may have wounded me in deep ways, but I can't say he failed me. He was still my father, even in his absence.

My papa raised me the way he raised my dad, and my dad reiterated those lessons of manhood. So I learned the type of man I should be: a good ol' boy, self-sufficient and able, strong and silent until it was time to be heard. I still have no real clue how a man like that is supposed to be a father. They say that the son grows up to be like his father. Maybe I never really learned how to be a son, never really learned the lessons of manhood handed down to me, never really learned how to become the image of my fathers. As I grow older the fact remains I never have been, and never will be, like the fathers I had in my life.

My papa and my dad were big men. They filled doorways and had hands that always engulfed my slender fists. I always needed them. I was always small around them, short of stature, more bone and lean fibers than muscle and strength. Even after my papa's death, or maybe because of it, he remains big and I am always a boy in the shadow of his memories. And my dad, I still can't fill his hat or his cowboy boots.

Now, I have a three-year-old son. He gives the best, biggest hugs. He really loves his race cars, his stuffed kitty, his mom, and his dog. Every time he says to me, "I love you, dad," my heart jumps in a way I never knew it could. I look at him and feel nothing but love and gratitude for this son, my firstborn, (currently) only son. To be sure, he frustrates the snot out of me at times. He is willful, has the childhood gift of selective hearing, takes an excessive amount of time to eat his lunch, and consistently taps into an endless reserve of energy moments before bedtime. He also loves reading, the classic film *Cinderella*, cars, Ironman, puzzles, and taking walks in the woods. He is such a fantastic little human being.

How am I supposed to be a father to this little guy? All I know of fatherhood is discipline. I know how to tell him he needs to do things himself and I will be there if he fails. I know how to regurgitate the actions and words of my papa, so my son can grow to be the kind of man I never was. Is that the truth of fatherhood, teaching your child how to be the person you never were? How can I teach my son to be what I can't ever be?

I love my papa and I love my dad, but I am not them. I never will be. I can't be. I am too emotional, too much in my head. People tell me that I remind them of my dead mother, not my distant father. Yet still this is my image of manhood, of being a father and raising my son, this image tied to strength, emotional detachment, being a good provider, discipline, and self-sufficiency. It is an image I can't shake, and it is a picture that is so foreign to who I am.

This is the core of my fear of fatherhood: I don't know how to enjoy who my son is because I am in constant shame for not being the man I was raised to be.

I can't be the fathers I knew. For all the good they poured into me, they stripped me of any knowledge I had that it's okay to just be me. With their respective absences and emotional detachment, I was always told I needed to be better to be embraced. I was secondary, left to learn my emotions, my personality, my humanity on my own. I taught myself how to shave and I taught myself how to survive in my insecurity. I taught myself how to date and how to stop cutting myself. I taught myself how to make new friends and how to fail and rise again. In these ways, I guess you could say I ended up becoming the man my papa and my dad were telling me to be after all: a self-made man.

They say that your relationship with your father gives shape to your idea of God. I really hate that my picture of divinity is shaped, in part, by shame for what I am not, shame for what I will never fully be. If God is like my fathers, I will never be understood. I will never be big enough to finally be called an adult. If God is like my fathers, then silence and aloneness will be the hallmarks of my faith, even as I try and humiliate myself to ask for help yet again.

Can God embrace me even though I am incapable of being anything other than this small child that I am? Will I continue to disappoint God because I don't know how to raise my son into this shape of manhood I am incapable of achieving? Will I ever be enough to be a man, to be a father? These are the questions that stick with me as I watch my son sleep. My son is full of wonder, humor, love, and excitement. My son loves cheese and crackers, hummus, and pears. My son makes creative patterns with his rows of cars. My son spells his name and calls himself awesome. My son is entirely himself. I wish I could be like my son, so secure in his skin, never expecting failure. My son, whose father loves him and is well pleased with him.

I wish I knew what it meant to be the son of God. I wish I understood what it meant for my Father in heaven to be pleased with me.

I've come to terms that my relationship with my father figures will never be what it could have been: my papa died a few years back, and my dad and I are too broken to do anything but move forward. But my God and I, maybe there is still a chance I can learn to be his son, even if I continue to be insecure about my ability to reach manhood.

I am a father now, and the dynamics I have with my son tell me more about God than any of my father figures could. Jesus once said, "If your earthly fathers wouldn't give you a stone instead of bread, why would you expect less from your heavenly father? If you human dads wouldn't give your kid a snake instead of a fish to eat, how much more goodness will God your father do?" (Matthew 7:11, NRSV. Author's paraphrase) I know how broken I am. I know the evil inclinations of my own mind and heart. I know how desperately I want to do the right things, and how often I do the exact opposite. I know how foreign true love feels to me, how hard it is for me to not feel like a failure as a father. Yet, even with all my brokenness, all my failure, I still have a son who loves me and for whom I would die. I have a son for whom I will walk to the store in the middle of the night to get medicine. I have a son with whom I will play cars. I have a son I will put down for naps when he is tired, whom I will lay beside and enjoy, whom I will teach to read, to write, and to wonder at the world. I have a son I will take care of with a paycheck and my presence.

How much more will God be my good father?

I might have a really bad understanding of fatherhood and manhood, but I still have a child, a son, whom I enjoy and who enjoys me. I know what it is to be a child, because I still feel like a child most days. That understanding may actually put me in a place to be a better icon of fatherhood to my son. Learning to let God redefine my ideals of fatherhood, learning to let him be my father figure, coming to a more complex acceptance of what it means to be a child of God (Romans 8:17-17) may even allow my son to better understand the deep metaphor of God as his father, even when his earthly father fails and tries again.

What I want to be is a father who loves his son as who he is, rather than trying to raise him in my image. The freedom that comes with knowing oneself—these lessons I'm learning thirty-three years into my journey—is what I pray my son finds. Maybe part of the way I can find it is in my relationship with him. Sometimes we can't escape our broken pasts. The things that wound and haunt us stay close to our hearts. The fear of passing on that broken heritage can't consume the life I am building with my son. Sometimes just admitting that we are both adopted children of the god Yahweh, that we both will spend our entire lives learning what it means to be a child—sometimes that is enough to break the cycles to shitty fatherhood and stunted adulthood. Growing up with my son may just be the fatherhood we both need.

Sacrifice
by Bryan E. I. Brown

Bryan lives in Denver, Colorado with his wife, Heather, and serves as a pastor.

My father is a pediatrician, and growing up I witnessed how busy a pediatrician's life can be. Besides working full-time as a pediatrician, my father was on call during the weekend to assist other physicians in the labor and delivery area of the hospital. Needless to say, he was a busy man, but that did not stop him from making his family a priority.

Growing up I can remember my father making it a priority to spend time with me. I remember playing catch with him in the backyard when he came home from work. I remember shooting a basketball with him in the front driveway and getting excited to show him that I could dunk. I can remember traveling to many sporting events to cheer on our favorite sports teams together, even if they were terrible. I have many fond memories of my dad spending time with me and being available if I needed to talk to him about something going on in my life.

Sometimes, just so he could spend time with me, he would pick me up from school and take me with him to the hospital as he made rounds checking up on his patients. He could not take me from room to room with him as he made his rounds, so he would drop me off at the hospital employee family waiting room area.

There was never anything special about the waiting room; it only had a small television in the right top corner, some uncomfortable couches to sit on, and occasionally, donuts. I think this is the place where I fell in love with donuts because I do not remembering eating many outside of the hospital. Even though my father was working during this time and I could not be there with him, I cherished the moments at the hospital with him.

His habit of making time for me continued as I grew. When I was fourteen years old I decided to become the neighborhood paperboy. My parents thought it was a good idea, so I could learn hard work and responsibility. One of my responsibilities was to deliver the paper on Saturday and Sunday mornings, but there was just one problem. I was not a morning person and I hated waking up early. But every Saturday and Sunday who was there to wake me up early? My father.

There were times when I can remember running from house to house and I could see my dad half asleep in the car waiting for me to return to get more papers to deliver. I think he sacrificed so much sleep that he could sleep anywhere, anytime. If delivering papers was going to teach me responsibility and hard work, then he was willing to sacrifice sleep for me to learn. It was valuable to my dad to spend time with me even if I had to wait in the hospital waiting room or he had to wait in the car while I delivered papers.

Because my father had to work on the weekends, I also went with him to the hospital on Sunday mornings before going to church. He had a busy schedule, but he would not disregard his faith because of work. We would make rounds together before church and we would head over to Sunday school after he was done. There was always time for us to attend a church gathering and my father taught me the simplicity of being consistent and faithful to the body of Christ.

My father's consistency was not just about showing up on Sunday morning, but also about reading his Bible and being a person of prayer every day before he cooked breakfast and got ready for work. Moreover, as an act of worship and thankfulness to God, he gave a portion of his finances every week to support the ministry of the church (and taught me to do so as well).

One Sunday my father forgot to give me my portion of his money to contribute before church, and instead of placing the money into the offering plate himself, he cut me off as I walked up to the front of the church and handed me the money in front of everyone. It was in front of the pastor, the deacons, and the entire church. I was horrified and immediately dropped it into the plate. I was in middle school then and I remember my embarrassment as the source of my financial contribution was exposed. I can look upon that time with laughter now, but also recognize that it was important to my father that I participated in supporting the church financially. And to be honest, without his example I would not be generous with my financial contributions to the church today.

When I reflect upon these times and how I saw him live out his faith, I think about the verse in Proverbs that says, "Train up a child in the way he should go; even when he is old he will not depart from it" (Proverbs 22:6 ESV). Quietly, my dad was setting an example for me and my family; nothing in life was more important than loving God, living a life of faith, family, and serving others.

I learned a lot about life, faith, fatherhood, and family from my father. He was an excellent example of a man who would sacrifice time, money, and sleep to do what was best for his family. I can remember the telephone ringing all hours of the night when he was on call and how he would answer the phone and go to the hospital to help a family deliver a healthy baby. You could see the joy he had in his life and it spilled over into his family, faith, and life. He is an example of the man of God that I want to be when I become a father someday.

I know that as an African American male that I am lucky to have a father who has been present all of my life. My father took time out of his busy schedule to be with me. I have no idea how many hours of sleep he lost doing this, but he did it quietly and passionately and I do not remember my life being an inconvenience for him. He became interested in what I was interested in, he watched television with me, and he went to all of my sporting events growing up. Even if he was going to be late for my basketball games or track meets, he made sure he was there to show support. It was as important to him as eating—and he loves eating. My dad wanted to be a present father and he genuinely loved watching me play and grow into the man I am today.

I say this because I have so many friends and family members who do not know what this is like. For many, their father was absent and still is absent. Some never knew who their father was or is. Others know that they have a father, but have only seen him for a small portion of their lives.

I know other people whose fathers are present in their lives, but spending time with their children isn't a priority. These friends feel neglected by and unimportant to their fathers, even if their fathers genuinely care about them.

As much as I am thankful for my father's love and presence, I am even more thankful that my father showed me the importance of keeping my faith at the forefront of my life. My father was so busy that he could have been selfish about his time because it was always in demand. But instead of thinking of himself only, he prioritized being a part of the church. He volunteered for events, served on the deacon board, and brought us to church every Sunday (whether we liked it or not), even on vacations. I believe the example he showed helped me become the man of God that I am today.

He was not the most knowledgeable when it came to the Bible, nor was he the most eloquent speaker, and he definitely did not need to be in the spotlight, but with humility he raised us to love God and love others. There is something significant in being a humble man of God who serves others and raises his family well. I say that it is significant because I think that many people view their daily grind of being present in a child's life and spending time with them as insignificant.

We never realize how meaningful our lives are in the short run, or if our lives are making any significant difference, but we are, even if we think no one notices. I think the moments where we are present in a child's life are the times where we are able to create the foundation for love, friendship, faith, and happiness that we all need.

As I reflect upon the man that I want to be, I know that I want to be like my father. No, he was not perfect, but that does not mean I didn't learn so much from him. I saw up close how he sacrificed his time for the important things in life. If it was important, he was going to be there and make time for it, no matter how tired he was. I learned that his faith was not a matter of lip service. He did not attend a church gathering to check it off of his list for the week. The church gathering was an important part of his faith and life as a believer.

When I think of my dad, I think of Matthew 20:28, when Jesus says, ". . . the Son of Man came not to be served but to serve, and to give his life as a ransom for many" (ESV). My father exemplified what it meant to serve, not to be served. No, my father did not give his life as a ransom for many, but he did give his life for the well-being and benefit of my family and others in his community.

He served us by working extra hours to put food on the table, clothes on our backs, and to provide a warm home to sleep in. He served us and taught us life by putting our well-being before his. He served me by spending time with me and hanging out with me at concerts, movies, and sporting events even if he occasionally dozed off. He served me by prioritizing me over himself and I am forever thankful for this.

If I am blessed to have children of my own, I want to raise them like my father raised me. Raise them in humility, with integrity, by sacrifice, and by living my faith practically in the day in, day out grind of life.

I want to thank my dad for being a man of faith who raised his family well. If I make my faith and family a priority, it will have a ripple effect for generations to come. My father's sacrifice has made an impact on me, and I hope to be the same man of God to my children as my father was with me.

Being a Dad of Faith:
One Dirty Diaper at a Time
by Michael Jimenez

MICHAEL JIMENEZ is a loving husband to Lluvia, father of Lucas and Raylan, and teaches history and theology at Biola University and Azusa Pacific University. He is a doctoral candidate at Fuller Theological Seminary working on a study of Karl Barth's historical lectures.

I recently heard the comedian Jim Gaffigan make a keen observation: "If you mess up being a dad, you mess up an entire person." Fatherhood is serious business. However, there is the prospect of being so serious that you might actually alienate your children. On the other hand, if you are going into fatherhood with the intention of being a cool dad you have just proven how absolutely uncool you really are. This is even more awful for parents of faith. Christian parents often have good intentions but sometimes do irreparable harm to their children and drive them light years away from the faith. Stern dad creates an atmosphere that tends to make Christianity too domineering, while cool dad makes it seem too lackadaisical. From my small life experience as a father I have tried to maintain a sense of humor about the responsibility I have as a father .

At the time I am writing this essay I have two sons: my oldest is two years old the younger is four months. Naturally, this means that I never get a full night of sleep. I always look for ways to squeeze a nap in sometime during the day, so, believe me when I say that one needs a sense of humor to survive. Nevertheless, it has been a tremendous joy watching my kids grow and develop. Before they were born I imagined myself leading my children in prayer by their bedside. Now I just try to basically hypnotize them into sleeping the whole night while I attempt to escape their bedroom without waking them. Fatherhood is hard but rewarding work. Fathers who do not take themselves too seriously will accept every role that comes with being a parent.

I cannot understand the father who is too manly to change a diaper. Granted, there is nothing glamorous in changing a diaper at two a.m. and observing the different color of green in each successive dirty diaper. Still, this is as much a part of fatherhood as playing backyard catch or reading the biblical Book of Proverbs. If you can change a diaper, mix baby formula, close and open a baby stroller (more difficult than it sounds), then teaching a child about your faith cannot be too hard. Unfortunately, the church often reinforces the false ideal of manliness in regard to fatherhood.

One of the biggest problems for a Christian father is that churches do not really help the process. Too often, Christian fathers are sold a one-size-fits-all formula for being a biblical parent. Some pastors may give a sermon pointing out various biblical figures as examples of fatherhood. They might say: "Here are the five steps of being a strong dad like King David." However, if we are really honest, we would take the call to follow the biblical example of fatherhood with a grain of salt. For instance, we call King David a man after God's own heart, but he was a terrible father (see the body count of his children in the book of Second Samuel). Jesus teaches us to call God our Father, yet this same Heavenly Father actually commands Abraham to sacrifice the son he always wanted, and let us not forget the other son Abraham abandons in the middle of the desert! Abraham is not much of a poster child for family values! Instead, the church should point out that the Bible depicts men as men with all of their frailties and failures. There is much talk among Christian leaders of how manliness is missing today in society because people have forsaken the so-called biblical model (which is consequently a not-so-subtle knock against women). I sometimes feel sorry for children raised in American Christian culture because it can be frustrating knowing one's role for both the parents and the kids.

During a sermon the pastor will talk about children being the gift of God, then in the next breath talk about them containing *el Diablo*. What a mixed message! Still the absolute worst sermon the kids have to endure is the "spare the rod" talk. Imagine sitting there quietly as a child while you listen to a sermon about your own demise. Other parents like to reference that verse constantly—"Spare the rod spoil the child" (Proverbs 13:24)—which sounds like something that happens to your food if it does not get proper refrigeration. I am always surprised how often people recommend I remember the importance of discipline. Frankly, if the first advice that you would give a new father like me is, "Make sure to be ready to hit your kid," then you have problems. Behind much of this advice is an unhealthy passive-aggressive guilt trip placed upon both children and parents for not fulfilling their alleged God-given roles.

I consider myself someone who survived the Christian fundamentalist sub-culture experience and was able to separate the good from the bad of this worldview. I realize it is cliché to say I got through my experience because of Christ, but his life helped navigate how I judged the advice I received as a child. For example, when spoken to directly by pastors, children are given the general warning to avoid the "ways of the world"—the most ill-defined term in the Christian dictionary. It was often suggested in Bible class when I was a kid that we "put on the whole armor of God" (pictorial illustrations were provided in case we did not know what armor looked like) so that we could defend ourselves in the world. However, there must have been chinks in my armor because I often wrestled with what I enjoyed in the world and did not think was necessarily bad. The way I eventually dealt with the mixed messages of Christian culture is to develop of sense of humor about it. I like to think most kids are that way and that they have not drunk all of the Kool-Aid.

One of my problems with Christian culture is that it tries to replace what it considers are the fun aspects of "the world" with a Christianized version of it. However, I am eternally grateful my parents never sent me to Christian summer camp or forced stuff like Christian music on me. (We did go to the Christian bookstore quite often, because my father likes to read theology.) I remember thinking that Christian music record labels had the worst sales pitch: "If you like Dave Matthews Band then you will love Newsboys!" What teenager listens to Dave Matthews ever anyway? To see Christian musicians go from big hair eighties bands (mullets sometimes included) to nineties grunge and alternative (flannel shirts always included), followed today by acoustic folk guy, was always good material for a family joke.

My parents were actually pretty transparent on how Christian culture is pretty cheesy, and this probably both saved my faith and kept my sanity. They were also pretty conservative and my dad could be especially intimidating to me as I was growing up (not too intimidating, because he also listened to a lot of opera). My brother and I would give each other "the look" as a warning that our dad was not in the mood to be around any horseplay. However, my parents had a sense of humor that was welcoming and gave us enough space to learn to laugh at life. I recall once getting caught with some fairly explicit rap music during my "gangsta dayz" only to be counseled by my pastor at the time to listen to wholesome Christian music instead. He just happened to recommend his own Christian barbershop quartet. Only my sense of humor helped me to survive that conversation. I appreciate that my parents' response to this talk was that they thought for sure that the pastor was only kidding, proving that even my parents could not believe anyone could be that naive. This brings me back to the topic of cool dad.

While I stated some reservations in the introduction, it is probably better to strive to be more like a wannabe cool dad like Phil Dunphy from *Modern Family* because at least there is something endearing about his character, especially in reaction to the stoic, meat-eating manliness touted in some evangelical churches. Phil's kids know he empathizes with them, even while he is often embarrassing to them. Sitcom families are often idealistic representations, but what I like about the Dunphy family is the way they get through their often mundane problems with humor. In short, the family that laughs together stays together (or at least finds a way to use humor to avoid uncomfortable situations).

So I approach fatherhood with the experience of living in a Christian home and surviving Christian culture with the help of humor. Whether I like it or not, these experiences will ultimately shape how I raise my kids. Sometimes it is the small things that make all of the difference. I remember my dad used to play a recording of Sir Laurence Olivier reading the Bible in dramatic fashion while my brother and I were sleeping, so now when I read the Bible I always hear it in a Shakespearean accent (try reading the contemporary-sounding New Living Translation that way—it doesn't work). Night after night of these recordings helped me to remember the stories well and really to understand the drama behind the stories. I have really fond memories of these stories. I hope to try something similar with my boys if they promise to actually stay in bed (of course I will also imitate the over-dramatic voices to them).

My brother and I have big imaginations, so the stories of the Bible really captured our attention. The fact that the four Gospels are four stories made it easy for me to fall in love with Christ. One of the reasons I think we like funny things is that they are often expressed through stories that connect to our own experiences. One of pleasures of parenthood is reading books to your kids with a ton of pictures. My oldest son actually loves a good story. His favorite books are about animals, like *The Very Hungry Caterpillar* by Eric Carle, or about superheroes like Spiderman. In fact, I'm reading him a book right now featuring Superman on how to use the potty (please don't judge me). He even pretends to fly around the house with his cape while humming the Superman theme. How can the Bible compete with that? Well, I recently discovered that the twentieth-century writer C. L. R. James wrote a number of children's stories for his son while he was in exile separated from him. These stories mix together humans, animals, famous pop cultural figures (for instance, Moby Dick and Mighty Mouse), heroes from Classical Greek literature and the Bible. He retells the biblical story of David and Goliath with a fun simplicity that illustrates how the absurdity of the story can be a humorous way to make the Bible relevant to a small child. An example of this is the way James describes the Philistines when he writes that they "were so awful that although this took place a long time ago, up to today when a person is really dumb and mean and cheap, people still call him a Philistine."[1]

Humor can be disarming, but only if you use its powers for good. I think this can be done without cheapening the stories from the Bible in a way that American Christian culture, in my opinion, often does. If I can manage to instill my faith values with a pinch of humor into my boys the way my parents and C. L. R. James does in his book, and not make them hate me in the process, then I think I am doing an okay job. Frankly, if I can provide a smile via self-deprecating humor then I am doing my own little part to ensure my sons do not become axe murderers.

---

1. C. L. R. James, *The Nobbie Stories for Children and Adults.* Lincoln: The Board of Regents of the University of Nebraska, 2006. 114.

The Blue Blanket

by Micah J. Murray

Once upon a time MICAH knew everything there was to know about God and the Bible. Then one day he found himself admitting that, despite having all the answers, he barely believed any of them anymore. With the few shreds of faith he had left, he clung to the hope that God was searching for him, and that he would someday be found. Being found is more of a journey than a destination, and this is where you'll find Micah today. Slowly picking through all the broken pieces of failed religion, looking for Jesus in the midst of it, being found by Him more and more each day. When he's not chasing his two small boys around the house, riding motorcycles with his wife, or overdosing on coffee, Micah attempts to scrawl out the words of this unfolding story on the pages of the internet.

I don't even remember now where we got that blue blanket. It seems like he's always had it.

When he was a ball of tears and dirty diapers in the arms of newlywed parents, there was the blue blanket. When he was learning to crawl and then walk and fall on his diapered butt and try again, he dragged the blue blanket behind him. When we moved across the country and then made long road trips back home to visit grandparents and great-grandparents, the blue blanket was draped over his legs in his car seat. When his little brother was born and he moved to a big boy bed, he had the blue blanket tucked in tight around him every night to help him fall asleep.

I wish to God I did know where it came from, because then I'd be able to write a happy ending to this story. But between baby showers and shopping trips to Target and a small apartment and a big house and a new baby, the details are lost in the clutter. I don't know where we got that blue blanket. He's always had it.

They warned me that being a dad would be hard, and three years and two boys into it I still don't believe them. These stinky, adorable little creatures sent straight from heaven with the explicit mission of destroying everything I own look just like me and I can't help but love them. Just when I'm ready to give one or the other up for adoption, they fall asleep and look like perfect angels and I fall in love with them all over again.

They said I'd go a year without sleep when the first one was born, but that didn't bother me much. I was a senior in college that year, so all-nighters were already part of my weekly routine. I just added bottles and diapers to papers and quizzes and made a second cup of coffee and carried on.

They warned me of the "terrible twos," but he's almost three now and I couldn't ask for a kinder, sweeter, more adventurous kid. I have no idea what I'm doing, and I'll be the first to admit that. All I know is love the kids one day at a time and hope it all turns out right. Maybe I'm naïve, but it doesn't seem that hard.

I love airplanes. Always have and always will. When I was young and my mind was full of dreams and every career path was created equal, I wanted to be a pilot. A jungle missionary pilot, more specifically. Partly because of Jesus and stuff, and partly because I figured those little jungle airplanes would be a lot more fun to fly than a big automated airliner. I never did become a pilot, but somehow I've managed to pass on my love of flying to my boys. There's electricity in an airport, intangible excitement buzzing along the security checkpoints and moving sidewalks and snack shops and baggage claims. There's a moment of thrill every time I feel the enormous body of the airplane creak and shudder, and then leap skyward, and when I look over at my boy seated next to me straining to see the sky outside his window, I can see in his eyes that he feels it too.

"Daddy we are in an airplane and the airplane is in the sky!"

He drapes the blue blanket over his lap and points at the clouds outside the tiny window. He loves it, all of it, and I love him.

But airplanes and airports are fickle things, and fragile. The return flight a few days later is delayed, then cancelled. So, two tired parents and two tired boys begin the long hike from Gate E-19 all the way back to the baggage claim, then the curb, then the shuttle, then a hotel halfway between nice and sketchy.

He loves the moving sidewalks. We "stand right" so the important busy people can "walk left." I stand, he sits on my feet and runs his hands along the glass as we move effortlessly through the terminal. As the end of the sidewalk nears, he stands up and grabs my hand. We count to three, he leaps into the air and lands on the carpet. The journey has a bit of rhythm: moving sidewalk, leap, carpet. Moving sidewalk, leap, carpet.

Soon we're at the baggage claim, then the curb. We meet Mommy there, and wait for the shuttle longer than they said we would, with two boys and a stroller and two iPhones and a diaper bag and two suitcases and two backpacks. But the shuttle eventually arrives and the driver scowls as she opens the door for us and drives us through the rain to the hotel paid for by the airline whose airplane broke down.

But the blue blanket is missing.

As we tuck the boys into fresh hotel beds for an overdue afternoon nap, Mommy and I unzip backpacks and dig through diaper bags. I already know we won't find it there. My mind races backwards, through the shuttle, the baggage claims, the escalator he begged to ride, the moving sidewalks and the carpets. He had it there, draped over his shoulder. I helped him hold onto it, as I juggled backpacks and rolling luggage. I realize now that he didn't have it when we got into the hotel shuttle. I turn to Mommy as my heart sinks, "It's gone."

"I need my blue blankie!"

It's what he says every night as I tuck him into bed, and he wants it now in the hotel for his afternoon nap. It's part of the routine, after all.

"Uh, it's not here right now. It went bye-bye. Here, use this one instead. It's nice and warm."

That seems to satisfy him, at least for now. Soon he's asleep, and then the little brother and Mommy are too. I'm on the phone pacing in the hallway of the hotel, leaving voicemails for airport lost-and-found numbers and hoping that there's hope.

The next day we're back at the airport to try again, and while Mommy takes the little brother through security, I visit all the lost-and-found spots in the airport, whispering so he doesn't hear and get upset. Of course they haven't seen anything, and my heart sinks lower. If anybody was going to turn it in, they would have by now. Surely, the overnight cleaning crew or somebody. But I know for sure it was lost somewhere between Gate E-19 and Baggage Claim C-1, and where else could it be? Retracing my steps, I scan corners, benches, escalators. He doesn't even know what we're looking for, and I don't tell him. He just wants to ride the moving sidewalks again.

He sleeps through most of the return flight, and we get home at bedtime. I'm putting him in his own bed for the first time in a week, and we go through our bedtime routine.

Do you want music?

Yes!

Do you want me to sing rock-a-bye baby?

Yes!

I sing rock-a-bye baby and rock him in my arms as if he's three months instead of almost three years old, like I do every night. He sings along, quietly because he doesn't quite know all the words.

Ok, goodnight. I love you. Have sweet dreams.

And just before I walk out the door and pause to hear him say I love you too, he remembers.

Daddy, I need my blue blankie!

Oh, buddy, your blue blankie went bye-bye.

Is it at the airport?

Yeah, I think it's at the airport.

Oh. Okay. Will you go get it soon?

He nestles into the blankets he has, as I try to piece together a coherent answer. But I'm all out of words, and I can't find a way to tell him that I've already looked everywhere I can and left half a dozen voicemails and that by now the airport is a thousand miles away and there's no way for me to go get his blanket, but that doesn't stop me from wanting to walk all the way back there and find it for him.

So I just mumble an answer and kiss him goodnight and close the door and as I walk away I'm realizing that they were right. Being a dad is hard, and it does suck.

They warned me about this part, that I would hurt my kids. That I would fail. That they'd realize I wasn't Superman.

But I hoped it wouldn't be this soon, before his third birthday.

My mind wanders back through the terminal one more time, trying to recall where I let the blanket slip away. I'm haunted by this innocence and trust in his voice as he asked,

Is it at the airport? Will you go get it?

Because there's no way for me to explain to him that I can't, and his little head already so full of thoughts and ideas has never considered that there are problems I can't solve.

Now the world feels a little bit darker, and scarier, and I'm small and weak too. My mind wanders forward to all the things he'll lose, and all the ways I'll hurt him, and it kills me that even now I know I can't protect him.

I won't be able to protect him from skinned knees and broken legs. I'll be helpless against the sting of defeat on the basketball court, or the deeper ache of rejection from a girl. Sometimes I'll be the one hurting him and I won't be able to protect him from myself. And when he asks me to fix it I won't even have words, because I'm supposed to be Superman but I'm helpless.

I can't even find his blue blanket in the fucking airport.

When I imagined God, I used to picture some sort of distant puppet-master pushing buttons and pulling strings to keep the universe humming along perfectly to some foregone conclusion.

But my own experience of fatherhood is changing my view of God, and I'm just beginning to realize the heartbreak that must be such a part of His love. How He knows that His children will experience pain and loss in the world.

And I used to think that He was behind the curtain pulling the strings to teach us a lesson through pain, but I don't think so anymore. No more than I allowed that blue blanket to get lost in the airport to teach my not-quite-three-year-old that life is hard sometimes.

No, I have to believe that the God who hears when I pray "Our Father" must cringe as He watches us grow up too soon, knowing we'll all lose something precious and learn that the world is too often a tragic place. His heart breaks for us too.

And when we don't even realize it, He's rushing through the airport trying to fix it, trying to find what was lost.

I'm not a theologian, I'm just a young dad. I don't know why God can't prevent pain from reaching us, but I know it breaks His heart when it does. And I believe that His love is driving him to search every last corner of every airport to find lost blankets and make happier endings come true.

A Small Heart Grew Three Sizes That Day

by Daniel Haugh

DAN is the director of Youth and Young Adults at The American Church in Paris. Before coming to Paris in 2011, he served as a youth pastor for ten years in New York. He has also served as an adjunct professor of youth ministry at Nyack College, Alliance Theological Seminary, and Andover Newton Theological Seminary.

Dan is ordained in the Christian and Missionary Alliance denomination and received his master of divinity in church development from Alliance Theological Seminary. Dan is a social media coach and leads workshops and seminars for youth workers with Barefoot Ministries. He has written for *Immerse Journal* and *Youthworker Journal* and authors the blog www.emergingyouth.com.

With a passion for the global reach of God's Kingdom and serving the less fortunate, Dan has traveled to over thirty countries. He serves as the director of global development for Orchids of Light Foundation and as a vice president for research and development for Air Calvary.

He is married to Lauretta and they welcomed twin boys, Jack and Blake, into the world on December 14, 2012.

It is astounding how one small word can have such a large impact. I will never forget the moment when my wife told me she was pregnant. We had been trying to conceive for close to five years, and, though I was still confident, my faith was beginning to waver slightly. On a brisk Easter morning during our traditional sunrise worship service, I vividly remember the Scriptures speaking about new life, and it was as if God spoke directly to me, reassuring me that shortly new life would be forming within my wife. Within two weeks we heard the great news that my wife was pregnant—with twins!

Now, having twins was not part of the plan. My emotions surged from sheer euphoria to panic. My mind instantly raced toward the thought of needing two of everything. I knew that raising an infant would be challenging but the gravity of raising two of them at the same time had never really crossed my mind. More diapers, more food, more toys, more clothes, and certainly less sleep. What kind of stroller would we need? Would it even fit in our elevator? What if one baby does not sleep while the other is sleeping? How is my wife going to feel carrying two babies? What if one is healthy but the other one is sick? My mind raced through a myriad of similar questions and I struggled for answers. To complicate matters, we were living in a foreign country and could not understand the language very well.

That is how fatherhood began for me. Overwhelming, to say the least. By God's grace, most of my initial questions and concerns were answered and our double stroller just fit in our small Parisian elevator.

I have been a father now for six months, but I will never forget the moment when the twins arrived and took their first breath. The sentence from Genesis, "and God breathed life into him" (2:7) took on entirely new significance when I witnessed Jack, and then Blake, breathe for the very first time. My two boys were born on December 14, right in the middle of Advent.[1] As a pastor I have led congregations through Advent and Christmas before, but that year the joy of Christmas and the miracle and mystery of the Incarnation of Jesus[2] took on new significance for me.

The idea that a divine God would take on the frailty, weakness, and utter dependence of a newborn infant marvels me. There is nothing more fragile and helpless than a newborn and that is the profound

---

1. Advent is a season observed in many Western Christian churches as a time of expectant waiting and preparation for the celebration of the Nativity of Jesus at Christmas. The term is an anglicized version of the Latin word *adventus*, meaning "coming."

2. The Incarnation is a fundamental theological teaching of orthodox (Nicene) Christianity, based on its understanding of the New Testament. The Incarnation represents the belief that Jesus took on a human body and nature and became both man and God. In the Bible its clearest teaching is in John 1:14: "And the Word became flesh, and dwelt among us."

truth of what occurs on Christmas. Wrapped up in swaddling clothes, babies are 100 percent dependent on the care and provision of their parents. I have never felt such responsibility in my life, but that is accompanied by the deepest sense of love. I never knew how much love I was capable of having. Perhaps with twins, God has increased my heart even more in order to share the love with both of my sons. This was tested recently as my wife and children traveled back to the United States for three months. Over the past two years my wife and I learned that living in a foreign country is challenging, especially when a language barrier exists. Trying to raise twins proved to be more challenging as we quickly discovered the difficulties of urban parenting and all its complexities.

More difficult, however, has been living apart from our extended family and not having their help and presence with our boys. We have been fortunate that our parents have come to visit on a few occasions, but we also desire for the rest of our families to get to know the boys. Despite their physical absence, our parents' support and example have assisted us in many ways as we learn how to parent.

My own father's story serves as an example of sacrificing personal ambition for the sake of children. The first big decision my father had to make, and for which I will always be grateful and inspired by, was a choice between his professional future or his young family and new son. He choose the latter. He chose our future, and not his own.

Newly married and studying for his PhD at the University of Notre Dame, my parents learned they were expecting their first child. In lieu of finishing his studies, my dad and mom moved back home to Massachusetts to have me, where he took a job with Analog Devices for about a year. He worked the late shift and during that year I was born.

My mom recalls that when she had me, my dad would work his shift, go to my Nana's house and rest for a bit and then come to the hospital to visit us. As she recalls, "He was tired, but so proud of his little boy."

My dad next took a job working at my uncle's fish store in Arlington and my parents eventually moved into the second story apartment of my grandparents' house to save money and be close to family. My entire family, including cousins, all lived within a fifteen-minute drive, and every holiday and birthday was celebrated together. I went to the same school as my cousins and my family was everything to me. That was my life and it was a great one.

With that as a backdrop, one of our sons was born with a minor condition that is not treated in France. After much prayer we thought it best for my wife to travel back to the United States for the eight to ten weeks of treatment required. It is in the midst of this time period that I write now and reflect on changes inside me as a father.

I knew that when my boys came into the world my life would change forever. It certainly did, but the first few months were so incredibly stressful and tiring that time for reflection simply did not occur. While my boys were adorable, tiny infants, everything seemed like a chore to me. At times I resented not having any time to myself for study, work, recreation, or sleep. I was still operating from my selfishness and my boys began to test and try that deep-seated aspect of me. All my boys seemed capable of doing was eating, needing diaper changes, crying, and (at times) napping. There was little real interaction and this was hard for me. But they were my responsibility and I knew that true love is accompanied by action and sacrifice.

Over next few months, my boys grew at a rapid pace and I believe my heart did as well. Seeing a simple smile from one of my sons or hearing my other son laugh uncontrollably warms my heart more than anything or anyone ever has. It is these images and memories I hold onto in their absence. The irony in them being gone is that now I have more freedom, with no parental responsibilities and all the time in the world for rest and recreation, yet I am miserable. My heart and identity now rests with my boys. Though I remain the same person, I am a father now. Even though currently my children are not with me, my heart and my life are with them fully. What amazes me is that I loved these children before they were even born, and when they entered this world that love increased exponentially. This love is not based on anything they have done for me now or what they may do in the future. No, this love is unconditional and solely based on who they are and not what they have done. They are my children, on loan to my wife and me from their Heavenly Parent.

The weight of this responsibility has probably not sunk in yet, but having served as a youth pastor for almost fifteen years, the thought of parenting two teenage boys terrifies me. I remember what I was like at that age and the hell I put my parents through. Now I see the challenges facing today's teens and shudder at the prospects that await us.

This life experience has also made me better appreciate my own father and understand the challenges and sacrifices he made for me and my sister. I never realized what sacrifices both of my parents made until I got much older. I also never realized what I did not have.

Growing up, it never once crossed my mind to compare what we had (and did not have) with my other friends. My younger sister Lauren came along a few years later and by the time I was twelve my parents were able to purchase their first home and so we moved to New Hampshire. My dad had to continue to work two jobs to provide for our family.

He managed a Friendly's restaurant by day and then worked the night shift at a UPS warehouse. I never thanked him for that back then because I was young and selfish and never understood the tremendous sacrifice he made for his family.

And yet despite putting in all those hours (and I am sure stressing over finances), my sister and I never once had an unfulfilled need. My dad never missed one baseball game and we made sure to take family vacations. Apparently, when I was younger my dad and I were talking and he mentioned something about working long hours—wishing he had had more time with me, and I said " Dad, even though you were busy—you always made the time to be there." And he did.

It is strange to think of my dad viewing and loving me the same way I do my sons, but that has helped me better understand the depth of love that God has for all of His children. This love is not based on what we have done or may do. In fact it is not based on anything about us at all, but rather on who God is. My sons are not old enough yet to get in trouble or do something wrong. That day will come quickly, and if they are like their dad, there will be many of those days. Though I have not had to discipline them yet or offer forgiveness and grace, I already know the abundance of grace and love that is welling up within me for them. There is nothing they could ever do or become that would make me love them less. Even now, as young as they are, my love for them, especially in their absence, continues to grow fervently. I believe this is God's love for us, for all people.

The day my boys were born my eyes were opened to a new reality. I remember walking to the bus station and looking into the eyes of each person I passed by, noticing them differently on this day. For understandable reasons my eyes were drawn toward babies, but I also noticed old men and women and even some crippled beggars on street corners and came to realize that they too were infants once. Scripture reminds us that we were known by God before birth and we are loved unconditionally by God as sons and daughters (1 John 3:1).

This is only the beginning of the journey of fatherhood for me, but my prayer is for God to grant me grace to love and care for my children and wife well and to see the world around me with new eyes of compassion and through the lens of the paternal. I am a work in progress but I thank God for the gift of fatherhood and for the lessons of family and faith that I am learning along the way.

Blessing

by Justin K. Coleman

JUSTIN COLEMAN is the lead pastor of the Gethsemane Campus of St. Luke's United Methodist Church in Houston, Texas. A native of Houston, he is a graduate of Southern Methodist University in Dallas and Duke Divinity School in Durham, North Carolina. Pastor Coleman has also served as a pastor at University United Methodist Church in Chapel Hill, North Carolina, the SMU Wesley Foundation, and in other college and youth ministry programs.

Last fall, while visiting a teenager I mentor, he shared with me about his substance abuse problems. I asked why he uses and he said, "Life is tough. I have a lot of problems with my folks and other stuff, and, you know, it helps." When I asked where he learned to smoke weed, he said he'd learned from his dad when he was about ten. This young man had learned from his father a poor coping mechanism, one that he knows hurts him, but one that he continues to let define him. The young man both mimics his father and resents him. The father who was meant to bless his son has wounded him instead.

My church is in a neighborhood in transition. People live on the edge day-to-day. Stresses are high due to poverty, healthcare challenges, educational frustration, and a myriad of other challenges, and not everyone knows how to cope with those stresses. Poor coping mechanisms, like the one displayed by the young man above, mean that verbal abuse, physical abuse, substance abuse, and abandonment are all too regular occurrences in some households. As a pastor, I see the impact of "father wounds" every day. "Father wound" refers to the hurt that a father causes, whether through abuse, absence, or modeling unhealthy behaviors, such as being emotionally distant or selfish. I hear too few stories of fathers blessing their children, and too many instances of wounding them. It is not just in my neighborhood, however. I hear stories of father wounds happening to people from all walks of life. We need fathers who are intentional about blessing their children rather than wounding them.

Blessing begins with language and is ratified through action. I have two great sons, Zan and Max. They are seven and four years old, respectively. It is amazing to watch kids grow in their knowledge and use of language. We weren't too far into elementary school before we had to address "potty words" with Zan. It's not that he was using them in school, but he'd hear them from friends and then come home to cautiously test them out with us. These were, I'm glad to say, the junior league of potty words, like "stupid" or "dang it," but they were, my wife and I felt, the linguistic gateway to cussing like a sailor. So we talked to Zan about words that hurt and words that heal. We talked about words that respect and words that disrespect. I must say that I was encouraged by his immediate recognition. He knew these potty words didn't quite fit the language he'd seen modeled by his family and much of the community that surrounded him. When he's older he will make choices about how he wants to use more colorful language in rhetoric, but these early lessons are vital teaching for him and good reminders for us as his parents that we must consider how we use language.

I sometimes hear people say, "I'm blessed" or "God has blessed me with (fill-in-the-blank)," meaning that the individual has received material goods, which they consider to be a sign of God's favor or blessing. In reality, sometimes such gifts are blessings and sometimes they are not. It is a Western presumption that the more one has, the happier one will be. It may also be the case that the more one has, the more one has to worry about. We must give great care to model good use of the word "bless."

What I am seeking to recover in my own family life is an understanding of blessing that is seen in scripture. Blessing, in the Christian tradition, is a particular speech-act that is given to the people of God. It means to offer happiness and welfare or a sense of *shalom*. *Shalom* is the Hebrew word meaning wholeness with peace and justice. The writer of the Book of Jeremiah says, "'For I know the plans I have for you,' declares the Lord, 'plans to prosper you and not to harm you, plans to give you hope and a future.'" The word that we translate as "prosper you and not to harm you" is *shalom*. "For I know the plans I have for you," declares the Lord, "plans for *shalom*, plans to give you hope and a future." My desire is to speak words of blessing and *shalom* over my children and to encourage other fathers to do the same for their children.

On the Sabbath, Jewish fathers bless their children. A father will typically speak these words over his sons: "May God make you like Ephraim and Manasseh." This phrase comes from Genesis 48:20. This may at first seem like a strange way to bless, but in scripture Jacob speaks this blessing over his grandchildren, Ephraim and Manasseh, because unlike his own children, they lived in peace together and cooperated well. A Jewish father will speak these words over his daughters: "May God make you like Sarah, Rebecca, Rachel, and Leah." He will pray this blessing because these were strong women who gave birth to and raised the people of God amid much difficulty. I want my children to hear the voice of their father saying "I love you" often, and I also want them to regularly hear the voice of their father speaking words of blessing over them, so that is what I do. I pray a blessing over my sons each day as I drive them to school. I pray over them each night with my wife and I mark the sign of the cross on their foreheads as a form of blessing before kissing them goodnight, a physical act of blessing in the Christian tradition, and it is a blessing for me to see them pray for others and say, "I love you Daddy," in return.

My father passed away in February of 2013 from cancer. My dad loved me and was proud of me and my siblings, yet he was of a generation where men were taught to be providers and disciplinarians to their children first and foremost. It was sometimes hard for him to show affection and affirmation. He didn't want us to be too soft, and he didn't want to seem too soft either, so he determined to be stern. When I was away at school, no longer living in the house, we exchanged more hugs and "love yous" (we dropped the "I" to make expressing care seem less intense) than we ever had before. I knew my dad loved me, and during his later years and his fight with cancer I heard him express it more often, but such expression was difficult for him after having spent a lifetime being "tough." After I had children of my own, he commented to me several times about how he delighted to see me express affection toward my kids, and that he wished that he had done the same with his children. That sentiment, in itself, was a blessing to me.

A few days before my dad passed away, his sons were gathered at his bedside. My eldest brother asked him if he would offer his sons a blessing. By this time, my dad was no longer able to speak, so my brother asked him to blink once if he wanted to offer this blessing. With all the strength he could muster, he gave one hard blink and then with tears in all our eyes we observed a holy moment of silence as the blessing that needed no words was imparted. A moment that I will never forget.

In addition to the blessings that I might offer my children by word or gesture, I want them to be blessed by observing me keeping the faith. It has been said that faith is often caught as much as it is taught. Children learn from and imitate those adults who are closest to them. This is a form of discipleship not unlike the disciples spending their days with Jesus. In our day-to-day, we are able to demonstrate ways of seeing, speaking, and being in the world that are the result of the in-dwelling presence of Christ in our lives. Such witness brings a blessing that will continue to benefit my children throughout their lives. It is a blessing that seeks recognition, not by words of thanks, but by emulation.

I am not the only Christ-like example that my children see. It is important that they observe others keeping the faith. My children get to see Christians of all ages seeking to live out their faith each and every week, not only on Sundays, but throughout the week. We take time to point out to our kids good examples of Christ-like living when we see it. We also delight at what they are seeing on their own, this faith that is sometimes more caught than taught. One day, while playing, Max hurled a toy car at Zan, narrowly missing his head. Zan simply said, "You didn't listen to the Holy Spirit, Max." My wife and I were quite tickled at this surprising statement. Where did he get that expression from? Well, he had learned it from our amazing children's ministry director, Mrs. Amy. She modeled faithful thinking in such a way that Zan understood that good choices are often results of the Holy Spirit's work in us and that poor choices, like throwing toy cars toward his brother's face, well, are not. The blessed witness of others to our children can be immeasurable gifts.

Likewise, we should not discount our ability to bless children who are not our own. At the beginning of my ministry in the parish in which I'm currently serving, one of our senior adults, a delightful woman named Tex, made an appointment to visit with me. She was eighty years old, walked with a cane, always had a twinkle in her eye that was a beautiful mix of grace and mischief, and had true grit. She said something to me that I will always remember: "Pastor, you are our spiritual leader. You are like a father to us. Love us like your children, and we will always follow you." An amazing moment and gift of pastoral wisdom. Tex passed away last year, and I wept for my sweet daughter, and mother, and friend. She had been all those things. She taught me how to view those in my parish as my children. I often call the youth in my parish, some of whom were suffering from the father wounds I mentioned earlier, "son" or "daughter." They have never asked me why I do so, but seem to know that it is because I care and want to bless them.

I offer you this blessing that I often pray over my children using the words of Psalm 1 and inserting the names of my children into the verses:

> Happy are [my children] who do not follow the advice of the
> wicked, or take the path that sinners tread, or sit in the seat of

scoffers; but their delight is in the law of the Lord, and on his law they meditate day and night. [My children] are like trees planted by streams of water, which yield their fruit in its season, and their leaves do not wither. In all that [my children] do, they prosper. Amen.

Someday, a Family
by Benjamin R. Moberg

BEN MOBERG is a twenty-something gay man hailing from the northern suburbs of Saint Paul, Minnesota. He writes a blog about being in love with Jesus, being a gay man today, and how the crumbling evangelical subculture isn't worth saving. He likes reading memoirs, fishing at the cabin, and hanging out with his friends and family, all of whom are pretty much the same people.

On a warm autumn night, we stood in a circle beneath the parking lot lights. We had just spent the evening watching my brother, Matt, and his wife, Lauren, sing their hearts out before hundreds at the edge of Lake Harriet. It was my parents' anniversary, but it was still strange when Matt swung out a small gift bag. We never did gifts on anniversaries and they were too eager about it. Their twinkled eyes betrayed their flopping poker faces. Something was happening.

"You didn't have to get us anything!" My mom sighed; she plucked through the tissue paper.

"A book?" She fished it out, extended it out into the light. My dad and she squinted closely. She read: "*A Minnesota Guide for Grand—*." And then a shriek and a gasp and so much laughter and tears. My mom was in disbelief. "Grandparents? *GRANDPARENTS*?!?" Arms flung down and out at her sides.

"You're going to be grandparents," Matt nodded and they both fell into his arms. We all took turns embracing and shouting and making a crazy enough commotion to alarm passersby. But we didn't care. This was bliss. This was a first for us all.

And I'm not sure what word describes the moments that followed for me. Bittersweet seems too sad, affecting, too fleeting; perhaps it's best to say that after the bliss came a slow dimming.

Ten minutes later it was emptiness. Half of me swept away like a sand castle too close to the sea. I felt a yearning ache ripple through me, unlike any I'd known, and all I could do was curl into the corner of my seat in the car, crying as softly as I possibly could.

It had been just under a year since I told my family that I was gay, and though the time since had been beautiful and spiritual and progressive, I came to the conclusion that I could never have a family of my own. Evangelicalism was loud and clear about what my life options were: marry the right *woman* or make a vow to celibacy. The former felt impossible and disastrous and wrong. The latter felt, well, less impossible and disastrous and wrong. So I went with that.

Celibacy and singleness are the technical terms; the real name is Loneliness.

And *God*, did I try to make myself belong there.

I would imagine all the glory and beauty of the single life. The trips I could take, all the money I could save, all the autonomy I could have unchained from another person's dreams. No kids to break the bank. No baby waking me up at three in the morning. No difficult departures when they went off to college. It was liberation, really.

But a few months later I started seeing that vacant side of the bed. I saw the blank walls and empty rooms that should have been filled with cribs and finger paintings. There would be no graduation or little league games. There would be no bedtime stories to tell or scraped knees to bandage and kiss.

I saw Christmas Eve at my parents' house; my nieces' and nephews' kids chasing each other around, my siblings holding their spouses, swaying to the holiday music. They would all go home and tuck each other in or sit by the fire and open one early Christmas day gift.

I would go home to dead air. A great emptiness. In bed, shivering, trying to painfully remind myself that this is what God preordained. For every damn day, for the rest of my long life.

It was the unavoidable emptiness that spiked my depression like a fever.

I'd be in the middle of a college lecture and suddenly begin packing my things, run to my car, and sob against the steering wheel. I'd be at a wedding, drinking until I was stupid and uncaring and emotionless. Television commercials could trigger tears. Families at the park would make me turn my head into my shoulder.

I was crying frequently and randomly, and one night I came home and told my parents I was drowning in it and I should go to the hospital. I told them I wanted a family, I wanted children, I wanted a life like everyone else could have. They calmed me; I spoke on the phone with a doctor and got a prescription for a needed emergency anti-anxiety medication.

My older brother and his wife, at the urgent call from my mom, came over to talk me through it.

He sat on the floor beside the bed and really did try his best to be helpful. He said, "Ben, I am looking forward to the day when your sexuality doesn't tear you apart like this. I am looking forward to it becoming just another part of your fabric."

I looked at him, brows fully arched.

"That is easy for you to say." I scowled, and I meant it. I clarified for him, "You're married, and you'll have children. I will have no one."

"Right." He said, looking down, feeling the bluntness of that truth. For a few very long seconds, no one said anything.

"You can *have* a family!" My mom burst.

An exhale after months of holding her breath. She had respected my reasons for celibacy, because this was my journey and she didn't want to interfere. But if it was going to kill me like this, over and over, day by day, it couldn't be worth it. Moreover, it couldn't be right. On a number of occasions she gave me her blessing to pursue a partnership with another man, saying I wouldn't have to win her love and support, she was already there.

I touch that hole in my heart and I think about how fiercely I tried to fill it. Squeezing in long lists of purity perks, romanticized visions of chasing adventure, and a conviction that even if the loneliness grew to unbearable pain, it was just part of it. It was my cross to bear.

But nothing could smother out the ache.

And I think it's because nothing was ever meant to.

When I look at the hazy road ahead, I feel those dreams, of having a partner and children, rising strong and vibrant, breaking out like light before me. And I remember the beautiful truth that I am made. That it was He who breathed me to life, sculpted and painted my heart. A heart with a finger-pressed hole, designed to be filled with family.

I no longer cling to celibacy, which isn't to say my faith and sexuality are neatly reconciled. My walk continues, my questions persist, and it's beautiful because I would rather be wrestling with God than sitting resigned in my own sad corner. What I do know is that I don't have to have it all mapped out now. I don't have to place limits on what my life will look like based on my understanding as a twenty-three-year-old with a brief list of life experiences.

I know that I'll have kids, and I can hardly wait. But I'm not sure if I'll find someone to raise my family with. I don't know if I can give my kids the benefit of two parents. But here is what I do know.

I will cherish them like they are the last sparks of light in a dimming world. I will do whatever it takes, no matter the cost. I will be the tee-ball coach, I'll head the PTA; I'll read them Berenstain Bears and teach them to throw a football. I will let them know it's okay to cry and I will make them feel brave. I will tuck them in at night with prayers in their ears and kisses on their crowns, the way my mom and dad always did for me. I will take them to the edge of the ocean where the water washes up on their feet, drive them to northern Minnesota where the stars come fully alive, carry them to the side of a mountain, walk with them beneath the Red Wood forest, just so they can glimpse the power of beauty. The beauty of a God who pieced and painted everything together, blissfully crying that it was all Good. A God who died so they could be who they are.

My little nephew Wyatt was born on the sunny spring day of April 30. As I'm thinking through this essay, he is squeezing my finger tight in his tiny fist. Only seven weeks old and he is already smiling in the warmest, most unique ways.

When my brother first wheeled Wyatt out of the delivery room, he was swaddled up and yawning. I peered down at him and he opened his eyes for a split second, and I felt something that I hadn't before. Love at first sight. It is, indeed, the strangest of feelings. He's my nephew, not my son, and I don't know who he is yet, but in that moment, I could not love him more than I already did. It was the dumbstruck, unquestionable, take-a-bullet-for kind of love that for most of my life I believed was something earned. Yet, here the kid was, holding my heart in his balled up fist and gazing at me with his ocean-blue eyes.

It's hard to understand now how such a beautiful blessing could have broken my heart less than a year ago. Gently, I lift him up, set his chubby cheek flat on my shoulder, and I am so happy. Unbelievably grateful for his life. But in my mind, I am leaping forward. It is just before bedtime and my kid is cradled around my neck, and I can't believe it's all real. I can't believe that this is my life.

Baby Wyatt taught me something about God that I hadn't been able to feel for a long time. My ache and hurt and loneliness compressed densely in between us and in one quick glance, in a hospital hallway, a beam of light punctured through my darkness. The way I look at this kid, my crazy love for him, is how God sees me always. It is sure and absurd and beautiful and completely unearned. It is love and it is keeping me forever.

My Daughters, My Teachers
by Scott Emery

SCOTT is an avid reader of both books and culture, has an ever-increasing affection for ecology and agriculture, and has spent time as both an Anglican and house church pastor. The past eleven or so years have taken him and his wife into many differing contexts and approaches to church planting, all of which have been opportunities to live more like Jesus. He began working with special education students eight years ago and his life and theology were forever changed. He blogs at scottemery.wordpress.com where he focuses on discipleship, mission, and community. Scott and his family (wife and three daughters) currently live in Syracuse, New York, where they are pursuing simplicity and sustainability.

I am a thirty-one-year-old man whose world is painted pink and in which echoes of princess' laughter resounds. This is of my own doing—to the extent that I had a part in the mystery of procreation. My wife and I have three beautiful, witty, strong-willed, and often challenging daughters. At the time of this writing, they are four years, two years, and eight months old. They have simultaneously become my sources of joy and frustration; I would like to say I have taught them much, but honestly, they have taught me more than I am even aware. That's where I'd like to take an extended stop: my daughters, my teachers. In particular, I'd like to focus on one vital and essential lesson they have taught me:

Vulnerability. Let me explain.

I grew up in a world heavily constituted and marked by the conservative Evangelical church. The Bible was taken at face value and beliefs were generally not questioned. Evangelism was at the fore of most reasons for being in the world. Republican politics were the primary means of being active in government, which was usually coupled with being conservative in public issues and life. And, above all, the goal of life was being saved in order to enter heaven after death. This mode of "doing church" became an overarching culture, which engendered the environs of my youth. It was pervasive and seeped into every pore of my being. Every social circle I found myself a part of—family, local church, school, friends—was indelibly affected by the flooding waters of this religious world.

The bubble seemed huge: it encompassed all I knew. The reality of the situation was that it was smaller than I could have imagined. Sure, everyone knew everyone. But that's what happens in an insular community. That's what we had, after all.

Right?

Community was a word often used but hardly ever realized. We had all the tokens of community: midweek dinners at church, a shared vernacular, friendly smiles, similar rhythms of life. Friends were friends from childhood; often with multiple siblings from different families. Basketball games, track meets, chorus concerts, and other activities filled our collective calendars.

This was the world I grew up in.

Faith tied it together. Faith bound us. Faith weaved a variety of people into one tapestry.

Not just faith, but faith in Jesus. The same Jesus who was born to a virgin on Christmas, died on Good Friday, and rose again on Easter. The same Jesus who died so I could be forgiven. The same Jesus who forgave me so I could go to heaven when I died. The same Jesus who I prayed to; the same Jesus who I sang to on Sunday mornings; the same Jesus who I went on mission trips for to make sure others could go to heaven someday.

Or at least this is what I was told. I have since learned this Jesus who wanted to save my soul for heaven wanted me to be placed in a community of love with both other people and the creation I am a part of. It is this Jesus that now I live with and for.

I should say for the sake of clarity that I am beyond grateful for this upbringing. I was introduced to Jesus here and was introduced to many facets of life I still continue in till this day. What I began to notice as I reflected upon the Evangelical conservative faith I was reared within, however, was its constant affinity for the individual. Jesus was the Savior of the individual due to an individual's prayer of conversion. An individual's piety was based on keeping a list of individualistic rules circling Bible reading and prayer. The songs we sang rallied around the emotive "I" and "my," not "we" or "ours," and were evenly matched by sermons of therapeutic self-aggrandizement.

There was a vulnerability to be had with Jesus, but vulnerability ended there. The scattering of this vulnerability throughout and unto our brother or sister wasn't always encouraged. Certainly, it happened in the proverbial mountaintop and valley experiences of life. However, it was not a sustained characteristic of life. In many ways, it seems to me, this allowed for the veneer of community to exist in lieu of actual community. We were tethered to Jesus, but not really to one another.

What is vulnerability then? It is the opening up of oneself to another, leaving the results to themselves. The actual Latin roots of "vulnerable" mean "able to wound," giving us the connotation of possible pain, anguish, or torment. In a very real sense, it is a relinquishing of power over others through an understanding of one's limitedness.

Vulnerability is the first step in learning. It allows us to make sense of our limited nature and hence the need for others. This is the essence of vulnerability: the limitedness in me needs the giftedness in you and vice versa. Interconnectivity and interdependence are found where vulnerability is flourishing.

Thus, we don't do this alone because we learn to see our weaknesses through others and community is cultivated. It is in our propensity to neglect opportunities for vulnerability that community breaks down.

I have never seen this to be truer than with my own children. There is something about living life with three little girls four years old and younger that allows me to perceive vulnerability. Not only theirs, but in a penetrating fashion, my own. (Try blowing up at your two-year-old and not immediately learning more about yourself than you might care to know.) I learn about faith and its correlates of vulnerability and community when my girls need my help. "Daddy, I can't do this. Can you help me?" is possibly the most explicit manifestation of faith I know.

This takes place every morning. Between six-thirty and seven o'clock, I wake up with my girls and take them downstairs. We do the same thing nearly every morning: we walk downstairs, they sit on the couch, ask me for their morning cups of milk, and then watch their favorite PBS cartoons. Recently, it has begun to hit me how much vulnerability it takes—albeit unknown to them—to ask for their food and drink. There is a realization of how unable they are to simply retrieve their milk, warm it up, and get the proper cups to drink from. Never mind their obvious lack of the income and transportation needed to get the milk into the house in the first place.

The entire process of enabling them to eat and drink is out of their hands. This is the basic necessity of life, and for them there is a constant reckoning with their need to be dependent upon others. Hunger creeps in and their bodies tell them it is time to eat. Or to quote my four-year-old, "My belly is telling me it's hungry."

This doesn't just happen with my "speaking" girls. My eight-month-old demonstrates her vulnerability in every moment. Her cries can be a constant in times of dire need. Hunger, sleeplessness, or diaper issues open her vocal chords in unique ways of expressing her vulnerability. And, I, her father, have grown to know her particular cry over the cries of others. I am hers and she is mine. We, along with her mother and sisters, are inextricably tied together.

This vulnerability is what I think Jesus was getting at when he beckoned the children unto himself:

> At that time the disciples came to Jesus and said, "Who then is greatest in the kingdom of heaven?" And He called a child to Himself and set him before them, and said, "Truly I say to you, unless you are converted and become like children, you will not enter the kingdom of heaven. Whoever then humbles himself as

this child, he is the greatest in the kingdom of heaven." (Matthew 18:1-5 NASB)

The disciples expected Jesus to answer their question by describing some great leader or great champion of the faith. They expected Jesus to give them a list of admirable qualities belonging to the "greatest in the kingdom of heaven." What Jesus gave them instead was a child. In doing so, Jesus flipped their expectations upside down. They asked a question about greatness and Jesus answered by pointing them to meekness and vulnerability. This must have really rattled the cages of his disciples. Even in the framing of their question it is apparent that the disciples had bought into the world's understanding of vulner-ability: being vulnerable carries no significance; it doesn't carry any weight; only through asserting one's power over others can one really be considered "great." True greatness, however, comes through being like a child. It isn't that the children are more holy; they are transpar-ently open to love. They are vulnerable in a beautiful, beautiful way.

And so as my children teach me of the vulnerability called upon by Jesus for life in the kingdom, I can't help but reflect upon how this vulnerability is needed between me and God the Father. I mentioned our morning routine above because after I get them their milk, I tend to sit with my coffee and a bowl of cereal as I watch them fill their bellies. Some mornings I busy myself to the point of being inattentive, but when I slow myself down and make myself present to them, I see how their simple acts of asking and receiving set me off on my day much more aware of my own needs. They have taught me that my in-dependence is something to be grateful for, but my interdependence is what saves me. And, again, vulnerability is at the core of this.

As my children ask for my help, I also should recognize my identity as a child of God. As such, it is natural to come to the Father in weak-ness, seeking out the divine Giver of Gifts. Jesus says in Matthew 7:11: "If you then, being evil, know how to give good gifts to your children, how much more will your Father who is in heaven give what is good to those who ask Him!" This is not because God is my genie, similar to how I am not my daughters' genie, but because in the kingdom of God, everything is God's.

Therefore, everything is a gift given to us in our interconnectivity and interdependence within the kingdom of God. We are never isolated from the gifts of God. Every sunrise, every bodily function, every plant and animal: all gifts within the ecosystem of God. We are ipso facto weaved into the very fabric of vulnerability in regard to creation and others. When I pay attention to my daughters, my eyes and ears are more attuned to this as I live life with others and find myself in need of creation's bounty.

As my daughters age and mature, it is my duty to protect their vulnerability in gracious ways. They will continue to teach me in ways seen and unseen as I do my best to do likewise. One thing I know for certain: as long as we allow for a reciprocal vulnerability we will allow for learning. They have taught me this and for that I am grateful.

The Fight of Our Lifetime: Winning the Fatherhood Battle

by Edrin C. Williams

EDRIN C. WILLIAMS leads MOSAIC, a community of youth and college students at The Sanctuary Covenant Church in Minneapolis, Minnesota. He's been married to Shanequa for seven years and they are parents to a beautiful, independent toddler, Taylor Elise. The family house is currently pet-free, but who knows what the future holds. Edrin is a Carolinian who loves Minneapolis, along with music, history, travel, and people!

Edrin is a graduate of the University of South Carolina in Columbia, South Carolina. He holds a masters of divinity degree in preaching and communication from Bethel Seminary in St. Paul, Minnesota. Edrin is an advocate of the local church, and he's very passionate about equipping leaders of all ages who will impact society with the Gospel of Jesus.

Edrin blogs about faith, family, and other familiar things at www.edrin-williams.com.

For the past eight years I've served as a pastor to youth and children in urban Minneapolis and the surrounding metro areas. In that time, I've had my fair share of battles, spiritual and physical. I've "gone to war" on behalf of young people battling with nearly every conceivable issue. I've seen young men lose their freedom to the justice system. I've seen young women have their lives changed as they become mothers before they are ready. I've seen students struggle with issues of sexual identity, body image, poverty, substance abuse, and mental health. Although the work has been hard, it's been my privilege to journey with these kids, experiencing breakthrough and victory on many occasions.

About four years ago, I was leading a small bible study at the local Baptist church where I was serving as youth pastor when I observed a reality that changed the trajectory of my ministry. I was sitting at the head of a semicircle of ten teenage, mostly junior-high, boys. I can't recall what I was teaching exactly, but the guys were really locked in and engaged. As I talked, I had one of those experiences where it seems like you're sitting someplace else observing what's actually happening around you. I can still see the guys and the order in which they sat—Carlos, Jeremiah, Benjamin, Shawn, Gabriel, Jonathan, Tim, Patrick, James, and Darian. I mentally worked my way around that circle and realized that only three of the ten young men there had a father living in the home with them. The other seven boys were being raised by single mothers, aunties, grandmothers, and other family members. In the middle of what I was teaching, a question came into my heart that changed my ministry. "God, where are the fathers?"

That night, I began to struggle internally with that question. I began to think back to my time teaching middle school and coaching B-team basketball in South Carolina a few years earlier. Why were there no fathers in the stands at our games? Why couldn't I recall ever having a father approach me about his son's lack of playing time or my bad play calling? That night caused me to think back to my experience as a pastor over the previous few years. I had spent hundreds, perhaps thousands, of hours with young men and women, but their fathers had no clue who I was or how I was interacting with their sons and daughters. That night also reignited some personal wonderings, as I wrestled with my own painful fatherless past. Those father wounds that I assumed were past began to feel fresh and especially painful again, although I was a married man approaching twenty-nine years old. Why had my father made the decision not to be a part of my life? How did he make that same decision four years later when my sister was born? Was there something wrong with me that contributed to this?

Despite the personal pain and the troubling realizations that came along with that night, I'm grateful for it because it set me on a different course. In trying to make sense of what was a reality for these young men and trying to find healing for myself, I jumped into research around the issue of fatherlessness and what I discovered broke my heart over and over again. I discovered that these young men were in very good company. There was a name for them. They were a part of the Fatherless Generation.

Organizations like The National Fatherhood Initiative provide some startling statistics:

This generation, the fatherless generation, included as many as 24,000,000 children whose fathers are physically absent.

Nearly 65 percent of black children, 35 percent of Hispanic teens, and 25 percent of white children live in homes absent their fathers.[1]

Just as startling as the sheer numbers of this widespread epidemic is the effect that it has on society. Fatherlessness contributes to nearly every social ill that we see in society. Fatherless children, specifically those living without their biological fathers, are believed to be, on average, at least two to three times more likely to be poor, to use drugs, to experience educational, health, emotional, and behavioral problems, to be victims of child abuse, and to engage in criminal behavior than their peers who live with their married, biological (or adoptive) parents.[2]

Even if I was restricted to reviewing the data, I would be pretty thoroughly convinced that the absence of fathers creates a vacuum in the lives of children that quite often leads to destructive and unproductive lives. I did not, however, have the luxury of simply reading about this in census reports or blog posts. Instead, my journey over nearly ten years brought me face-to-face with this ugly epidemic.

There was Robert, who appeared in court eight to ten times in the years that I was his youth pastor. He missed the birth of his son because he was sentenced to several years in jail. There was Angelo, whose mom struggled to keep him away from the older guys in the neighborhood. He's serving five years for armed robbery because he

---

1. National Fatherhood Initiative, "Facts on Father Absence." Accessed October 20, 2013 http://www.fatherhood.org/media/fatherhood-statistics.
2. Ibid.

was with a guy who robbed an older man in the neighborhood. There was Cherise, who thought that the way to respond to the care and attention that she received from men at church was to offer herself to them physically. There was Leonard, who felt so distant from his estranged dad and so angry over past hurt that he actively worked to transform himself into a girl. Behind every number in a statistic, there is a real person, often someone suffering because of the absence of a father.

Spiritually, the outlook is even more troubling. I could not help but believe that fatherlessness affects a child's ability to see God as God desires to be seen. The greatest danger associated with fatherlessness is that it seems to make it extremely difficult, nearly impossible, for a fatherless child to grasp the concept of "God as The Good Father." Matthew 6:9-13 highlights some foundational truths about God and how we, God's children, relate to God through prayer. Verse 9 begins, "Our Father in heaven. Hallowed be your name." We're presented a powerful image of God as Father, or more accurately, *abba* or daddy. It is a term of intimacy, familiarity, and trust. If God is to be seen in that way, what is the plight of a fatherless child who has only known fathers to be absent, inconsistent, and sources of pain?

For years, I've counseled students and even adults as they work through questions that are rooted in fatherlessness. Fatherless kids struggle mightily to establish or maintain faith. Since that night in 2009, I've taken on the issue of fatherlessness, and I've used my ministry as a platform to address this problem. Because I saw fatherlessness as a direct threat to many of the kids that I serve ever becoming disciples of Jesus Christ, I felt obligated to address the issue head on.

Ministry to fatherless kids for me has taken a two-headed approach. On one hand, I've admonished the churches that I serve to care for "orphans and widows," with James 1:27 offering this up as the standard that proves our religion to be acceptable, pure, and faultless. In my experience, the orphans have almost always been children and teens who were abandoned by their fathers. What has this ministry looked like, though? The key has been to embed care for fatherless children into every area of the church, as opposed to creating a separate, stand-alone ministry. One example is when our men's ministry challenged men without sons to "adopt" fatherless boys, providing rides to church functions, attending that boy's activities, and being a regular connection between that young man and the rest our church family. The ideas will vary based on context and circumstance, yet the underlying intent is always to give fatherless children a larger network of support than they would otherwise have in the absence of their father.

Beyond what I've done to help churches develop a means of ministering to fatherless kids, I've placed an even greater emphasis on influencing churches to do a much better job of equipping and raising up the next generation of fathers. Our society expends tons of time, energy, and resources teaching young boys how to play sports, how to drive, how to ask a girl out, how to apply to college, and the like. Yet, most young men never get the proper instruction they need to become good fathers. How can a young man learn to be a good father unless someone teaches him and models it for him? I would argue that the best way to fix fatherlessness is to stop it before it starts. We can eradicate fatherlessness by equipping young men long before they become fathers, and I believe that the church is uniquely suited to lead here. Being so, I'm constantly asking certain questions. Where are the older men in the church who are willing to mentor teenage boys and college students long before they become dads? What are the essential lessons of fatherhood that any young man needs to have? Who are the experienced fathers who are willing to offer up their wisdom as a means of influencing the next generation of fathers?

Looking, again, at my own journey, it was God's grace and the efforts of a number of faithful, blue-collar men in my family and my home church that allowed me to avoid the pitfalls of growing up fatherless. These heroes of mine were men who worked in logging companies, on farms, and in factories, yet took the time to mentor and guide me and the many other fatherless boys who came together at that small Baptist church in the Lowcountry of South Carolina. These men had very little material wealth, but they were rich in wisdom and responsibility, allowing us to learn much from them. I'm forever indebted to these men, and I'm confident that what they did for us is still the simplest yet most effective way of addressing issues of fatherlessness.

There is no shortage of issues and causes that flood our ears and eyes, demanding a response of us. I believe that in many cases, these issues find their roots in a society that is becoming increasingly fatherless. In 2009, I realized that there was a choice to be made. I could expend all of my time, energy, and resources simply attending to these symptoms, or I could work to alleviate the root causes, including the fatherless epidemic. I decided that a part of my calling is to help raise up of a generation of fathers. My sincere prayer throughout these past four years has been an echo of Malachi 4:6, that God would "turn the hearts of the fathers to their children, and the hearts of the children to their fathers." Lord, let it be so. Amen.

Basketball and the Brown Towel

by Tyler Johnson

TYLER JOHNSON is a writer and actor living in Los Angeles, California. The son of an amazing pastor and father, Tyler grew up in Texas and Georgia. As an adult, he's worked at jobs in far-flung places such as New York, Frisco, Texas, and Los Angeles, all while pursuing his creative career. Tyler's father taught him that worship doesn't stop at the church door; you have to live it. Writing and acting are what bring Tyler the closest to God in his own life.

My dad can't sing. Or rather, he doesn't sing. At least not outside of church. He's got about a three-note range, and none of them fall squarely on the musical scale.

When I was a kid, of course I demanded he sing lullabies at bedtime. After all, Mom sang, so why should he be off the hook? Bedtime means story, prayers, and lullabies. In that order, no exceptions.

He'd do it, too. He didn't sing the song the way Mom did, which was confusing to my brothers and me. Doesn't everyone know the words to that lullaby? There are like six words in the whole thing. Get it right, Dad.

At least his version was consistently wrong to the point it became his own version. A funny thing happened to me, though, every time he sang his cockeyed lullaby. As he sang, the image of a brown towel hanging in a bathroom appeared in my mind. I had a decent imagination, so it struck me at the time as a very boring thing to imagine.

When I tried to think of something else, however, the brown towel remained fixed in my mind.

I told my mom about the brown towel hanging on a rack one day, in an offhand, isn't this weird sort of way. And then she told me what it meant. I didn't think such a thing could have a meaning, much less one that anyone would know about, but of course, moms know everything. But that's another essay.

This, then, is the meaning behind the picture in a little boy's mind that appeared every night when his father who could not sing sang to him.

When I was three years old, I got sick in the middle of the night. Dry heaves. Sheer terror. I ran into my parents' room. Three o'clock in the morning, maybe. This would happen often. The first several times, my parents bundled me up and took me to the emergency room only to sit with me, waiting, for an hour. My sickness would pass, and I'd sit sleepily on the doctor's table while my parents tried to explain why I was brought in. They'd get a prescription for medicine that tasted like bananas and sadness and would be out 150 dollars for the visit. After this happened several times, my dad just drove me to the hospital parking lot, waited fifteen minutes or so for me to settle down, and drove home. I guess he was able to get the banana sadness medicine refilled without the doctor visit.

Sometimes I would come into my parent's room with a hacking dry cough that would continue until it felt like my lungs collapsed and I couldn't draw in another breath.

Dad took me to the bathroom. He ran the shower, shut the door, and let the steam build up. We would sit for what seemed like a long time. Interminable. I cried and wretched up nothing and was scared. And Dad sang to me, holding me with my head on his shoulder. In that tiny bathroom, with my head on my father's shoulder, I stared at a brown towel hanging on the rack as his broken lullaby and the steam from the shower eased my lungs, sending me back to sleep.

Growing up, my dad made a herculean effort to be as involved in all of his three sons' lives as he possibly could while leading a large church as its senior pastor. Anyone who has ever served in that position knows the demands on their time are strenuous at the very least. And yet, he played catch with us whenever we wanted, built us a backyard basketball court, and coached my church basketball team and my little brother's Little League team.

I loved baseball so much that it didn't matter I wasn't any good at it. My passion for the game in no way made up for my lack of talent, but it did blind me to it. My dad worked with me in the street in front of the house where I grew up, catching my lightning-fast thirty-mile-an-hour speedball and my nonexistent curve ball. And he sent me to really cool baseball camps where I learned the fundamentals from amazing coaches. He took us all out for batting practice on Saturday mornings and bought us donuts and 7-11 Big Gulps afterwards.

He did all those amazing things, and what did I take away from it for most of my young life, up through my high school years? My dad didn't love me as much as my little brother. How did that screwed-up thought get into my brain? Because my dad coached my *basketball* team instead of my baseball team. I just knew that if my dad wasn't so busy coaching my little brother, who was extremely talented and played on tournament teams up through high school, and put his time and energy into my baseball career, I could have been the next Nolan Ryan. A little nepotism was all that kept me from greatness, and I resented him for it.

I think about the brown towel hanging on the rack and about the way the image stuck with me. I think about the angry little boy whose father gave him so much that went unappreciated because he wanted something different than what was given. I think about what these stories mean to me now, and how they point toward a truth all fathers should know about their children.

That truth is this: no matter what you do as a parent, even if, on paper, you do everything to earn that Father of the Year mug, you have absolutely no control over how your children take it in and apply it to their lives. And they may get screwed up for a while before they figure it out. And by "for a while" I mean their whole lives in one way or another.

My dad's co-pastor is fond of saying that children are excellent observers and terrible interpreters of information. Put another way, kids are sponges, and there's no telling what they will do with the information they absorb. For that reason, it is important for a father to carefully monitor, contextualize, and model the lessons he wants his child to learn. But I believe it is also important that he does so with the understanding that he will most certainly fail in some way.

I don't mean to say the job of a parent is futile. I'm pretty sure I turned out okay. I mean, I'm thirty, single, I'm an actor, I sing in a band, and have no children of my own, but I don't hold that against my father.

In all seriousness, my dad encouraged my gifts and my desire to chase a dream, pursuing a career in which 98 percent of its practitioners are out of work at any given time. He would occasionally, however, try to dissuade me from that path by presenting what he felt were viable alternatives. I could be a pediatrician, or an entertainment lawyer, or something related to the entertainment industry that had a paycheck and stability. These were basketball-coach moments. I had to remind myself that those words, though unappreciated at the time, came from a place of love and concern for my well-being.

On the other hand, every time he held back on sharing his fears and hesitations, and spoke life into me, that was a brown towel moment. He came to every play I was in in high school, no matter how terrible. He wrote tuition checks to an expensive private university so I could get a degree in theatre performance. He moved me into my first apartment in New York City. Brown towel moments, all. These moments gave me strength and courage to go out and dare myself greatly.

This isn't written to make you second-guess the decisions you make as a father, or to get you to try to avoid those basketball-coach moments altogether. You can't. You'll do something selfless for your son, and he'll look at that selfless act and think to himself, "If my father really loved me, he would have done x instead of y." We think this sort of thing of God quite a bit, so it's reasonable to expect your sons to think it of you, too. I wonder if parents appreciate this insight, those who have experienced it, when they glimpse how God must feel in His relationship with us when this sort of thing happens.

And there is our hope and encouragement. As I said, I don't want you to live in fear that some benign thing you do is going to screw up your kid. It's hard enough, broken as we are, to avoid screwing your kids up outright. Looking back, the basketball and the brown towel are the same. My father didn't console me as a child in the bathroom with the brown towel because I was a sick child, he did it because I was *his* child. My dad didn't coach my basketball team because he believed I had special athletic ability. I think maybe, just maybe, he did it because I was his son and he loved me.

Why Fathers Matter
by Michael McBride

PASTOR MICHAEL MCBRIDE (known as "Pastor Mike") is a native of San Francisco and has been active in ministry for over twenty years. Throughout the years, Pastor McBride's commitment to holistic ministry can be seen through his leadership roles in both the church and community organizations. A graduate of Duke University's Divinity School, with a master's in divinity and an emphasis in ethics and public policy, Pastor McBride launched The Way Christian Center in West Berkeley, where he presently serves as pastor. In March 2012, he became the director for the Lifelines to Healing Campaign with the PICO National Network, a campaign led by hundreds of faith congregations throughout the United States committed to addressing gun violence and mass incarceration of young people of color. Recently, Pastor McBride was selected as the #9 Top Clergy Leader in the United States by the Center for American Progress. He is married to Cherise McBride and they have two beautiful daughters, Sarai and Nylah.

During a science class in fifth grade, our teacher asked everyone in the class to share what they would like to be when they grew up. I was one of three students of color in this predominantly white private Southern Baptist school in San Francisco. As many students shared their goals of being doctors, lawyers, pastors, teachers, and the like, I boldly declared I would be an astronaut or fighter jet pilot. You must understand and appreciate that during the 1980s, *Star Wars* and *Star Trek* had so captured my imagination that all I could think about was flying in airplanes or spaceships. I loved planes, building models, math, and science. I loved going to parks to sit in the old jets that were constructed as part of the playground and imagine I was flying through the air. And to this day, I still vividly remember the teacher laughing at me and saying in front of the whole class, "Michael, that is not possible—maybe you should think of being something that is more realistic. People from your community don't become astronauts."

I was crushed, and my mother, who taught music instrumentation at this same school, heard about the incident and communicated this to my father. This stands out as one of the many incidents where my dad would show up in my life—whether at school or in the neighborhood or in my daily decisions—*to reaffirm my purpose, defend my dignity, and redirect my energy*. Not only did my dad show up to the school to challenge this teacher's assertion, but he reassured me that whatever I wanted to be, with the help of God, I could become. This was the first time that a biblical principle taught to me by my family, my church, and even this school came alive: I can do all things through Christ who gives me strength. This is the most enduring impact of my father in that he made truth concrete in my life both through his words and by his actions. He was present…and active!

Growing up in the Bayview-Hunter's Point neighborhoods of San Francisco during the crack-cocaine epidemic has left an indelible mark on my life. As I came of age, the unique and active presence of my father began to stand out and differentiate me among my peers. There was a time I got so mad with a teacher in class who was picking on me that I turned on the Bunsen burner, unaware of the risk I was causing. Some of the older guys quickly intervened and said, "Mike, you know if your dad has to come up to this school, it will be all bad!" I was sent to the principal's office and when I explained what happened, one of the male teachers in the school who knew my dad and me was called in to intervene, saving me from suspension, expulsion, or much worse. Whether at school or in the neighborhood, everyone knew my dad, or a caring male mentor or protector was not too far away. I never had the feeling I had to fend for myself.

As an adult engaging in a life of ministry and service, I have witnessed firsthand the crippling impact that the lack of fathers and caring men have had in our communities. Whether I'm performing the funerals of young men and women; visiting the jails where they are housed; or working with them to succeed in underfunded and unwelcome schools, I am always met with the same question: Why are there not more men like you around? Who will protect us? Does anyone care?

It is very clear to me that the active presence of my dad, and other men of integrity and character, was not only critical to my physical safety and emotional well-being, but also my spiritual vitality. The confluence of my personal life experiences and current realities convince me that an ecology or network of caring men, whether fathers, mentors or protectors, is one of the most important vocations any man alive in this contemporary moment must answer.

My best example of a father has been my dad, James McBride. My dad was raised in Golsboro, North Carolina during the social unrest of the civil rights movement. He was the oldest of six siblings, and was raised in a home characterized by physical and sexual abuse. He eventually was drafted by the army for the Vietnam War and upon his return from the war, found himself relocated to California, where my grandmother was forced to move the family to escape the abuse of my grandfather.

I know all this because my dad regularly sat us down and shared the tragedies and triumphs of our family history. He shared with us very important and intimate insights about our family's vices, including violence, alcohol addiction, sexual brokenness, and physical abuse. He imparted to us the rich spiritual heritage of my great-grandfather, a Classical Pentecostal bishop, who started a now-defunct Pentecostal denomination during the early decades of the 1900s. He made sure that all of us were familiar with our story and understood the unique call of God in our lives to be what he and my mom said they were: cycle breakers.

Knowledge of such a history forced me to contend early on with the vices that threatened to overtake my life. I recall instances when my brothers or I were engaged in destructive behavior, or at risk of being consumed by others' destructive assumptions about us, and my dad used those as teachable moments to remind us of both the angels and demons that exist in our lives. He constantly reminded us how we were not like everyone else. And that it was his job to make sure we never forgot it!

I remember when one of my friends gave me a copy of the NWA hip hop record, "F*#K tha Police," my dad went ballistic. He sat us down and explained how vulnerable we are as black males and taught us how to respond to police when treated unfairly. He forbade us to internalize these messages of rage and reminded us that we would be forces of good and redemption in the world. These kinds of "fatherhood interruptions," I am confident, literally saved my life. Many of my friends who responded to the realities expressed in the music, culture, and lived experiences of urban life with rage, apathy, and rebellion are dead or in jail. But today, all of my siblings are ordained clergy pastoring congregations, engaging in faith-based social justice, or providing social services to alleviate poverty, crime, and hopelessness.

It's important to also appreciate that my dad did not limit his "fathering" to just me and my siblings. There were many young men who were friends of ours who would live with us for weeks, months, and even years at a time due to their own family situations. This left an indelible mark on who I considered "my responsibility to care for." Perhaps this was grounded in my dad's role as Sunday School National President for our church denomination. One favorite lesson he taught us was that of Abraham, and this song embodies the way we understood our friends and community:

> Father Abraham, had many sons . . . many sons had Father Abraham.
>
> I am one of them, and so are you, so let's just praise the Lord.

His modeling of manhood, masculinity, and consistency became my blueprint for fatherhood as I found myself in positions of influence for young people in our community, schools, and churches. It was clear that most of the youth in my circle of influence grew up without fathers, mentors, or protectors who were connected to the wisdom and values instilled in me through my dad and a larger ecology of caring men. So although anger, fear, and pain were all common experiences in the lives of these young men and women, learning how to process or deal with it constructively proved to be an elusive skill set. To this day, I liberally pass on the fatherhood lessons that I learned. The need for these lessons has never been in greater demand.

A young man in my neighborhood came to me recently, filled with rage and quick to respond to real and imaginary slights with an all-consuming fire of destructive language and sometimes physical violence. Drawing from the many conversations my dad had with me when I was young, I explained to this young man why controlling his rage, anger, and frustration is so important.

"You must understand that God gives us feelings, and these feelings are what make us human. And we also know that since we live in such a dangerous neighborhood or move about in such an uncaring world, these feelings can consume us and threaten to get the best of us. The question is, can you learn to control the fire that burns within you? Or will this fire control you? Back in the day, lamps provided light using the flame of fire. And this fire was fueled by oil inside the lamp that was controlled by a dial. You turn the dial up and the oil would increase, making the fire more bright. You turn the dial down and the oil would decrease, making the fire less bright. If you turned the dial all the way down, the light would cease to exist and the lamp would be nonfunctional. If you turned the dial up too high and too fast, the oil would ignite the fire and it would consume the lamp and sometimes the person holding it. What you must learn, young fella, is how to turn the necessary dials of passion and emotion up and down in such a way where you are not useless because of apathy. Nor are you destructive to yourself and those around you because of the intensity of the fire that is burning."

By sharing this truth, as told to me by my father, I was able to bridge the gap between us, a gap of both generation and wisdom. In this way, my dad demonstrated the biblical truth of our tradition as communicated by James the brother of Jesus: True religion is this:

to care for the orphans and widows and remain undefiled before the world! These kinds of lessons saved not only my life, but the lives of young folks I've interacted with in my last twenty years of ministry.

This is the legacy of fatherhood and why I believe fathers matter the most: We create undeniable truths and experiences that are hard to leave behind. This can be both a blessing and a curse; for if the truths and experiences are life-giving, they are indeed the gifts that keep on giving. But if they are filled with pain, betrayal, and disappointment, then they re-inscribe themselves for generations until cycle breakers emerge. My hope then for Christian men in general, and Christian fathers in particular, is that we embrace the generational impact of our own call to father children. Whether we have functional marriages or mixed families, may we appreciate the uniqueness of fathering the children we have created or inherited; may we realize that fathers matter.

Pursuing My Children

by Jason Poon

JASON POON is married to his best friend, TJ, and is father to two beautiful daughters, Eden (pronounced AY-DUHN) and Ariella. He is a graduate of the University of Texas at Austin and is currently on staff with Epic Movement, a ministry of Campus Crusade for Christ, serving as national conferences and events coordinator. Outside of his family and faith, Jason has two other loves in his life: soccer and steak. In fact, he has a Tumblr about the steaks he eats: http://mysteakbook.tumblr.com.

"He won't know how to be a good father."

"What do you mean?"

"How can he, if his own father isn't a Christian?"

There was a long pause.

"Am I wrong? How will he know how to be someone when no one has shown him how to become that person? He won't be a good father."

During my college years, I had an older friend, Randy, whom I looked up to immensely. He was very much the older brother I always wanted but never had. He taught me so much, from negotiating the price on my cell phone plan to changing the tile on the bathroom floor. He taught me how to grill, build a computer, throw darts, hustle someone in foosball, use Photoshop, and break into a home. In our defense, the last one was us breaking into his own home because he got locked out, but that was still a lesson learned.

I hung onto every word he had to offer. He was kind and patient when dealing with me, but quick to deliver a firm hand when I needed it. Even though I was a Christian prior to meeting Randy, he taught me how to read the Bible, to look at the text within its proper context. He humbled me when I made snap judgments about people and called me out when I was rash and immature. Randy was smart and funny and I am very, very proud to call him my friend and mentor.

Out of everything he taught me, one of the greatest lessons he imparted was to always be a learner and to spend time learning and perfecting something, anything. A shortcut to learning, he taught me, was to learn by observing others and mostly to pay attention to their mistakes and to make sure I didn't repeat them. A classmate's phone is confiscated by the professor because the ringer went off? Take that moment to make sure my ringer was off. Friend got a parking ticket for being too close to the fire hydrant? Take note of how close he was and make sure you don't park that close to a fire hydrant next time. Defender blocked my teammate's jumper? Pump fake next time that defender is on me.

The conversation at the beginning of this essay was a conversation between an ex-girlfriend and her father, talking about me. Not long after, that conversation became one of several reasons that she broke things off with me. In their father-daughter dynamic, she was rarely free to make her own decisions. Our relationship ended and he became another in a string of fathers who served as examples to me of what not to do when I became a father myself. In the three short years since my first child was born, I've made attempts to carefully observe fathers of all ages, from those with infants and toddlers to those with adult children. I even took notes on what my father was like to me growing up and how he is with me now. Across all the life stages, the common thread that appeared was one of fathers struggling to connect to their children on the child's level or interest.

This relationship dynamic has been particularly true between me and my father. When I was a child I was really into video games. I liked the interactive puzzles and challenges that each level brought on and the increasing difficulty as you progressed further and further. It challenged your agility, mind, and wit to hone and master whatever techniques you learned from the previous level. Sadly, in my home I was alone in this interest. I remember many nights when I would practically beg my father to join me for a few minutes. Most nights he would decline and on the rare night of acceptance, he would do so very reluctantly. My father wasn't very good and I knew that. That wasn't why I asked him to play with me. I just wanted to connect with him and the thing that came most naturally as an eight-year-old was to ask him to pick up a Nintendo controller. Not surprisingly, my relationship with him mirrored most Chinese-American father-son dynamics where the father was physically present and provided for the family's physical needs but was largely absent emotionally and rarely engaged his son in anything other than schoolwork. My father was pretty distant and aloof for most of my life and rarely took an interest in anything other than the grades I was earning. Even though this was the norm for many of my friends and their relationships with their fathers, it still didn't change the fact that I hoped for more than that status quo. That became even more evident when Randy entered my life and showed me how someone pursues a relationship and values you outside of what you do and what you bring to the table.

During my college years I longed for a closer relationship with my father so I started throwing myself more into a few things that I knew he was into, including social drinking. If there was one consistent thing about my dad that I could count on while growing up, it was that every time he returned home from work he would crack open a beer, open a bottle of wine, or pour himself a dram of whiskey. He would always stop after one or two drinks, but it was clearly something that he really enjoyed at the end of a long day. When I turned twenty-one a few friends took me out for a celebratory beer, but I couldn't finish it. I really disliked the taste, but I made a conscious decision to acquire it. If I were to reconnect with my father, I knew I had to meet him on his terms and that would mean sharing a drink with him. So I spent the next eight months with a drink in hand each night over dinner, slowly trying to acquire the taste so that I could surprise my dad at Christmas with a bottle of scotch and two glasses. My dear old friend Randy didn't like drinking himself, but he would often have a drink with me in support of my attempt to connect with my father.

I was successful, and when my father and I connected during that break, we ended up having many great late-night conversations over a drink. I learned many things about him, my grandparents, my great-grandparents, his hopes and dreams—mostly things we had never talked about before. I do not regret taking up his hobby, but there is sadness that it was me, the son, who had to find ways to connect and relate to him. He never pursued me in the same way.

I know I'm not alone in having this type of story to tell. I've seen plenty of sons being pushed into football because their father had been an all-state player, even though it was evident to everyone around them that the boy was a scholar and not an athlete. I've seen a son ridiculed for his interest in computers and technology by his tech-averse parents. And the list goes on. The narrative keeps pointing to a growing number of fathers who try to make their children a reflection of themselves, rather than seek out and deliberately foster the development of the type of person God wired their children to be.

I had an eye-opening experience in my early twenties regarding fatherhood when I was taking a class on the Book of Psalms. The professor was a decorated theologian and scholar with multiple PhDs to his name. His wife was equally impressive and probably had the same number of credentials.

He shared with the class how he was blessed to be a family of six, with three boys and a girl, and that his three sons were what God created them to be: firefighters. Naturally he fielded many questions about how he felt about being such an educated man himself with three boys who never took a single college level course. Even though it's almost been a decade since, I still remember very clearly his response:

"My children owe me nothing. They are not mine. They belong to the Lord. I am nothing but a steward of their lives and because of that I owe them and God everything to raise them to be who God made them to be. And God made them to be heroes who save people out of burning buildings."

My ex-girlfriend's father was right that my father didn't necessarily show me how to be a godly father, but he underestimated the people around me and my ability to learn and observe from others. Randy taught me to observe others and learn from them. Fathers everywhere showed me what not to do, and that professor showed me something so profound about fatherhood that it became a sort of motto for me. My children belong to the Lord and I am nothing but a steward for their lives. I am charged with discovering their interests, their skills, and their gifts, and giving them every possible opportunity to fine-tune those things so that they can live out their adult lives in the way God always meant for them.

I have two little girls: one is three, the other is eight months. It's a bit too early for me to determine what kind of person my youngest is, but I have am getting a picture for who my oldest might turn out to be. At eighteen months old she was doing puzzles meant for kids twice her age. For "fun" she pulls out a map of the United States and memorizes the states. She routinely beats her parents at games of memory because she never misses matching cards after she has seen the image once. God has clearly wired my child with an active mind and one that I need to make sure I consistently challenge and develop.

She invites me daily to do puzzles with her, to pull out the map and study it, and to build blocks together. None of those are really my thing, but I am thankful to have developed a mature understanding of my father's lack of engagement with me. It has taught me how to respond to her requests: With great enthusiasm and without a moment's hesitation I drop everything and sit down with her as though she just invited me to the party of the century. As far as my children are concerned, I hope many years from now that they'll remember my enthusiasm for them and their interests. That I was a father who engaged with them on their terms and didn't withhold relationship and intimacy because they weren't into what I enjoyed. I want them to know their father was someone who pursued them, especially in the areas where we lacked common ground, because that was the same way Randy pursued and supported me as a friend. I wasn't blessed to have a father model for me how a father pursues his children, but I had the next best thing: someone who showed me what I didn't want to become.

Waiting for Dad to Come

by Cedrick Valrie

CEDRICK VALRIE is a ministry leader and a professor of practical theology at Southeastern University in Lakeland, Florida. He is currently pursuing a doctor of ministry at George Fox University. Cedrick and his wife, Sarah, have three children: Antonio, Julius, and are expecting baby girl in July, 2014. They serve on staff at Bay Chapel, a church plant in Wesley Chapel, Florida.

Fathers possess incarnate, God-given sparks to ignite a son's capacity to love deeply, give generously, and to be a private and public success at home and in the workplace. Today, my father and I laugh like old neighborhood friends, and shoot the breeze while sipping iced tea and eating sausage sandwiches. Even a heartfelt "I love you" from time to time comes over the phone as we share stories and sometimes Scripture concerning the latest happenings in our lives. But this is a new, restored relationship—it was not always this way for me and my dad, as I grew up in a fatherless home in the inner city.

Throughout my childhood and teenage years my grandmother often reminded me that though my father was not actively involved in my life, he was still my father. She would not tolerate insults to him or my own self-pity. I can vividly remember sipping my Kool-Aid on the front porch in the afternoon Alabama sun, eager with anticipation because I had heard my daddy was coming to visit. As the moon made its appearance in the night sky, my mom would redirect my attention to dinner—a classic peanut butter and jelly sandwich. Something inside me wanted to hold out hope that he would show up for me as planned for once. Yet his face grew fainter in my memory because of his continued absence. Those experiences compounded and gave root to disappointment, bitterness, insecurity, and a critical attitude. It seemed all I knew of my dad was his name. Though we only lived thirty minutes apart, I spent no more than thirty minutes with him total as kid. I wanted to know simple things about him. What did his laugh sound like? What type of cologne did he wear? Did he eat as much PB and J as I did? Did he like to listen to my favorite songs by Kool and the Gang or KC and the Sunshine Band?

At an early age, we moved in with my grandmother. She worked her fingers to the bone making decent provisions for the family. From sunrise to sunset, the city bus was her second home. On most warm Alabama evenings, my siblings and I would meet grandma at the bus stop to help bring the groceries home for dinner and to see if she had goodies for us. Soon I realized that my grandmother's work ethic, Southern cooking and hospitality, early rising, and a bulldog tenacity to treat people right, were well-stitched characteristics in her personality and that they had become part of me also. Shucking corn and peeling potatoes with grandma was a rich pastime. Some of my most notable, unsolicited run-ins with common sense and practical wisdom were imprinted on me when assisting with food prep for community BBQs, family reunions, or birthday parties. She would issue provoking statements such as, "Son, it is just as easy to do the right thing as it is to do the wrong thing" or "Your business ain't everybody's business." Such talk felt like a Sunday morning message from the preacher that I would receive at the weekly Sidewalk Sunday school that we attended.

Although we did not cling to a certain denomination in my home, most of my family members claimed to be Baptist. Yet the weekly Sidewalk Sunday school was at a Pentecostal church. There was a respect for God in our home. Spirituality looked like listening to Gospel radio stations or searching the TV for some good, soul-stirring Gospel music while we participated by snapping our fingers or tapping our feet to the rhythm of the drums. As a family, we were not avid churchgoers. Often, the kids were sent to church alone and had to reflect with the adults on the experience once back home.

As I progressed into the preteen years, I was a bit impatient, believing that the Burger King motto, "Have it your way," was my calling. This smug attitude began when the relationship severed between my mother and grandmother. Inadequate communication skills and feeding many mouths with few resources were constant tensions and put a wedge between the women. As a result, I had to part ways with the only home I knew. With no credit, money, or apartment rental know-how, my mother could not secure a stable place for us to live, so we temporarily moved in with some of her friends. I missed the conversations and interaction with my grandma; I had difficulty feeling comfortable around my mom's acquaintances. Their conversations were often dark and misguided. Sadly, the family environment in which growth, wisdom, and encouragement took place was being replaced with an atmosphere of uncertainty, anxiety, and misery.

My mother eventually managed to find an apartment in the Orange Grove public housing community of Alabama where I was introduced to Mrs. Ann Stacey. This warm-hearted woman invited me to attend the Yogi Bear Sidewalk Sunday School located behind the local Boys and Girls Club. She had my attention when she mentioned games and candy. It did not seem to matter to me or the other kids that the huge open field where we met was riddled with trash, broken beer bottles, used condoms, and candy wrappers. Beneath the shade of deep navy blue tarps, hundreds of kids from the local project areas assembled weekly to enjoy the fun games, Bible stories, and a sweet treat at the end for good behavior. One particular Thursday stands out in my mind. A bird puppet named Patty Pigeon helped tell the Bible story. I found myself intently repeating Patty's prayer, "Oh Lord, I'm yours and I'm glad to be. Take my heart. Take my life. Take all of me."

Years passed and my family struggled to survive in Orange Grove. We were not accustomed to hearing multiple shootings, witnessing prostitution and drug dealing, barely having food to eat at times, and neighbors stealing the clothes off the clothesline. We were in serious survival mode and learned to adapt. By this time Ann had moved back to New York to continue her education. The director of Yogi Bear, Bill Gray, built a relationship with me and became my mentor and father figure. At this point in life, I was doing very well as a senior in high school, despite my community influences. JROTC, the National Honor Society, and the Men of Distinction Club were three of my favorite outlets. Each group contained respectable men who mentored me in leadership, relationships, and how to rise above my circumstances. I appreciated them helping me to develop good character.

The night before I moved to Florida for college, the local congregation that had provided me with practical ministry experience asked me to preach about forgiveness and healing. I had no idea what awaited me in that service. I was a mere fifteen minutes into preaching, when a man walked in late through the side door. His stature caught my attention: it was my dad. The timing proved quite providential, as I was in the middle of challenging the people to allow God to transform their lives with inner healing through extending forgiveness. That was likely the last clear thought I uttered; I was in disbelief that my father would show up at such a moment. Filled with anxiety, I abruptly closed the service in prayer and quickly dismissed the congregation. After saying my goodbyes to the various church members, I noticed that the one person lingering in the parking lot was this man I struggled to forgive.

He began the conversation by telling me that he heard from a family member that I was leaving for college the next morning. Interestingly, he expressed that he once lived in the city I was headed to. He graciously offered to help me to drive my first long road trip and pay for gas; without hesitation I took him up on it. His offer dramatically shifted the weight of the moment. I suddenly felt like he was extending his approval to me. Though we did not have a storybook moment of a father-son reunion with a forgiving embrace and time to talk through the past, it still was a freeing moment. I was able to acknowledge with him that though we could not make up for lost time, we could use this time to build a relationship. That experience was an answer to prayer, and the drive to college made it even better. I felt like God smiled on that trip, as I had a chance to finally learn what type of cologne my dad wore and about his favorite foods.

Today, I can say without reservation or hesitation that I love my dad. The night that he reentered my life truly was a new start for us, and there has been no looking back. Over the last twelve years we have consistently visited each other and talked on the phone. About seven years into our newfound father-son relationship, I heard my dad tell me he loved me for the first time. Honestly, I had no words; it was my wife who initially replied, "We love you, too." Over the years I have also learned that it was my dad's original aspiration to become a preacher, but his decisions led him down a different path. Nevertheless, he has opened his heart again to the Lord and is actually considering becoming a deacon in the local church.

Such restoration has refreshed my soul. In the years since our turning point, I have continued with my education, now pursuing a doctorate. My wife, Sarah, and I have been happily married for six years. God has provided me numerous role models to demonstrate healthy marriages and families, and I have taken time to glean lessons from them. I am also a proud father to our two-year-old son, Julius. We are privileged to have both my grandmother and my father still involved in our lives. Though I once feared becoming an insecure, incompetent, emotionally distraught father, with God's help and much soul healing, I have been able to counteract these previous thoughts with new realities and truth. The character traits I most focus on modeling to my family are being generous, authentic, fully present, diligent, and maintaining an atmosphere where we can laugh at ourselves. It warms my heart to already see my son displaying qualities of gentleness, care, and compassion. I am continually grateful for the opportunity for my family to write its own new story while still building on our life experiences.

About the Editor

DR. R. ANDERSON CAMPBELL lives and writes in Portland, Oregon where he is an Assistant Professor of Christian Studies at George Fox University. He is a lover of story, student of metaphor, spiritual pilgrim, and mentor to others along The Way. He has served as a deacon at Theophilus Church in southeast Portland, responsible for the community's creative liturgy. He enjoys speaking on matters of faith and narrative and exploring new metaphors for spiritual formation. In his spare time he likes brewing beer, getting tattooed, and blogging at thecrookedmouth.com.

I Speak for Myself series

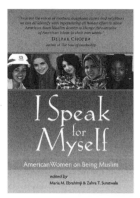

VOLUME 1

I Speak for Myself
American Women on Being Muslim

ISBN: 978-1-935952-00-8 / $16.95

VOLUME 2

All-American
45 American Men on Being Muslim

ISBN: 978-1-935952-59-6 / $16.95

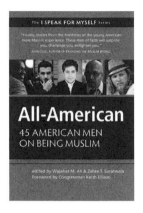

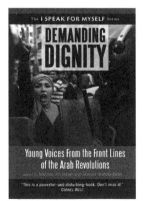

VOLUME 3

Demanding Dignity
Young Voices from the Front Lines of the Arab Revolutions

ISBN: 978-1-935952-71-8 / $16.95

VOLUME 4

Talking Taboo
American Christian Women Get Frank About Faith

ISBN: 978-1-935952-86-2 / $16.95